Literary Lives

Founding Editor: **Richard Dutton**, Professor of English, Lancaster University

This series offers stimulating accounts of the literary careers of the most admired and influential English-language authors. Volumes follow the outline of the writer's working lives, not in the spirit of traditional biography, but aiming to trace the professional, publishing and social contexts which shaped their writing.

Published titles include:

Felicity Rosslyn ALEXANDER POPE	*Joseph McMinn* JONATHAN SWIFT
Ira B. Nadel EZRA POUND	*Leonée Ormond* ALFRED TENNYSON
Richard Dutton WILLIAM SHAKESPEARE	*Peter Shillingsburg* WILLIAM MAKEPEACE THACKERAY
John Williams MARY SHELLEY	*David Wykes* EVELYN WAUGH
Michael O'Neill PERCY BYSSHE SHELLEY	*Caroline Franklin* MARY WOLLSTONECRAFT
Gary Waller EDMUND SPENSER	*John Mepham* VIRGINIA WOOLF
Tony Sharpe WALLACE STEVENS	*John Williams* WILLIAM WORDSWORTH
William Gray ROBERT LOUIS STEVENSON	*Alasdair D. F. Macrae* W. B. YEATS

Literary Lives
Series Standing Order ISBN 0–333–71486–5 hardcover
Series Standing Order ISBN 0–333–80334–5 paperback
(*outside North America only*)

You can receive future titles in this series as they are published by placing a standing order. Please contact your bookseller or, in case of difficulty, write to us at the address below with your name and address, the title of the series and one of the ISBNs quoted above.

Customer Services Department, Macmillan Distribution Ltd, Houndmills, Basingstoke, Hampshire RG21 6XS, England

Samuel Taylor Coleridge

A Literary Life

William Christie

First published in 2007 by
PALGRAVE MACMILLAN
Houndmills, Basingstoke, Hampshire RG21 6XS and
175 Fifth Avenue, New York, N.Y. 10010
Companies and representatives throughout the world.

PALGRAVE MACMILLAN is the global academic imprint of the Palgrave Macmillan division of St. Martin's Press, LLC and of Palgrave Macmillan Ltd. Macmillan® is a registered trademark in the United States, United Kingdom and other countries. Palgrave is a registered trademark in the European Union and other countries.

ISBN-13: 978–1–4039–4066–7 hardback
ISBN-10: 1–4039–4066–5 hardback

This book is printed on paper suitable for recycling and made from fully managed and sustained forest sources.

A catalogue record for this book is available from the British Library.

Library of Congress Cataloging-in-Publication Data

Christie, William, 1952–
    Samuel Taylor Coleridge : a literary life / William Christie.
        p. cm. – (Literary lives)
    Includes bibliographical references and index.
    ISBN 1–4039–4066–5 (cloth)
        1. Coleridge, Samuel Taylor, 1772–1834. 2. Poets, English – 19th century – Biography. I. Title. II. Series: Literary lives (Palgrave Macmillan (Firm))

PR4483.C524 2006
821'.7—dc22   2006046063
[B]

10 9 8 7 6 5 4 3 2 1
16 15 14 13 12 11 10 09 08 07

Transferred to digital printing in 2007.

For my mother
Diana Christie (née Silcock)
with love

Contents

Acknowledgements

My greatest debts are to Coleridge's biographers: to Coleridge himself, in his autobiographical letters to Tom Poole of 1797–8 and in the *Biographia Literaria*, and thereafter to a host of dedicated Coleridgeans, from Joseph Cottle and James Gillman through to Richard Holmes's generous double volume biography, which straddles Rosemary Ashton's scrupulous account in the Blackwell Critical Biographies series. To these last two, in particular, and to the many editors of The Collected Works of Samuel Taylor Coleridge, Bollingen Series LXXV, I am deeply indebted.

This could not have been written without the advice and encouragement of many of my colleagues here at the University of Sydney, but again I single out two: Deirdre Coleman and Margaret Harris have been especially attentive and generous.

I am also indebted to the Research Institute in the Humanities and Social Sciences (RIHSS) here at the University of Sydney for a fellowship granting me relief from some of my teaching during a vital period of the study's gestation.

Paula Kennedy at Palgrave Macmillan has been enthusiastic about the project from the beginning and helped make it all worthwhile, and my old teacher, Geoffrey Little, kindly offered to read through the final draft.

Finally, thanks to my wife Patrice and daughter Ellen for (on top of everything else) making the trip to the UK without me to allow me to finish the book, and to my other daughters, Francesca and Vita, and to my grandson Archie, for putting up with less time than they deserve.

Abbreviations

References to the following will be found in parentheses within the body of the text:

BL   *Biographia Literaria or Biographical Sketches of My Literary Life and Opinions*, The Collected Works of Samuel Taylor Coleridge, 7, ed. James Engell and W. Jackson Bate, in 2 vols (Princeton, NJ: Princeton University Press, 1983).

CL   *The Collected Letters of Samuel Taylor Coleridge*, ed. Earl Leslie Griggs, in 6 vols (Oxford: Clarendon, 1956–71).

CN   *Collected Notebooks of Samuel Taylor Coleridge*, Bollingen Series L, ed. Kathleen Coburn, with Merton Christensen and Anthony John Harding, in 5 double vols (New York, Princeton, and London: Princeton University Press and Routledge & Kegan Paul, 1957–2002).

N   *Coleridge's Notebooks: A Selection*, ed. Seamus Perry (Oxford: Oxford University Press, 2002) [the text of Perry's edition is preferred for all those notes included in his selection].

References to the following will be found in the endnotes:

Ashton	Rosemary Ashton, *The Life of Samuel Taylor Coleridge* (Oxford: Blackwell, 1996).
Church and State (CC)	*On the Constitution of the Church and State*, The Collected Works of Samuel Taylor Coleridge, 10, ed. John Colmer (Princeton, NJ: Princeton University Press, 1976).
Coleridge: The Critical Heritage	*Coleridge: The Critical Heritage*, ed. J. R. de J. Jackson (London: Routledge & Kegan Paul, 1970).
Essays on His Times (CC)	*Essays on His Times in* The Morning Post *and* The Courier, The Collected Works of Samuel Taylor Coleridge, 3, ed. David V. Erdman, in 3 vols (Princeton, NJ: Princeton University Press, 1978).
The Friend (CC)	*The Friend*, The Collected Works of Samuel Taylor Coleridge, 4, ed. Barbara E. Rooke, in 2 vols (Princeton, NJ: Princeton University Press, 1969).
Gillman	James Gillman, *The Life of Samuel Taylor Coleridge* (London: William Pickering, 1838).

HCR	*Henry Crabb Robinson on Books and Their Writers*, ed. Edith J. Morley, in 3 vols (London: J. M. Dent & Sons, 1938).
Holmes, *Darker Reflections*	Richard Holmes, *Coleridge: Darker Reflections* (London: HarperCollins, 1998).
Holmes, *Early Visions*	Richard Holmes, *Coleridge: Early Visions* (London: Hodder & Stoughton, 1989).
Lamb Letters	*The Letters of Charles and Mary Anne Lamb*, ed. Edwin W. Marrs Jr, in 3 vols (Ithaca, NY: Cornell University Press, 1975–8).
Lay Sermons (CC)	*Lay Sermons*, The Collected Works of Samuel Taylor Coleridge, 6, ed. R. J. White (Princeton, NJ: Princeton University Press, 1972).
Lectures 1795 (CC)	*Lectures 1795 On Politics and Religion*, The Collected Works of Samuel Taylor Coleridge, 1, ed. Lewis Patton and Peter Mann (Princeton, NJ: Princeton University Press, 1971).
Lectures on Literature (CC)	*Lectures 1808–1819 On Literature*, The Collected Works of Samuel Taylor Coleridge, 5, ed. R. A. Foakes, in 2 vols (Princeton, NJ: Princeton University Press, 1987).
Lectures on Philosophy (CC)	*Lectures 1808–1819 On the History of Philosophy*, The Collected Works of Samuel Taylor Coleridge, 8, ed. J. R. de J. Jackson, in 2 vols (Princeton, NJ: Princeton University Press, 2000).
Marginalia (CC)	*Marginalia*, The Collected Works of Samuel Taylor Coleridge, 12, ed. H. J. Jackson and George Whalley, in 6 vols (Princeton, NJ: Princeton University Press, 1980–2001).
Opus Maximum (CC)	*Opus Maximum*, The Collected Works of Samuel Taylor Coleridge, 15, ed. Thomas McFarland, with Nicholas Halmi (Princeton, NJ: Princeton University Press, 2002).
Oxford Companion to the Romantic Age	*An Oxford Companion to the Romantic Age: British Culture 1776–1832*, ed. Iain McCalman (Oxford: Oxford University Press, 1999).
Poetical Works (CC)	*Poetical Works*, The Collected Works of Samuel Taylor Coleridge, 16, ed. J. C. C. Mays,

in 6 vols (Princeton, NJ: Princeton University Press, 2001) [All quotations from Coleridge's poetry are taken from this edition].

The Prelude William Wordsworth, *The Prelude, 1799, 1805, 1850*, ed. Jonathan Wordsworth, M. H. Abrams, and Stephen Gill (New York: Norton, 1979) [All quotations from *The Prelude* are taken from this edition].

Shorter Works (CC) *Shorter Works and Fragments*, The Collected Works of Samuel Taylor Coleridge, 11, ed. H. J. Jackson and J. R. de J. Jackson, in 2 vols (Princeton, NJ: Princeton University Press, 1995).

Table Talk (CC) *Table Talk Recorded by Henry Nelson Coleridge (and John Taylor Coleridge)*, The Collected Works of Samuel Taylor Coleridge, 14, ed. Carl Woodring, in 2 vols (Princeton, NJ: Princeton University Press, 1990).

Thomas Poole and His Friends Mrs Henry [Margaret E.] Sandford, *Thomas Poole and His Friends*, in 2 vols (London: Macmillan, 1888).

The Watchman (CC) *The Watchman*, The Collected Works of Samuel Taylor Coleridge, 2, ed. Lewis Patton (Princeton, NJ: Princeton University Press, 1971).

Wordsworth Letters: The Early Years *The Letters of William and Dorothy Wordsworth*, I, *The Early Years 1787–1805*, second edition, ed. Ernest de Selincourt, rev. Chester L. Shaver (Oxford: Clarendon, 1967).

Wordsworth Letters: The Middle Years 1 *The Letters of William and Dorothy Wordsworth*, II, *The Middle Years*, Part 1, *1806–1811*, second edition, ed. Ernest de Selincourt, rev. Mary Moorman (Oxford: Clarendon, 1969).

Wordsworth Letters: The Middle Years 2 *The Letters of William and Dorothy Wordsworth*, III, *The Middle Years*, Part 2, *1812–1820*, second edition, ed. Ernest de Selincourt, rev. Mary Moorman and Alan G. Hill (Oxford: Clarendon, 1970).

Wordsworth Letters: The Later Years 1 *The Letters of William and Dorothy Wordsworth*, III [for IV], *The Later Years*, Part 1, *1821–1828*, second edition, ed. Ernest de Selincourt, rev. Alan G. Hill (Oxford: Clarendon, 1978).

Wordsworth Letters: *The Later Years 2*	*The Letters of William and Dorothy Wordsworth*, V, *The Later Years*, Part 2, *1829–1834*, second edition, ed. Ernest de Selincourt, rev. Alan G. Hill (Oxford: Clarendon, 1979).
Wordsworth Poetical Works	*The Poetical Works of William Wordsworth*, revised edition, ed. Ernest de Selincourt and Helen Darbishire, in 5 vols (Oxford: Clarendon, 1952–9) [All quotations from Wordsworth's poetry, other than from *The Prelude*, are taken from this edition].
Wordsworth Prose Works	*The Prose Works of William Wordsworth*, ed. W. J. B. Owen and Jane Worthington Smyser, in 3 vols (Oxford: Clarendon Press, 1974).

Chronology

1772	(21 October) Coleridge born Ottery St Mary, Devonshire	William Wordsworth two years old; Dorothy Wordsworth one year old
1774		Robert Southey born
1775		Charles Lamb born; Jane Austen born
1776		American Declaration of Independence
1778	Coleridge attends Ottery Grammar School	William Hazlitt born
1781	Coleridge's father dies	
1782	Coleridge to Christ's Hospital	
1785		Thomas De Quincey born
1787	Coleridge's elder brother John, an army captain, dies in Madras	
1788		George Gordon (later Lord Byron) born
1789	Coleridge introduced to Bowles' sonnets at school by Thomas Middleton	The Fall of the Bastille initiates the French Revolution
1790	Coleridge's elder brother Luke, a surgeon, dies	Edmund Burke *Reflections on the Revolution in France* published
1791	Coleridge's sister Ann (Nancy) dies; enters Jesus College, Cambridge	Tom Paine *Rights of Man* published; mobs attack Joseph Priestley's house in Birmingham
1792	Coleridge's brother Francis, a lieutenant in the army, dies in India; Coleridge wins Browne medal for an ode on the slave trade	Percy Bysshe Shelley born; Mary Wollstonecraft *Rights of Woman* published
1793	Trial of William Frend at Cambridge; Coleridge enlists in 15th Light Dragoons as Silas Tomkyn Comberbache	Louis XVI of France executed; war declared on England and Holland by France; William Godwin *Political Justice* published; Marie Antoinette (French queen) executed
1794	Coleridge meets Robert Southey at Oxford; pantisocracy planned; Coleridge to London for treason trials; begins publishing 'Sonnets on Eminent Characters' in *Morning Chronicle*; to London and the Salutation and Cat with Charles Lamb	Robespierre executed; state trials for treason of Thomas Hardy, John Horne Tooke, John Thelwall (acquitted)

1795	Coleridge brought back to Bristol by Southey from London; delivers his lectures on politics, on revealed religion, and on the slave trade; pantisocracy abandoned; *A Moral and Political Lecture, Conciones ad Populum, The Plot Discovered* published; Coleridge marries Sara Fricker	John Keats born; the 'gagging acts' introduced in parliament
1796	Coleridge launches his periodical *The Watchman; Poems on Various Subjects* published; son Hartley Coleridge born; *Sonnets from Various Authors* published (with Lamb and Charles Lloyd); Coleridge to Nether Stowey	England threatened with invasion
1797	Coleridge to Racedown, Wordsworth and Dorothy to Alfoxden House near Nether Stowey; Lamb and John Thelwall visit Stowey; *annus mirabilis* begins	
1798	Coleridge meets William Hazlitt; accepts the Wedgwood annuity; *Fears in Solitude etc.* published; son Berkeley Coleridge born; *Lyrical Ballads* published; to Germany with the Wordsworths	Irish uprising; Napoleon invades Egypt; Nelson wins the Battle of the Nile
1799	Coleridge's son Berkeley dies; Coleridge to the University at Göttingen; returns to Stowey; Coleridge's first tour of the Lake District; meets and falls in love with Sara Hutchinson; to London to begin work for the *Morning Post*	Napoleon becomes First Consul of France
1800	Coleridge's translation of Schiller's *The Piccolimini* and *The Death of Wallenstein* published; Coleridge moves to Greta Hall, near Keswick; son Derwent Coleridge born	Highland clearances; the Union of Great Britain and Ireland
1801	a second edition of *Lyrical Ballads* ('by William Wordsworth') published; Coleridge in London (briefly) writing for *Morning Post*	Prime Minister William Pitt resigns; Henry Addington's ministry begins; Napoleon signs Concordat with the Pope
1802	Coleridge at Humphry Davy's lectures on chemistry in London; writing for *Morning Post*; 'Dejection: An Ode' published on William and	Peace of Amiens (peace with the French); Napoleon becomes Consul for life; foundation of the *Edinburgh Review* and of William Cobbett's

	Mary Wordsworth's wedding day (4 October); tour of Wales with Tom Wedgwood; daughter Sara Coleridge born	*Weekly Political Register*; French army invades Switzerland
1803	Coleridge in Somerset with Tom Poole and the Wedgwoods; *Poems* (1803) published; visits by Hazlitt, Sir George and Lady Beaumont at Greta Hall; tour of Scotland begun with Wordsworth and Dorothy, completed alone	Britain declares war on France
1804	Coleridge to London; embarks for Malta; private secretary to Sir Alexander Ball, governor of Malta; visits Sicily	Code Napoléon; Spain declares war on Britain; Pitt's second ministry
1805	Coleridge appointed Acting Public Secretary in Malta; learns of death at sea of John Wordsworth; tourist in Naples and Rome	Napoleon declared King of Italy; Nelson's victory at the Battle of Trafalgar
1806	Coleridge in Rome, befriends American painter Washington Allston; visits Florence and Pisa; returns to England, lingers in the south; to Keswick to effect separation from his wife; joins Wordsworths at Coleorton	Pitt dies; 'Ministry of all the Talents' formed under Lord Grenville; Charles James Fox dies
1807	Coleridge at Coleorton hears Wordsworth read the 13-book *Prelude*; to London, then Bristol and Stowey; meets De Quincey; returns to London	Portland ministry; abolition of the slave trade; bombardment of Copenhagen by British fleet; war on the Spanish peninsula begins
1808	Coleridge's first literary lectures at the Royal Institution; Wordsworth to London; Wordsworths moves to Allan Bank, Grasmere; Coleridge to Allan Bank	Convention of Cintra signed; Napoleon invades Spain
1809	Coleridge begins publishing his periodical *The Friend*	Foundation of the *Quarterly Review*; Spencer Perceval forms ministry
1810	*The Friend* folds; Coleridge to London; quarrel with Wordsworth; moves in with John and Mary Morgan and Charlotte Brent	Napoleon annexes Holland; George III goes mad
1811	Coleridge contributes to *The Courier*; literary lectures at Scot's Corporation Hall	Prince of Wales declared Regent; Luddite uprisings begin

1812	Coleridge makes last journey to the Lake District; literary lectures in Willis's Rooms; relations with Wordsworth resumed	*Childe Harold's Pilgrimage*, cantos I and II; prime minister Perceval shot; United States declares war on Britain over trade restrictions; Napoleon invades Russia, then retreats
1813	*Remorse* opens at Drury Lane for 23 nights; *Remorse* published (3 editions); Morgan bankrupt, escapes to Ireland; Coleridge to Bristol, lecturing; suffers major breakdown	Austria declares war on Napoleon; Southey becomes Poet Laureate; Jane Austen *Pride and Prejudice* published; Leigh Hunt imprisoned for libel; Wellington's peninsular campaign successful
1814	Coleridge under medical care for his opium addiction; literary lectures in Bristol; rejoins the Morgans, and they move to Calne in Wiltshire	Allies invade France; treaty with Austria, Prussia, and Russia against Napoleon; Napoleon defeated and exiled to Elba; Wordsworth *The Excursion* published; Walter Scott *Waverley*, Byron *The Corsair* published; Congress of Vienna; America and Britain at peace
1815	Coleridge dictates his literary life	Napoleon escapes from Elba (The Hundred Days); the Battle of Waterloo; Napoleon imprisoned on St Helena
1816	Coleridge accepted as patient and boarder by Dr James Gillman at Highgate; *Christabel Kubla Khan, and Pains of Sleep* published; *Statesman's Manual* published; attacked by the reviewers, notably Hazlitt	Byron goes into exile; Roman Catholic relief rejected in Lords; Jane Austen *Emma* published; Spa Fields riot
1817	*A Lay Sermon* (Coleridge's second) published; *Biographia Literaria* and *Sybilline Leaves* published; meets disciple and amanuensis Joseph Henry Green; *Zapyola* published	*Blackwood's Edinburgh Magazine* ('Maga') founded; Roman Catholic relief rejected in Lords again; Jane Austen dies
1818	Coleridge publishes a preliminary 'Treatise on Method' in the *Encyclopædia Metropolitana*; literary lectures at the London Philosophical Society; meets disciple Thomas Allsop; a new, reorganized and rewritten *Friend* issued; lectures on the history of philosophy and on literature at the Crown and Anchor Tavern, Strand	Agitation and vote (rejected) for reform of electoral system; Mary Shelley *Frankenstein* published
1819	Coleridge's lectures continue	Byron *Don Juan* begins; the Peterloo Massacre

1820		George III dies; accession of George IV; Cato Street conspiracy; revolution in Spain and Portugal; trial of Queen Caroline; Keats *Lamia and Other Poems*, Shelley *Prometheus Unbound*, Wordsworth *The River Duddon* sonnets published
1821		Keats dies in Rome; Napoleon dies; Greek War of Liberation begins
1822	Coleridge's 'Thursday-evening class' begins; Mrs Coleridge and daughter Sara visit Coleridge at Highgate; nephew (later son-in-law) Henry Nelson Coleridge begins recording Coleridge's table talk	Shelley drowns in Italy; Castlereagh suicides; Protestants and Catholics clash in Ireland
1823	Coleridge sets himself up in the attic bed and bookroom in the Gillmans' new house	War between France and Spain
1824	Coleridge elected Royal Associate of the Royal Society of Literature, with 100 guinea annuity	Byron dies at Missolonghi in Greece
1825	Coleridge *Aids to Reflection* published; lecture 'On the *Prometheus* of Aeschylus' delivered to Royal Society of Literature and published	
1826		First crossing of the Atlantic under steam
1828	Coleridge *Poetical Works* (in 3 volumes) published	Repeal of Test and Corporation Acts
1829	Coleridge *On the Constitution of the Church and State* published	Agitation for Catholic Emancipation; third Catholic Relief Bill passed by Lords; Humphry Davy dies in Switzerland
1831	Royal Society of Literature annuity withdrawn	Bill for reform of the electoral system (the famous Reform Bill) introduced into parliament and preoccupies the nation
1832		Reform Bill finally passes through both houses
1834	Coleridge dies at Highgate (25 July)	Lamb dies five months later

Prologue
Literary Life, 1815

Anyone attempting a literary life of Samuel Taylor Coleridge must come to terms with the formidable precedent set by Coleridge himself in his own 'Literary Life' – the famous *Biographia Literaria*, subtitled 'Biographical Sketches of My Own Literary Life and Opinions' and eventually published in 1817. For the literary scholar writing at any time after the institutionalization of 'English' as a core secondary school subject and university discipline, the *Biographia* represents one of the seminal texts – if not *the* seminal text – of literary criticism in English. It is an account of the growth of Coleridge's own mind, one in which he records his exposure of the empty regressions of the materialist philosophers who had dazzled him in his youth and his discovery of the German philosophic idealism that would allow him to reconcile reason and faith and affirm the will and dignity of humanity in a God-ordained universe. The literary critical corollary of this philosophical revelation and maturation in the *Biographia* is Coleridge's discovery and characterization of the poetry of William Wordsworth – the poet who, as friend and co-author with Coleridge of the *Lyrical Ballads* of 1798 and as the object and terrain of the *Biographia* as a critical quest romance – will remain associated with Coleridge throughout literary history.

It was Wordsworth's poetry, according to the *Biographia*, that inspired Coleridge to seek to isolate the distinguishing faculty of poetic genius – the imagination – a term that will remain no less associated with the name of Coleridge in the English-speaking world than will the name of Wordsworth:

To find no contradiction in the union of old and new; to contemplate the ANCIENT of days and all his works with feelings as fresh, as if all had then sprang forth at the first creative fiat; characterizes the mind that feels the riddle of the world, and may help to unravel it. To carry the feelings of childhood into the powers of manhood; to combine the child's sense of wonder and novelty with the appearances, which every day for perhaps forty years had rendered familiar;

> With sun and moon and stars throughout the year,
> And man and woman

this is the character and privilege of genius (*BL* I, 80–1)

Coleridge is credited with having made the imagination central to any adequate account of what it means to be human and the two volumes of the *Biographia* pivot on a definition of imagination which, however imperfectly understood, has been more often quoted and venerated and been more influential than any equivalent passage of English critical prose:

> The IMAGINATION then I consider either as primary, or secondary. The primary IMAGINATION I hold to be the living power and prime agent of all human perception, and as a repetition in the finite mind of the eternal act of creation in the infinite I AM. The secondary I consider as an echo of the former, coexisting with the conscious will, yet still as identical with the primary in the *kind* of its agency, and differing only in *degree*, and in the *mode* of its operation. It dissolves, diffuses, dissipates, in order to re-create; or where this process is rendered impossible, yet still at all events it struggles to idealize and to unify. It is essentially *vital*, even as all objects (*as* objects) are essentially fixed and dead. (*BL* I, 304)

An immethodical miscellany

For an influential autobiography by a pre-eminent philosopher-critic, however, Coleridge's *Biographia Literaria* is an uneven, indeed an unlikely text – as Howard Mumford Jones's indictment of its 'lack of formal structure' reminds us:

> Familiarity with famous passages in the *Biographia Literaria* (1817) probably leads readers to overlook its hodge-podge make-up. Besides the sections on the imagination and on Wordsworth as a poet, the book includes some letters written from Germany, an imaginary dialogue, a good deal about Coleridge's school years, 'remarks on the present mode of conducting critical journals', a set of Italian madrigals in that language, ten theses on a proposed 'Dynamic Philosophy', a lengthy footnote concerning someone whose venom Coleridge discusses on only 'hearsay evidence', an anonymous letter advising him to revise the *Biographia Literaria*, a defense of the church establishment, a discussion of landscape painting, an argument intended to show 'why the hand of Providence has disciplined all Europe into sobriety', and much else. Of course the subtitle is 'My Literary Life and Opinions', but *Tristram Shandy* is not more capricious and a story by Jean Paul Richter, Hoffmann, or Tieck can scarcely be more anarchical in structure.[1]

Jones's exasperated anatomization is a salutary reminder of the *Biographia*'s heterogeneous – or 'hodge-podge' – nature. 'The *Biographia Literaria* is the greatest book of criticism in English', wrote Arthur Symons in his introduction to an abridged edition of 1906, 'and one of the most annoying books in any language'.[2] Coleridge himself anticipated the exasperation of Jones and Symons in a characteristic attempt to disarm criticism by apologizing in the fourth chapter for foisting 'so immethodical a miscellany' upon the public (*BL* I, 88). Coming from the author of a projected treatise on method – a treatise that itself remains, characteristically, a suggestive 'preliminary'[3] – the phrase has an obvious, if ironic resonance and marks the *Biographia* as something of a cobbler's child.

Composed, or rather dictated, in the spring and summer of 1815, nearly two years before it was eventually published, the *Biographia* is the work of a 42-year-old writer in desperate circumstances and at a critical point in his career. It inherited the fragments of all of Coleridge's many, many unborn prose works, shored against his imminent ruin: 'the Reservoir of my Reflections & Reading for 25 years past' (*CL* V, 160). Ideas, images, and whole passages from his unpublished lectures, letters, marginalia, and notebooks – as well as passages, indeed continuous pages, plagiarized from the writings of others – found their way into what began as a brief autobiographical preface to a volume of his collected poems.

Over the course of that spring and summer, as Coleridge warmed to the task of talking about himself and Wordsworth to his willing amanuensis, John Morgan, the autobiographical preface soon expanded. By the end of July 1815, Coleridge had dictated all of the reflections on his own creative life – with its host of characters who conspire to discipline and naturalize his early poetry, up to and including the advent of Wordsworth – and all his reflections on Wordsworth's own poetry and on the document with which the two poets (to Coleridge's discomfort) had become identified in the periodical press: the Preface to *Lyrical Ballads* (1800).

> The necessity of extending, what I first intended as a preface, to an Autobiographia literaria, or Sketches of my literary Life & opinions, as far as Poetry and *poetical* Criticism is concerned, has confined me to my study from 11 to 4, and from 6 to 10, since I left you.—I have just finished it, having only the correction of the Mss. to go thro'.—I have given a full account (raisonnée) of the Controversy concerning Wordsworth's Poems & Theory, in which my name has been so constantly included. (*CL* IV, 578–9)

It was at this point that Coleridge, having completed his literary reminiscences and his revisionary criticism of Wordsworth, decided to extend his 'literary life and opinions' to include a history of his own philosophical development and a statement of his metaphysical convictions (chapters 5–13), convinced that 'the application of rules, deduced from philosophic principles, to poetry and criticism' required no less (*BL* I, 5). These chapters, filled out with material plagiarized from a number of German philosophers and philosophical historians unavailable in English at the time, are the ones that, along with material traced to August Wilhelm Schlegel in his literary lectures after 1811, offer a standing threat to Coleridge's reputation as a philosophical critic.

As it turned out, Coleridge himself was obliged to abandon them, interrupting a long and abstruse dissertation on the postulates of philosophical Idealism that he had borrowed from Friedrich Schelling (chapters 12–13) with a letter claiming to be from an interested friend and warning him of the likelihood that his discussion would annoy 'the great majority of your readers' (*BL* I, 301). It was Coleridge himself, in fact, not any pretended friend, who had written the letter. The whole charade of offering to relieve the reader of a hundred pages of dense philosophizing while at the same time leaving the incomplete argument standing as a taste of what might have been said – and, more to the point, of *how* it might have been said – is a typical piece of late-Coleridgean desperation and cunning. Instead of following through with a philosophic exposition in which he could not quite believe, in other words, Coleridge chose comically and quixotically to abbreviate it midthought, while retaining the fragment in order to preserve its intellectual authority and rhetorical force. It is one indication among many that the fragmented and apparently disparate forms and discourses in the *Biographia* need to be read ironically, as variations on a larger personal and cultural theme. For this is exactly what the *Biographia* amounts to. What had begun as a preface to a collection of poems became 20-odd chapters – some of them very odd indeed – of tendentious critical and cultural commentary, underwritten by a selection of self-consciously impenetrable philosophy.

As unlikely as it seems, moreover, this 'immethodical … miscellany' salvaged out of much grander ambitions and many years of 'Thinking, Planning, and Resolving to resolve' (*CL* IV, 611) has proved one of the most influential, if controversial documents of British Romanticism and made the poet-critic Samuel Taylor Coleridge synonymous with the dream and discipline of English Literature.

An immethodical life

One explanation for the apparent derangement of the *Biographia* has always been, appropriately, biographical. The two years leading up to its composition had been the worst years in a life that in truth had known only a few brief periods of unalloyed happiness and sustained productivity. Only a year and a half before its composition, Coleridge could be found holed up in an attic bedroom in the Grey Hound Inn on the outskirts of Bath, overdosed on opium and in a fever of self-recrimination for recent offences in what seemed to him a long life of shameful dereliction and dependency. Coleridge had recently secured a cottage for himself, Mary Morgan, and her sister, Charlotte Brent, in the tiny village of Ashley, near Box, intending to return to the cottage on weekends after delivering lectures in Bristol. The Morgans, Mary and her husband John, had offered Coleridge a home on and off since his separation from his wife, Sara, and their three children in 1807 and his subsequent rupture with the Wordsworth household in 1810. Throughout his life, Coleridge, ever the orphan (even while his own family were alive and well) would live as a more often than not honoured and welcome guest with families not his own, until finally settling for the last eighteen years of his life in the household of Dr James Gillman of Highgate, just outside London.

Coleridge and the Morgans had recently survived the privation and ignominy of Morgan's bankruptcy, during which Morgan had had to flee to Ireland and Coleridge had taken upon himself the support of the embattled household with a resolution that was heroic in one so emotionally dependent and so heavily addicted to opium as he had become since the turn of the century. The Coleridge who at the time could not rally in support of his own children, refusing to acknowledge their needs and to answer, even to open their letters, had been able to find the time and energy to lecture and borrow on behalf of the destitute Morgans. Indeed, in spite of his losing half the annuity of £150 granted him in 1798 by the Wedgwood family (of pottery fame) late in the previous year, 1813 had witnessed something of a resurgence in Coleridge's literary reputation, starting with the resounding success of his play *Remorse* at Drury Lane Theatre in January and culminating in a successful lecture series in Bristol in October and November, with some energetic borrowing in the West country on behalf of the Morgan household.

Having settled Mary and Charlotte at Ashley in early December, however, and for reasons about which we can only conjecture, Coleridge did a King Lear, histrionically abandoning the cottage and his surrogate daughters one foul night on 5 December 1813 to make his way through a storm to Bath – 'very unwell with a violent cold', he wrote to a friend, Josiah Wade, 'I was obliged to walk to Bath thro' *such* a Road, Slip or Slop, Mud or Mire, the whole way' (*CL* III, 462) – before finally collapsing at the Grey Hound. He was hallucinating from fever and persistent overdosing on brandy and opium, a condition which would almost certainly have been compounded by the usual crippling side-effects of constipation and abdominal cramps that tormented him all his adult life. He lay prostrate, incoherent, violently depressed, and threatening suicide: 'sunk', according to his biographer Richard Holmes, 'in one of the loneliest and most desperate periods of his entire existence'.[4]

It was, as Holmes says, one of his loneliest and most desperate periods, but it was only one among many. In the most intriguing and perceptive pen portrait of Coleridge to have come down to us from his contemporaries, William Hazlitt recalled the young 25-year-old Coleridge visiting a Unitarian church at Shrewsbury in January 1798 to offer a sermon that amounted to a trial of his talent and commitment as a preacher:

> When I got there, the organ was playing the 100th psalm, and, when it was done, Mr Coleridge rose and gave out his text, 'And he went up into the mountain to pray, HIMSELF, ALONE'. As he gave out this text, his voice 'rose like a steam of rich distilled perfumes', and when he came to the two last words, which he pronounced loud, deep, and distinct, it seemed to me, who was then young, as if the sounds had echoed from the bottom of the human heart, and as if that prayer might have floated in solemn silence through the universe.[5]

The solemn and forbidding silence of a radically incommunicative universe, through which Hazlitt imagines Coleridge's lonely prayer floating unanswered, recognizes in the poet an isolation that, while arguably profoundly representative, was also acutely personal. At the same time as Coleridge reached out of his solitude in the church at Shrewsbury that day he was writing in *The Rime of the Ancient Mariner* what is surely the greatest poetic allegory of alienation and existential isolation in our language. Indeed, with its awed vowels and eerie sibilants, Hazlitt's language knowingly alludes to the 'silent sea' of Coleridge's masterpiece, the site of the Mariner's 'supernatural, or at least romantic' estrangement (*BL* II, 6):

> Alone, alone, all, all, alone,
> Alone on a wide wide sea!
> And never a saint took pity on
> My soul in agony.
> (*The Rime of the Ancient Mariner*,
> ll. 232–5)

Coleridge was haunted by a sense of his own isolation, returning to it frequently in notebook jottings and random marginalia made throughout his life:

> I stand alone, nor tho' my Heart should break
> Have I, to whom I may complain or speak.
> ('Lines Inscribed in Benedetto Menzini',
> ll. 1–2)

It lay behind the despair and dread that drove (and threatened) his mental activity, behind his self-destructive search for love and friendship, behind his addiction to opium, and behind his yearning for a religion and a poetry able to reconcile 'the heart with the head' and bring the 'whole soul of man into activity' (*BL* I, 25; II, 15–16). Isolation for Coleridge was a condition of the *psyche* – the mind and soul – a condition to be overcome. Again and again, one traces in his poems a wish-fulfilling movement from isolation to community and redemption, effected most often by an unselfconscious act of love that is also, at the same time, an act of *imagination* in the exalted sense that we have inherited from Coleridge himself:

> O Lady! we receive but what we give,
> And in our life alone does nature live:
> Ours is her wedding garment, ours her shroud!
>   And would we aught behold, of higher worth,
> Than that inanimate cold world allow'd
> To the poor loveless ever-anxious crowd,
>   Ah! from the soul must issue forth,
> A light, a glory, a fair luminous cloud
>   Enveloping the Earth—
> And from the soul itself must there be sent
>   A sweet and potent voice, of its own birth,
> Of all sweet sounds the life and element!
>   ('Dejection: An Ode', ll. 47–58)

It was at Greta Hall near Keswick in the Lake District, where he wrote his 'Dejection: An Ode', that Coleridge had finally succumbed to the self-exacerbating habit of 'opium eating', as it was called. What that meant for Coleridge was swallowing larger and larger doses of laudanum, a standard, over-the-counter liquid analgesic in which opium was dissolved in alcohol for easy consumption and to potentiate the narcotic. The promise of his early career was over and he was finding it far easier to dream of grand literary projects than to write them. 'This Lime-Tree Bower My Prison', 'Frost at Midnight', 'Kubla Khan', and *The Rime of the Ancient Mariner* – all written during an *annus mirabilis* from 1797 to 1798 that had been crowned by the publication with Wordsworth of the *Lyrical Ballads* – stood as testament to his extraordinary poetic powers. These are poems of great worth that no one has ever tried to take away from Coleridge. In spite of a second surge of creative activity in 1800, however, *Christabel* was – and would remain – unfinished. So, too, would the *Life of Lessing* he had promised the Wedgwoods, for which he had travelled and settled temporarily in Germany in 1799–1800. So, too, would his 'Imitations from the Modern Latin Poets', the history of the German peasantry, the account of Pantisocracy, strictures on the philosophy of William Godwin, *The Brook*, epic poems on the origin of evil and on 'Mahomet', the 'Bibliotheca Britannica' (a history of English literature, including writings in Welsh, Saxon, and Erse), a translation of Goethe's *Faust*, and scores and scores of other exciting prospects announced in letters and notebooks until we come to his final, unfinished opus maximum: the *Logosophia*. Some, like the *Life of Lessing*, could and should have been written; some were inspired fragments that were never likely to progress beyond fragments;[6] most were exhausted by their annunciation.

From 1801, Coleridge became progressively less able to face, let alone to meet, the demands of the literary life he had set in train for himself, and for which he had accepted patronage. Oscillating in the opening years of the century between dreams of poetry and ambitious literary projects in the Lake District and the hand-to-mouth existence of the journalist in London, he soon sank into a prolonged illness and depression from which a journey to Malta and Sicily from 1804 to 1806 failed to rescue him. Back in England, his health broken, in deeper bondage to opium and out of love with his wife – all the while harbouring desperate but unmanageable feelings for the sister of Wordsworth's wife Mary, Sarah Hutchinson – Coleridge began on the unsettled existence of his drugged and guilt-driven middle years, making what money he could to supplement the Wedgwood legacy by occasional lecturing and journalism and periodically spiralling into the paralysis of addiction and depression.

Coleridge, then, was no stranger to suffering and despair. Still, the two weeks spent in the Grey Hound in Bath in December 1813 under the salutary superintendence of a Dr Charles Parry – 'who was called in by accident (for I was too wild with suffering to direct any thing myself)' (*CL* III, 464) – were probably the worst of his existence. Arguably, these crucial weeks can also be seen to represent the beginning of a turn around. They initiate a spate of self-flagellating essays in confession and renunciation in which Coleridge faces his own predicament for the first time and shares it with a few, select friends. A resolve grows within him to put himself in the hands of a sympathetic medical practitioner like Parry, who did indeed become the first of a series which culminated in the kindly and intelligent Gillman with whom Coleridge spent the remainder of his life. Within weeks of his breakdown, Coleridge found himself installed in the large guest room of Josiah Wade, one of his oldest friends from the days of his triumph as a political lecturer and controversial essayist in Bristol in the mid-1790s. With Wade's physician Dr Daniel in attendance, a manservant to restrain him from opium and self-harm, and all the sharp instruments removed from the room, Coleridge began an agonizing regime of self-restraint and self-abasement over the early months of 1814, from which he would emerge after numerous relapses in April. It is the one period of his life from which no letters of his have survived. 'I had been crucified, dead, and buried, descended into Hell', he wrote from Wade's to the Morgans in Ashley Cottage in May, 'and am now, I humbly trust, rising again, tho' slowly and gradually':

> By the long long Habit of the accursed Poison my Volition ... was compleatly deranged, at times frenzied ... so that I was perpetually in a state, in which you may have seen paralytic Persons, who attempting to push a

step forward in one direction are violently forced round to the opposite. ... The worst was, that in *exact proportion* to the *importance* and *urgency* of any Duty was it, as of a fatal necessity, sure to be neglected. ... In exact proportion, as I *loved* any person or persons more than others, & would have sacrificed my Life for them, were *they* sure to be the most barbarously mistreated by silence, absence, or breach of promise. ... What crime is there scarcely which has not been included in or followed from the one guilt of taking opium? Not to speak of ingratitude to my maker for the wasted Talents; of ingratitude to so many friends who have loved me I know not why; of barbarous neglect of my family; excess of cruelty to Mary & Charlotte, when at Box, and both ill—(a vision of Hell to me when I think of it!) I have in this one dirty business of Laudanum an hundred times deceived, tricked, nay, actually & consciously LIED.— And yet *all* these vices are so opposite to my nature, that but for this *free-agency-annihilating* Poison, I verily believe that I should have suffered myself to have been cut to pieces rather than have committed any one of them. (*CL* III, 489–90)

Coleridge would never entirely shake himself free from opium, as it turned out, but he would learn to keep its control of him under control. And the new and deeper spirituality that grew out of this period of intense suffering would instigate and inform the prose works of his later years, his 'lay sermons' on the need for the careful balance and integration of religion, culture, and politics to resist the rampant commercialism and materialism of a modern mass culture. Coleridge, in his old age the sage of Highgate Hill, would talk wisdom on the other side of personal dissolution and despair.

Composing a life

Before all this eventuated, however, and his celebrity in life and reputation after death could be affirmed, a textual and intellectual economizing had to take place, one inspired by Coleridge's urgent need for psychic economy and (to quote J. H. Haeger) 'personal authentication'.[7] This is where the *Biographia Literaria* came in. In 1815, at Calne in Wiltshire and back again with the Morgans, Coleridge not only wrote his life, he also wrote *for* his life – or, more accurately, *talked* for his life. After the many dark nights of his adult existence, he finally began the autobiographical essay that he had projected in a notebook entry as early as 1803.[8] In a literary life that appeared to him, to his friends and patrons, and to the literary world at large, to be deranged and disintegrated, Coleridge was determined to discover or recover the 'unity' of intrinsic form and purpose that from a very young age he had sought in the universe. In the *Biographia Literaria*, his 'Literary Life', Coleridge sought to compose himself: to compose an idealized image of himself, that is, and at the same time, more simply, to regain composure.

Indeed, Coleridge's famous definition of the secondary Imagination in the thirteenth chapter quoted earlier can be applied to the *Biographia* itself as an essay in therapeutic and existential self-composition. 'Dissolved', 'diffused', and 'dissipated' over the early years of the nineteenth century by the failure of his career and of his marriage and by physical and mental illness and their exacerbating 'anodyne' in opium – desperate 'to salvage something from a spendthrift career of erratic brilliance, humiliating dependency, and steady marginalization', to quote Jerome Christensen[9] – Coleridge in the *Biographia* strove to recreate himself in his own ideal image from the biographical, as well as textual and intellectual, *disjecta membra* of those lost years. And 'Where this process is rendered impossible', still he 'struggles to idealize and to unify' (*BL* I, 304).

In this, as in so many things, the *Biographia* is Coleridge's prose counterpart to Wordsworth's famous autobiographical epic, *The Prelude*, 'a long poem upon the formation of my own mind':[10]

> I had hopes
> ... that with a frame of outward life
> I might endue, might fix in a visible home,
> Some portion of those phantoms of conceit,
> That had been floating loose about so long,
> And to such beings temperately deal forth
> The many feelings that oppressed my heart.
> (*The Prelude* [1805], I, 127–33)

Both *The Prelude* and the *Biographia* are elaborate, biographical introductions – *The Prelude* to Wordsworth's 'moral and Philosophical Poem' on 'Nature, Man, Society', *The Recluse*;[11] the *Biographia* to an equally ambitious work called 'the *Logosophia*' or 'PRODUCTIVE LOGOS human and divine' (*BL* I, 263, 136) in which Coleridge would prove Christianity to be the key to all philosophy. Both *The Prelude* and the *Biographia* are attempts to justify the ways of genius and imagination to man, and throughout both can be heard the question that opens and drives the earliest version of *The Prelude*: 'Was it for this?'[12] Where in *The Prelude* Wordsworth recreates his discovery, first, of nature, and then of his own imaginative powers, Coleridge in the *Biographia* recreates *his* discovery of *Wordsworth's* mental powers[13] – along with his discovery of a philosophy and a philosophical language able to discriminate and characterize mental powers themselves.

Typically, however, in recording his own intellectual and imaginative formation, Coleridge appears to have experienced what Michael Cooke has called 'a breakdown in the process of self-construction',[14] leaving to posterity yet another Coleridgean fragment, or tissue of fragments. The result, as Howard Mumford Jones points out, is a formal mess: a text that is autobiographical, metaphysical, and critical by turns, with a promiscuous variety of footnotes and digressions; pleas, prayers, and plagiarisms; self-defensive threats and self-addressed envelopes. Since its publication in 1817, the *Biographia*'s editors have often responded to the book's miscellaneousness either by offering more or less extensively abbreviated versions of the text as it was originally published or by endeavouring to fix an otherwise unstable text with extensive biographical and scholarly annotation. George Sampson, for example, showed no compunction about offering his edition of chapters 1–4 and 14–22 in a popular abbreviation of 1920:

> Coleridge's *Biographia Literaria* is a work of which a part is greater than the whole. It is fragmentary and discontinuous—a series of beginnings, with a conclusion that fits none of them. The separate presentation of its better portions is therefore an act of kindness to many readers, and especially to students, who (being young) dutifully endeavour to read the whole book, and find themselves dismayed, if not defeated, by the mass of imported metaphysic that Coleridge proudly lumped into the middle.[15]

As life writing, moreover, the *Biographia* has always been a frustrating document, a more than usually unstable mixture of autobiographical recovery and autobiographical cover-up. Few of its details and interpretations are trustworthy. James Boyer, for example, the head of Christ's Hospital and Coleridge's teacher in his final years before going up to Cambridge, was simply not like that, either in himself or as he appeared to Coleridge as a schoolboy and an adult. It was not that Coleridge had forgotten Boyer's wilful insensitivity and obtuseness or the nightmares that Boyer's vicious regime of corporal punishment had occasioned. But Boyer had an argumentative function to perform in Coleridge's revisionary account of his own early years and that function was not allowed to be complicated by the facts.

Again, notoriously, Coleridge the young radical of the 1790s largely disappears from the record. We will see that in the turbulent decade following the revolution in France in 1789, as political opinion in Britain swayed with and against French fortunes before war between the two countries was declared in 1793 and in Britain a political reaction set in, Coleridge was a prominent force in the culture of religious and radical dissent, communicating and mixing on equal terms with leading public intellectuals like William Godwin and John Thelwall. First as a university student and then as a freelance lecturer and writer, the poet whose name is now not unjustly associated with imaginative and narcotic withdrawal and introversion was at least momentarily at the centre of a more socially various political stage than any Britain had previously known, a product of the economic changes and reformist agitation of the late eighteenth century. For journalists of all persuasions and certainly for the reactionary cartoonists of the thriving pamphlet and periodical culture of the 1790s, Coleridge was a radical firebrand. For the *Biographia*, on the other hand, he was throughout these years a sane

voice in an insane world – when he was not a poet engaged in genteel dialogue with commonsensical, paternalistic teachers and sympathetic reviewers
(*BL* I, 187).

Even the revelation Coleridge claims to have experienced on his introduction to Wordsworth as the greatest poet of the age – perhaps as accurate a
biographical record as any in the *Biographia* – even this is modified in retro-
spect in line with the critical quest romance identified earlier, with imagination as the Holy Grail. (So, too, the shifts in the author's philosophical
allegiances had to be reconfigured.)

Literary life in 1815

Yet in spite of the *Biographia's* heterogeneity and in spite of its sometimes
cunning censorship, the materials for a literary life are all there, if only (as
the word 'sketches' in the subtitle suggests) in cartoon form. There is, after
all, a good deal in the *Biographia* that engages directly as well as indirectly
(anecdotally) with the cultural and material conditions of the writer in early
nineteenth-century Britain. (Chapters 10 and 11 on his own publishing experience and the often-overlooked 21st chapter on contemporary reviewing are
only the most obvious examples.) A new literary life of Coleridge must not
only revise some of the *Biographia's* priorities – in spite of its author, so to
speak – it must also restore other priorities on its author's behalf.

1815 was the year of Coleridge's cathartic self-composition: the composition of his literary life out of fragments and, with that, the effective consoli-
dation of his career as a public intellectual, especially as a cultural
commentator, later to become the venerable sage of Highgate Hill. (Within
eight months of his completing the *Biographia*, he had moved in with James
Gillman.) 1815 was also the year that began the equally painful and equally
necessary reconstruction of Britain after the Battle of Waterloo, with its con-
comitant political and class conflict. Issues of social, legal, religious, and
electoral reform – all effectively occluded by the Tories in the name of the
war with France – now resurfaced. The first of Coleridge's attempts at periodical publishing he had entitled *The Watchman*, and in the more circum-
spect and conservative *Biographia* we find him watching still and reflecting
upon his own period in ways that are not always obvious.

I see the task of Coleridge's literary biographer as one of interpreting and
revising Coleridge's tendentious 'self-composition' over the summer of 1815,
of critically rereading his life *through* his famous literary autobiography as a
complex, often anxious response, not just to the suffering and isolation of a
dysfunctional adult life, but also to the suffering and fragmentation of a dysfunctional nation. Having said that, at the risk of stating the obvious I should
also say that Coleridge as an individual and writer can never be reduced to
the culture and politics of any one or more of the periods in, or on which, he
wrote – or to the culture and politics of any one or more of the interest

groups with which he was associated during his lifetime, whether the Dissenting radicals or the Tories (conservatives). For one thing, Coleridge's politics were never that straightforward. As Coleridge himself protested, more and less ingenuously, his politics were more idiosyncratic than was ever allowed either by his anti-Jacobin (reactionary) critics in the mid-1790s or by his liberal and radical critics when, later in life, and especially after the *Biographia*, he was hailed as an apostate among many apostates.

Keeping faith with Coleridge, however, requires more than just deferring to the complexity or inconsistency of his political opinions at any one time. A literary life of Coleridge must strike a balance between, on the one hand, the private, withdrawn world of acute apprehension and compulsive specu-lation, crowded sometimes to suffocation with images and ideas – this is the world recreated in his 70-odd notebooks, published in a massive edition by Kathleen Coburn over the last half of the twentieth century – and, on the other hand, the public world of the political journalist and controversialist who played a fitful but influential part in what was an aggressive and often conflicted political and print culture. His poetry inhabits both worlds, some-times separately, sometimes simultaneously, sometimes alternately, and very often uneasily – like Coleridge the pedestrian, veering unsteadily from one side of the footpath to the other.[16] If to his credit it meant that he didn't get stuck in a rut, it was and still is often hard to know where to have him. When his poetry worked for him, however, as it did for a brief period in the late 1790s, he created miracles of rare device. It is for this handful of astonishing poems that Coleridge will and should be remembered, and for a literary criticism of rare insight and compelling beauty that apes and inspires the creative apprehension it describes and exalts.

1
'The Discipline of His Taste at School': Christ's Hospital and Cambridge

A literary life begins with a literary education. In the *Biographia*, Coleridge is content to reach no further back than the classroom in the Classical Sixth Form at Christ's Hospital School, where an eccentric James Boyer, headmaster and head teacher, channelled his aggression into enforcing principles of 'GOOD SENSE' as the foundation of all writing, principles which the literary autobiographer identifies, belatedly, as fundamental to his own creativity and career.

> In our own English compositions (at least for the last three years of our school education) he showed no mercy to phrase, metaphor, or image, unsupported by sound sense, or where the same sense might have been conveyed with equal force and dignity in plainer words. Lute, harp, and lyre, muse, muses, and inspirations, Pegasus, Parnassus, and Hippocrene, were all an abomination to him. In fancy I can almost hear him now, exclaiming *'Harp? Harp? Lyre? Pen and ink, boy, you mean! Muse, boy, muse? your nurse's daughter, you mean! Pierian spring? Oh 'aye! the cloister pump, I suppose!'* (*BL* I, 9–10)

The account of Boyer's classroom activities that Coleridge offers in the *Biographia* suggests genuine intellectual obligations. Beyond these, however, Boyer has certain argumentative and ideological functions to perform. For example, Boyer's Johnsonian impatience with the ingenuities and mannerisms of fashionable poetry – in short, with cliché – becomes the point of departure for Coleridge's own literary pilgrimage. And though the pilgrim will lapse painfully – 'My judgement was stronger, than were my powers of realizing its dictates' (*BL* I, 8) – the lessons of the master are seen to constitute a stabilizing force in the evolution of Coleridge as both poet and critic.

Coleridge the man will grow beyond James Boyer and Christ's Hospital, however, as Coleridge the poet and critic will grow beyond the eighteenth-century tradition of 'good sense' that his old schoolmaster represents. In the hierarchy of mental faculties that Coleridge seeks to promote – each faculty a spiritual refinement of the last – good sense is seen as primary and vitally necessary, but hardly sufficient:

GOOD SENSE is the BODY of poetic genius, FANCY its DRAPERY, MOTION its LIFE, and IMAGINATION the SOUL that is everywhere, and in each; and forms all into one graceful and intelligent whole. (*BL* II, 18)

There is, moreover, an important sense in which, even before he arrived at the school, Coleridge had already grown beyond Boyer and Christ's Hospital, beyond the educational institutions available to him in the late eighteenth century. In an account of Coleridge's life this incommensurability is a defining characteristic, both of the education on offer at that time and, more importantly, of the boy himself.

Wunderkind

By his own and everyone else's account, Coleridge was a child prodigy:

I was fretful, and inordinately passionate, and as I could not play at anything, and was slothful, I was despised & hated by the boys; and because I could read & spell, & had, I may truly say, a memory & understanding forced into an almost unnatural ripeness, I was flattered & wondered at by all the old women—& so I became very vain, and despised most of the boys, that were all near my own age—and before I was eight years old, I was a *character*—sensibility, imagination, vanity, sloth, & feelings of deep and bitter contempt for almost all who traversed the orbit of my understanding, were even then prominent & manifest. (*CL* I, 347–8)

The fourteenth and last child of Rev. John Coleridge, the 53-year-old Anglican minister of the town of Ottery St Mary in rural Devonshire, and the tenth and youngest of John Coleridge's second wife Ann, née Bowden, Coleridge was clever and, if not charming exactly, certainly engaging and captivating. Having acquired reading and writing skills very early, as young as the age of three, he was 'wonderful' in the strict sense – a wonder. 'I was flattered & *wondered at* by all the old women'. The word would be used of him again and again as a child *and* as a man, a characterization finally sealed by an elegiac note of Wordsworth's on the occasion of Coleridge's death: 'Many men have done wonderful things – Newton, Davy &c., but S.T.C. is the only wonderful man I ever knew'. And the child wonder was petted for it – by his father, especially, and by the other villagers of every estate, high and low.

Coleridge's parents

Coleridge remembered his father as a naive, benevolent, and eccentric character, likening him 'in learning, good-heartedness, absentness of mind, & excessive ignorance of the world' to Parson Adams in Henry Fielding's novel *Joseph Andrews* (*CL* I, 310). Parson Adams is a rural clergyman touting his unreadable sermons with him about the countryside in search of a publisher and betrayed into one scrape after another by his own well-meaning and generous ineptitude. He is one of the more distinguished and enduring children of Don Quixote peopling eighteenth-century literature and life, and some of the anecdotes that survive about the Rev. John Coleridge might have come straight out of the pages of a Fielding novel. On one occasion, for example, sitting around the dinner table, John Coleridge is said to have stuffed the apron of his bishop's daughter down his trousers, mistaking it for his own, untucked shirt.[1]

Unlike Parson Adams, however, John Coleridge had managed to see a handful of his works into print. The schoolmaster in him – he was the headmaster of the local, King Henry VIII Grammar School (the King's School) – published a textbook (1758) and a Latin grammar book (1772); the preacher, a selection of sermons; the domestic theologian, a *Dissertation on the Book of Judges* (1768). For the university educated, as all parish priests had to be, publication of this kind was hardly remarkable. The only thing remarkable about this list, perhaps, is the absence of a volume of poems, for poetry, too, was the burden of the educated class, no less than it is today. John Coleridge published by subscription, a form of publishing common in the eighteenth century, especially in the provinces, in which members of the community to whom the author was known or recommended put up the money for a publication, to have their names immortalized in the opening pages if they chose. During a century in which professional writers frequently bewailed the passing of patronage and their dependence on the marketplace – as Coleridge would do – patronage was in fact alive and well, having survived in the collective form of subscription publishing, often the first recourse of the aspiring amateur with a manuscript volume of sermons under his arm. (Another way of publishing was to pay for it yourself and publish 'on commission', as John Coleridge did with his *Fast Sermon* on the outbreak of the American War of Independence.[2]) Once the list was filled and as long as the subscribers were as good as their word, subscription left publisher and author alike without risks.[3]

Coleridge, too, would seek subscribers to defray the cost of his two ventures in periodical publishing, *The Watchman* (1796) and *The Friend* (1809–10), but periodical publications unfortunately required the interest of the subscribers and the readership to continue over an indefinite period, certainly beyond the concerted effort of the first issue. While like the vast majority of people who publish, then and now, Rev. John Coleridge made no money from his writing, his son managed to lose money. And Coleridge, as he reminds his readers in chapter 11 of the *Biographia*, no doubt with his own father in mind, had no church living to fall back on.

Later in life, Coleridge would take on much of what he remembered as his father's benign eccentricity and use it in his own writing against a perverse, unpredictable, and calculating world (as does Fielding with his Parson Adams). Looked at from another point of view, however, John Coleridge's career was an astonishing success story. The son of a bankrupt weaver, he had left home at fifteen to become, first, an usher (assistant), then a teacher at the local school. Though married with four daughters, he went up to Cambridge at the age of 28, becoming what we would call a 'mature age' scholar. And a very good scholar, too, good enough for a fellowship had he not been married and thus disqualified, good enough to receive as a living the parish of Ottery St Mary with its fine church and grammar school, and good enough to go on to publish a respectable collection of works testifying to his professional commitments. 'The truth is', wrote Coleridge, 'my Father was not a first-rate Genius' (*CL* I, 310) – implying that here the analogy between himself and his father must end. To aspire to education and office, however, and to gain promotion and preferment as he did, John Coleridge must have applied himself with determination and industry and focus – more determination, industry, and focus, certainly, than Coleridge could find when he went up to Cambridge 44 years after his father.

The loveable eccentricity dear to his son's heart was perhaps a product of declining age and the relaxation that attends upon it, but perhaps it was also a product of the contrast Coleridge found between his father and his mother. There is no doubt that Coleridge's having lost his father at age nine, and the dramatic changes this effected in his young life, influenced his feelings towards his father, 'ensuring that his son's memory of him would remain rose-tinted', to quote Rosemary Ashton.[4] John Coleridge died suddenly and unexpectedly in 1781 on his return from placing Coleridge's brother Frank as a midshipman in the Royal Navy in Plymouth. Coleridge's mother had the misfortune to survive her husband.

Already ambitious for her many sons (Coleridge had only one full sister and had little to do with his half-sisters), Ann Coleridge must have felt an acute sense of responsibility for securing her youngest child's future after John Coleridge's death. Even before his death, she seems to have expressed her affection in practical, rather than openly in tactile or verbal ways. Only one letter written to his mother from school in London survives. In the letter, the 12-year-old Coleridge is prolific in disseminating his compliments amongst his neighbours and his 'kind love' and 'kindest love' amongst family members and servants, while in painful contrast signing himself with exaggerated restraint 'your dutiful son' (*CL* I, 1). Indeed, after Coleridge's transfer to boarding school in London just before his tenth birthday, his mother seems to have had little to do with him. There is no evidence of her having gone up to London to visit him throughout the entire length of his schooldays, nor that he returned to her in Ottery St Mary more than two or three times. Nor is there any evidence that she was anxious for his return. Before he even began at Christ's Hospital, Coleridge was dispatched to her brother's in London for ten weeks.

In truth, beyond commending her energy in 'aggrandizing' her large and impoverished family, none of Coleridge's biographers has much to say in Ann Coleridge's favour, least of all Coleridge himself. (His father 'had so little parental ambition' that he would have been happy had his children been blacksmiths, according to Coleridge, 'but for my Mother's pride & spirit of aggrandizing her family' [*CL* I, 354].) The very lack of evidence and the paucity of references to her in his correspondence appears to have condemned her.

On the other hand, Coleridge did say that as a very young child he was his mother's darling (and that this exposed him to the rivalry of his brother Frank and Frank's nurse). On one occasion that seems hard to read too much into, the seven-year-old Coleridge stayed out all night after a fight with his brother Frank, which ended with Coleridge's running at his brother with a knife and being intercepted by his mother. In fear of a 'flogging' and 'thinking *at the same time* with inward & gloomy satisfaction, how miserable my Mother must be!', Coleridge stayed out all night, while the village was mobilized in search of him. The adult Coleridge, for whom the state of his own body and mind was a source of endless fascination, blamed many of his chronic illnesses on his exposure that night but the child Coleridge got exactly what he wanted: 'My mother, as you may suppose, was outrageous with joy' (*CL* I, 352–4).

All this comes from a series of autobiographical letters written at Nether Stowey in 1797 to his friend and neighbour Thomas (Tom) Poole at Poole's behest (from which most of our information about Coleridge's attitude to his family derives). Elsewhere in the same series, however, after having talked at length about his father, Coleridge has only this to say: 'My Mother was an admirable Economist, and managed exclusively' (*CL* I, 310).

Helluo Librorum

Ann Coleridge may have been an unaffectionate mother but it is doubtful that any amount of affection could have satisfied the hunger of her youngest son, whose appetite for food, for books, for love, and for *admiration* was insatiable. (Adulthood would add only opium to the list.) These needs were entrenched well before his father died, the need for admiration increasing with all the admiration so freely conferred upon him. Coleridge was, as I have said, a precocious reader. 'I took no pleasure in boyish sports but read incessantly', he writes to Poole:

> My Father's Sister kept an *every-thing* shop at Crediton—and there I read thro' all the gilt-cover little books that could be had at that time, & likewise all the uncovered tales of Tom Hickathrift, Jack the Giant-killer, &c &c &c &c &c—/— ... At six years old I remember to have read Belisarius, Robinson Crusoe, & Philip Quarle—and then I found the Arabian Nights' entertainments ... and I distinctly remember the anxious & fearful eagerness, with which I used to watch the window, in which the books lay— and whenever the Sun lay upon them, I would seize it, carry it by the wall, & bask, & read. (*CL* I, 354)

So, later, as a London schoolchild, after a misunderstanding in which 'his hand came in contact with a gentleman's pocket' – in the story as he gave it to James Gillman, Coleridge claimed to be imitating Leander swimming the Hellespont – the same 'gentleman' indulged Coleridge's appetite as a '*helluo librorum*' ('devourer of books') by making him 'free of a circulating library in King Street, Cheapside'. 'I read *through* the catalogue', Coleridge told Gillman, 'folios and all, whether I understood them, or did not understand them, running all risks in skulking out to get the two volumes which I was entitled to have daily'.[5]

The two things that strike us most about his youthful reading are its voracity and its escapism: 'My whole being was, with eyes closed to every object of present sense, to crumple myself up in a sunny corner, and read, read, read'.[6] A child as sickly and fretful as Coleridge is driven by more than just intellectual and imaginative curiosity, he 'takes refuge in early & immoderate reading' (as Coleridge later told William Godwin).[7] Like all Romantic questing, Coleridge's youthful voyage through 'strange seas of Thought, alone' was a profoundly ambiguous one in which strategies to avoid some unacceptable or unbearable reality can just as easily be identified as concentration and curiosity.[8] It would remain that way all his life, not just with his reading but also with his thinking. The 'philosophizing' in which he was wont to take such defensive pride, he was on other occasions as likely to dismiss as a form of indulgence and escape: 'At a very premature age, even before my fifteenth year, I had bewildered myself in metaphysicks, and theological controversy' (*BL* I, 15).

It was not Coleridge's reading that struck his contemporaries as prodigious, however. Before anything else, Coleridge was from infancy a talented and intellectually precocious *talker* (the significance and irony of which become clear when we recall that the original meaning of the word 'infant' is 'speechless'). William Hazlitt records meeting Coleridge – 'the only person I ever knew who answered to the idea of a man of genius' – at the height of his powers in 1798:

> He was the first poet I ever knew. His genius at that time had angelic wings, and fed on manna. He talked on for ever; and you wished him to talk on for ever. His thoughts did not seem to come with labour and effort; but as if bourne on the gusts of genius, and as if the wings of his imagination lifted him from off his feet. His voice rolled on the ear like the pealing organ, and its sound alone was the music of thought.[9]

This truly wonderful facility in what Coleridge himself called '*Oneversazioni*' – as distinct from *conversazioni* or 'conversations' – reflects the paradoxical relationship Coleridge would maintain throughout his life with society, private and public (*CL* VI, 790). The ten-year-old Coleridge's success in captivating the mixed audiences of his London Uncle Bowden's neighbourhood just before going up to Christ's Hospital is, like so many of Coleridge's childhood reminiscences, both engaging and disturbing:

> He received me with great affection, and I stayed ten weeks at his house, during which time I went occasionally to Judge Buller's. My Uncle was very proud of me, & used to carry me from Coffee-house to Coffee-house, and Tavern to Tavern, where I drank, & talked & disputed as if I had been a man—/. Nothing was more common than for a large party to exclaim in my hearing, that I *was a prodigy*, &c &c &c—so that, while I remained at my Uncle's, I was most completely spoilt & pampered, both mind & body. (*CL* I, 388)

The need, beyond everything else, to engage an audience and enforce a recognition of his undoubted genius accounted at once for his compulsive social inclinations and at the same time for his ultimate and inevitable isolation. It is this need for social recognition that arguably kept Coleridge sane and alive when, deeply addicted and imaginatively withdrawn, he did not take his own life but instead reached out for help. Coleridge, all his life alone, needed people desperately – needed their approval and their confirmation of his genius, of his very existence.

The Anglican establishment

John Coleridge's death left his widow comparatively poor and dispossessed. She and thirteen-year-old Ann (Nancy) and nine-year-old Samuel were obliged to quit the large Vicarage and Schoolhouse and, at the indulgence of the local patrician Sir Stafford Northcote, to move temporarily into the humbler lodgings of the Warden's House attached to the Church. But if the Coleridges were poor they were still sheltered to some extent by the Anglican establishment that the Rev. John Coleridge had adopted and defended in political sermons during his lifetime – and that Coleridge himself would readopt and defend later in life after years in the wilderness as a political radical and a Unitarian. Sir Stafford Northcote's gift and other exertions on behalf of the Coleridges are a case in point. Prior to that, John and Ann Coleridge had been able to find preferment for their sons in the genteel professions of the army and the church.

On the death of her husband, accordingly, Ann formally appealed to Christ's Hospital, a London charity school founded by Edward VI in 1552 for the sons (and originally the daughters) of the poor and funded largely by City of London philanthropists. In Coleridge's time, Christ's Hospital specialized in supporting children from families of clergymen in the Church of England who had been 'orphaned' by losing at least one of their parents. An 'Orphanotrophium', its charity was designed, in Coleridge's memorable phrase, 'to catch the falling':

> It is to preserve, in the same rank in life in which they were born, the children of reputable persons of the middle class, who either by the death or overwhelming calamities of their parents must otherwise have sunk down to a state, which *to them* would be penury and heart-breaking, because alike unfitted to their bodily and their mental habits.[10]

Unlike the great public schools, which by 1800 had become elitist institutions more interested in taking paying boarders and less and less interested in local students 'on the foundation' – at Eton, for example, fee-paying students outnumbered the subsidized students by six to one[11] – Christ's Hospital retained a strong commitment to its charitable origins. It was also a long way from the aristocratic anarchy and class privilege of Eton, Harrow, Rugby, Charterhouse, Westminster, Shrewsbury, St Paul's, Merchants Taylors', and Winchester, as Richard Holmes reminds us: 'There were no riots, no underground magazines, no tutorial friendships between boys and masters, no freedoms outside school hours'.[12] Pride taken precisely in *not* being one of the cradles of the gentry and the aristocracy seems to have been encouraged by the school. The radical poet and essayist Leigh Hunt goes on at length in his *Autobiography* about the egalitarian ethos encouraged at the school, which recognized only the cleverest boy, 'let his father be who he might':

> Christ's Hospital is well known and respected by thousands, as a nursery of tradesmen, of merchants, of naval officers, of scholars, of some of the most eminent persons of the day; and the feeling amongst the boys themselves is, that it is a medium, far apart indeed, but equally so, between the patrician pretension of such schools as Eton and Westminster, and the plebeian submission of the charity schools.[13]

But Hunt's pride in the school's egalitarian compromise was another pupil's shame, and Christ's Hospital transferred to some of its pupils the class insecurity that its very existence symbolized. Faced with authority generally and the aristocracy in particular, Coleridge certainly alternated all his life between self-abasement and self-defensiveness.

The family friend Judge Buller, a former pupil of Coleridge's father, in the first instance had actually talked of sending Coleridge to Charterhouse, before the idea had to be abandoned and the family were obliged to throw themselves on the charity of the Governors of Christ's Hospital. On the instigation of Buller and with the support of Coleridge's godfather, Mr Samuel Taylor, and of John Coleridge's successor at the Ottery St Mary vicarage, the Rev. Fulwood Smerdon, Ann Coleridge petitioned the Governors to extend their 'usual Pity and Charity to distressed Men, poor Widows, and fatherless Children' and admit young Samuel to the school, 'there to be Educated and brought up among other poor children'.[14] Like half the other pupils at the endowed Christ's Hospital, Coleridge would be a 'charity boy', which in his case also meant conceding 'the right of the Governors of Christ's Hospital to apprentice her son' in the event of his academic inconsequence. The guardianship and future of the nine-year-old Coleridge thus lay with the school and its place within a network of establishment institutions. From Christ's Hospital, Coleridge would be passed on to Jesus College at the University of Cambridge with a selection of scholarships and awards that, had he continued to apply himself, would eventually have seen him through to a fellowship at one of the colleges or, like his father before him, to one or more church livings.

In other words, what the Coleridge of the *Biographia* had belatedly learned from his experience at home in his father's church and school, and later at Christ's Hospital, was more than just 'the discipline of his taste', it was also an integrated and hierarchical national culture in which the institutions of land, religion, politics, education, law, and the military cohered and collaborated. Coleridge would come to value and promote this interdependence in *On the Constitution of the Church and State* (1829), his last address to a conflicted society, and would come to conceive of a place within the system for what he called a 'clerisy' of intellectuals like himself.[15] It was in the interests of the Anglican establishment that Coleridge in the *Biographia* offered his carefully edited and sanitized version of his own formal education.

Christ's Hospital

Christ's Hospital was the largest school in the nation with over a thousand pupils. Rather than being a single school, however, it was a composite of different schools, each with a different syllabus, different teachers, and a different object in mind. The Writing School, for example, was designed for boys intending – or, more likely, intended – to go on to a commercial apprenticeship at age 14 or 15. The (Royal) Mathematical School was actually founded separately – by Charles II in 1673 – to train mathematicians and navigators who would progress into careers as Naval officers or merchant seafarers or (by Coleridge's day) in the East India Company. The Mathematical School, accordingly, had its own Royal Charter and its own very distinct culture. Charles Lamb's account of 'the king's boys', as they were called, in his 'Recollections of Christ's Hospital' (1813), describes them as generally older and more athletic than the boys at the other schools and goes on to offer an archetypal image of institutionalized school bullying. Themselves subject to 'frequent and severe punishments', says Lamb, the King's boys were 'hardy, brutal, and often wicked', 'a constant terror to the younger part of the school'.[16]

Later to become famous as an essayist and, with his sister Mary, author of a set of durable prose renditions of *Tales from Shakespeare* (1807), Charles Lamb was Coleridge's younger contemporary and lifelong, if often exasperated, friend. He was also Coleridge the poet's staunchest *and* shrewdest defender. It is to Lamb that we turn for a more accurate (and disquieting) account of life at Christ's Hospital than we are offered in the *Biographia* – and in the other, better-known essay 'Christ's Hospital Five and Thirty Years Ago', for a more accurate account of life from Coleridge's own point of view. Lamb was a city boy with easy access to his family, whereas the narrative voice of that essay, 'alone among six hundred playmates', is the voice of a dislocated country boy modelled on Coleridge: 'O the cruelty of separating a poor lad from his early homestead! The yearnings which I used to have towards it in those unfledged years! How, in my dreams, would my native town (far in the west) come back, with its church, and trees, and faces! How I would wake weeping'.[17]

The Grammar School

As we might expect of two boys who would go on to become famous writers – and to these we could add Leigh Hunt, the poet, political journalist, and friend of Keats from whose *Autobiography* I quoted earlier, and Thomas Barnes, later editor of *The Times* – Coleridge and Lamb were not in the Writing or Mathematical Schools, but in the more academic Grammar School. (Lamb did go on to work for the East India Company all his life, however.) Coleridge's career at school was distinguished and auspicious, though it just as easily might not have been. He failed to thrive in the junior school under an indifferent Mr Field, who could not see past the child's abstraction. Coleridge was only brought to the attention of James Boyer by the lucky accident of being discovered reading Virgil for pleasure by Thomas Middleton, a senior student and later Coleridge's 'patron and protector' (*BL* I, 13). Coleridge then – probably in 1785, aged 12 – graduated into the Classical Sixth Form under Boyer with other gifted students, to become, first, a 'Deputy Grecian' and later one of the three or four scholars (called 'Grecians') who each year went up to Oxford or Cambridge.

The burden of the Grammar School at Christ's Hospital was to teach the Classical languages: Latin, first and foremost, but also Greek. It was almost exclusively Latin and Greek that a boy would have been taught at any one of the 700 traditional grammar schools from amongst the 4167 'endowed' schools in England, which around the time of the *Biographia* in 1816 – when the reforming MP Henry Brougham organized and headed the first ever parliamentary select committee on education – were responsible for the education of 165,433 pupils.[18] ('Endowed' schools, as the epithet suggests, were schools subsidized by the Church or by a charitable bequest that usually originated with the Church or the Monarchy.)

Instituted, to quote Dr Johnson's *Dictionary*, 'for teaching grammatically the learned languages', this is what, before anything else, traditional grammar schools set out to do.[19] It is what the vast majority of them did before offering what would come to be called 'literary appreciation', for example – at least according to the Romantic satirist Thomas Love Peacock: 'The instructors of youth aim only at communicating the knowledge of the words and rules of a language, without exciting the taste of the student to penetrate into the beauties of the authors who have written it'.[20] Though a few of the grammar schools over the eighteenth century took the initiative of introducing elementary mathematics, modern languages, bookkeeping, and dancing, if these were available at all it was more often than not as extra-curricular subjects (which meant that additional fees were involved).

It is worthwhile also reminding ourselves that learning 'grammatically the learned languages' was what Coleridge had been doing at least since the age of six when he left the local Dame school to attend his father's grammar school in Ottery St Mary, and what he would be expected to continue doing later, at university. To this extent, you could argue that Coleridge was fortunate in having James Boyer as his teacher. In Boyer's class, as well as looking at the Greek and Latin poets, 'he made us read Shakespeare and Milton as lessons' (*BL* I, 9). The truth is, even if we confine ourselves to the traditional education of the Romantic poets – Wordsworth at Hawkshead Grammar, Shelley at Eton, Byron at Harrow – there seems ample evidence of other texts besides classical ones entering the school classroom and other topics of discussion besides the 'Quippe-quare-quale-quia-quidditive Case!' dear to Rev. John Coleridge's heart (*CL* I, 310). Still, with the exception only of mathematics, and here only at certain schools, nothing other than the learned languages was systematically studied.

The Scottish universities and the Dissenting academies

The extreme narrowness of the formal educational curriculum was not centrally prescribed, of course, because education would not become compulsory until 1870. It was encouraged or constrained by the universities and the clergy they educated, who in turn became the teachers of the next generation.

It was also – and would remain, at least until the First World War – an ideological battleground. Outside the Anglican establishment, a modernization of the syllabus had taken place in the eighteenth century and radically different methodologies were applied. The differences between the Scottish universities – St Andrews, Glasgow, Aberdeen, Edinburgh – and the two English universities, for example, could not have been more marked, with Scotland teaching 'new' empirical or experimental sciences, like chemistry and physics, and the vocational disciplines, law and medicine. It is telling and characteristic that nearly all the recognized thinkers of the eighteenth-century Scottish Enlightenment – Francis Hutcheson, Adam Smith, Hugh Blair, Thomas Reid, William Robertson, Adam Ferguson, John Millar, Joseph Black, Dugald Stewart – spoke and wrote out of the universities.

So with the more progressive Dissenting academies. Excluded by the Test and Corporation Acts of the late seventeenth century from the grammar schools and the two universities, the Dissenters (originally Independents and Presbyterians, Baptists, and Quakers; later Unitarians and others identifying themselves as *rational* Dissenters) had been obliged to develop their own academies. There were over seventy of them, most of them a cross between a 'private venture' (or private) school and a university. (Though they could take students from quite a young age, they also trained students for the Dissenting ministry, as Oxford and Cambridge trained students for the Anglican ministry.) Their significance for our purposes is that many of them offered a sophisticated syllabus and an educational system that exploited their want of charter to encourage a vigorous, independent-minded religious and secular education.[21] Their syllabuses, for example, were often extensive and comprehensive: French and Italian; history and political theory; geography; a version of English literature and, most notably, the new physical sciences – all on top of the Classical languages and literatures with which the establishment schools and universities remained preoccupied.

Dissenting academies varied considerably amongst themselves, it should be said, and were only as good as the teachers who taught in them. As it happens, though, their teachers included some of the most progressive intellects of their respective periods, people like the Unitarian Joseph Priestley at Warrington, whose name and works will come up again in our discussion of Coleridge's radicalism in the next chapter. (At Warrington, Priestley taught chemistry, anatomy, history, geography, languages, and *belles lettres*.) 'Freethinking' academies like those at Hackney and Hoxton became at different times extreme in their 'rational dissent', stressing the moral and rational aspects of Christianity and downplaying or even scoffing at the mysterious and liturgical aspects. (Indeed, in many cases, the teaching was too freethinking for the Calvinist elders who sent their sons there to train as Nonconformist ministers.) The more progressive academies turned out students trained to approach all subjects with an enquiring and sceptical eye and taught their pupils to judge social and cultural institutions on their merits, rather than with an uncritical admiration for the authority they derived from tradition.

This speculative and questioning side of the teaching of select academies became especially problematic later in the century as religious dissent became synonymous with political dissent – or 'Jacobinism' as it was called, after the extreme left faction in the republican French parliament. The conservative polemicist Edmund Burke wrote of the Hackney Academy as 'the new arsenal in which subversive doctrines and arguments were forged' and it is easy to see why, for conservative writers like Burke – and, later, for Coleridge himself – the more famous Dissenting academies were nurseries of radical reform, if not of out and out revolution.[22] 'The intellectual route from opposition to the Test Acts', writes Kenneth Johnston, 'through doubts about the Trinity, to Unitarianism, and thence to republicanism, was the intellectual fast track of the era'.[23]

It is this Dissenting tradition that we need to bear in mind – this and the enlightened modernism of Scottish liberal intellectuals – when reading Coleridge's tendentious and edited account of his own education in the *Biographia*, written *after* he had embraced and abandoned Unitarianism and political radicalism. The respect for authority argued and enacted in those pages – the same sense of reverence and wonder that the author of the *Biographia* demands of his own readers – became more and more important to the ageing apologist for orthodox religion and more and more central to his attack on the Enlightenment and its English and Scottish heirs:

There are indeed modes of teaching which have produced, and are producing, youths of a very different stamp; modes of teaching, in comparison with which we have been called upon to despise our great public schools, and universities

> In whose halls are hung
> Armoury of the invincible knights of old—

modes, by which children are to be metamorphosed into prodigies. And prodigies with a vengeance I have known produced! Prodigies of self-conceit, shallowness, arrogance, and infidelity! Instead of storing the memory, during the period when the memory is the dominant faculty, with facts for the after exercise of the judgement; and instead of awakening by the noblest models the fond and unmixed LOVE and ADMIRATION, which is the natural and graceful temper of early youth; *these* nurslings of improved pedagogy are taught to dispute and decide; to suspect all, but their own and their lecturer's wisdom; to hold nothing sacred from their contempt, but their own contemptible arrogance: boy graduates in all the technicals, and in all the dirty passions and impudence, of anonymous criticism. (*BL* I, 12–3)

By the time of the *Biographia*, the 'threat' from the Dissenting academies was in truth well and truly over, the academies themselves having succumbed to the pressure of political reaction in the 1790s. Some had been undone by theological sectarianism, others by their political sympathies. The 'anonymous criticism' of the Scottish intellectuals associated with the *Edinburgh Review*, on the other hand, was coming into its own as a political force. Fifteen years later, they would help bring the Whigs into power, initiating a set of electoral and other reforms that would threaten the Anglican establishment Coleridge defends in his later works.

The inspired charity-boy

Though not itself one of 'the great public schools', Christ's Hospital in the *Biographia* stands for a whole inherited, hierarchical system of Anglican education against the incursions of the 'nurslings of improved pedagogy'. There is no indication of the narrowness and partiality of that system and only a hint of its entrenched brutalities (*BL* I, 11). Not all contemporary accounts of the great public schools were acrimonious, of course, and feelings as to their educational and national significance were mixed.[24] Indeed, brutality was actually on the decrease in the late eighteenth century. Violence and the threat of violence amongst the boys themselves was excessive, however, and corporal punishment was taken for granted. In the hands of figures like James Boyer it could be a form of licensed sexual sadism, as Coleridge recognized unofficially in a remark to Charles Lamb on Boyer's death:

> Perhaps we cannot dismiss him better than with the pious ejaculation of C[oleridge] when he heard that his old master was on his death-bed; 'Poor J.B.! — may all his faults be forgiven; and may he be wafted to bliss by little cherub boys, all head and wings, with no *bottoms* to reproach his sublunary infirmities'.[25]

Boyer was not only a serial flagellator, he also had a habit of holding pupils aloft by their ear, leaving a traumatized Coleridge with a rich set of images to haunt his adult nightmares. Coleridge 'said he dreamt of the master all his life', Leigh Hunt was told, 'and that his dreams were horrible'.[26] Occasional notebook entries support this (*CN* I, 1250, 1726).

The school routine at Christ's Hospital, moreover, was a Spartan affair for the spoilt country boy, especially immediately after he arrived from ten weeks with his uncle Bowden and six at the more indulgent preparatory school at

Hertford. With sixteen to a dormitory, six o'clock rising, only three weeks a year summer vacation, a lot of thin porridge, little meat, more fat, few fresh vegetables, and aggressive nurses charged with keeping hundreds of boys free of nits and attending to all the poxes of the boarding house, it cannot have been easy (*CL* I, 387–9).[27] On top of all this, the 'charity boys' were constantly being reminded of their obligations. In 'Frost at Midnight', his more than usually eloquent version of the gospel according to William Wordsworth written years later in 1798, Coleridge prays for his son Hartley to escape the alienation and confinement he had known as a city schoolboy for 'the lakes and shores' and 'mountain crags' which are the 'eternal language' uttered by God.

The truth is, however, that Coleridge soon made a life for himself at Christ's Hospital, adapting, as children are wont to do, to the alien routines and to the various demands that were made upon him, however arbitrary or perverse. Early on, it is true, he was lonely and prone to escape into books and daydreams, wandering the streets alone on 'whole-day-leaves' when boys without family were cast adrift in London, and no doubt desperate to engage the attention and admiration of a passerby. Later in life, the emptiness and unhappiness of these days would return to him in his dreams along with memories of corporal punishment. But Coleridge did not feel compelled to protest, as his later friend Robert Southey did against Westminster, getting himself expelled for writing against flogging,[28] or as Percy Bysshe Shelley did against the brutal fagging system at Eton.[29] Coleridge did not feel resentful enough – nor, admittedly, would he have felt confident enough – to challenge authority in this way. There was, besides, a good deal about the school for him to take pride in, and occasional things outside the school to take pleasure in, like the family of his first love, Mary Evans, the first in a long line of adoptive families.

Moreover, he was able to distinguish himself academically, and the school had built a deferential system around the academically distinguished. Coleridge was, after all, a clever child, and never tired of being reminded of it. The most famous pen portrait of Coleridge during this period – Lamb's – certainly gives no indication that Coleridge was suffering unduly as a schoolchild, not while he was talking at least:

> Come back into memory, like as thou wert in the dayspring of thy fancies, with hope like a fiery column before thee—the dark pillar not yet turned— Samuel Taylor Coleridge—Logician, Metaphysician, Bard!—How have I seen the casual passer through the Cloisters stand still, entranced with admiration (while he weighed the disproportion between the *speech* and the *garb* of the young Mirandula), to hear thee unfold, in thy deep and sweet intonations, the mysteries of Jamblichus, or Plotinus (for even in those years ye waxed not pale at such philosophic draughts), or reciting Homer in his Greek, or Pindar——while the walls of the old Grey Friars re-echoed with the accents of the *inspired charity-boy!*[30]

Self-education

Where did Coleridge come by this arcane knowledge with which he 'entranced with admiration' the 'casual passer through the Cloister' at Christ's Hospital? Homer and Pindar we can confidently assume to be an extension of his classroom training, but the neoPlatonists Plotinus and Iamblichus? These he presumably borrowed from the King Street or the school library and pored over in his spare time. There is no reason to doubt Lamb's recollection because Coleridge was all his life 'entranced with admiration' for the neoPlatonists, from the third to the seventeenth centuries. And what better philosophy for a schoolboy to conjure with than the abstruse – the nearly but not quite intelligible – yet at the same time poetic sublimities of the neoPlatonists?

> We must not run after it, but fit ourselves for the vision [of the Intellectual Principle] and then wait tranquilly for its appearance, as the eye waits on the rising of the sun, which in its own time appears above the horizon— out of the ocean, as the poets say—and gives itself to our sight.
>
> This Principle, of which the sun is an image, where has it its dawning, what horizon does it surmount to appear?
>
> It stands immediately above the contemplating Intellect which has held itself at rest towards the vision, looking to nothing else than the good and beautiful, setting its entire being to that in a perfect surrender, and now tranquilly filled with power and taking a new beauty to itself, gleaming in the light of that presence.
>
> This advent, still, is not by expectation: it is coming without approach; the vision is not of something that must enter but of something present before all else, before the Intellect itself made any movement. Yet it is the Intellect that must move, to come and to go—going because it has not known where it should stay and where that presence stays, the nowhere contained.
>
> And if the Intellect, too, could hold itself in that nowhere ... it would remain forever in the vision of its prior, or, indeed, not in vision but in identity, all duality annulled.[31]

The same sun – warmer, though; less abstract and less literary – would reappear in the closing lines of 'This Lime-Tree Bower My Prison', annulling difference and duality. It reappeared out of the ocean of Coleridge's immense reading, begun with the Bible at age three and carried on crumpled up in one sunny (or sunless) corner after another throughout his life, largely if not exclusively *outside* the classroom. Before we turn to Coleridge's translation to at the University of Cambridge, then, it is worth revisiting the issue of Coleridge's literary education and looking at it in the broader context, first, of Coleridge's *whole* intellectual and imaginative life, and then of the cultural life of the nation at large, bearing in mind the ideological battle over the syllabus being waged at the time and carried over into the pages of the *Biographia*.

Education as an Enlightenment project – the broad cultivation of the mind and heart, fitting one 'to perform justly, skilfully, and magnanimously all the offices, both private and public, of peace and war', according to John Milton[32] – had from the beginning always been larger than mere schooling. Indeed, the great educational theorist, John Locke, had doubted the efficacy of sending a child to school.[33] In the late eighteenth century, before the Mechanics' Institutes and the Society for the Diffusion of Useful Knowledge and long before the Elementary Education Act of 1870, there arose a large and colourful contingent of working class autodidacts (self-teachers), some of whom, like William Cobbett and Horne Tooke, would become famous.[34] If we start referring to every child who is educated away from an educational institution as an 'autodidact', however, we are going to have to include very many of the upper classes (about a quarter of the aristocracy and half of the gentry were educated at home, by private tutors or governesses or by their own parents).[35] If, on the other hand, we use the word 'autodidact' to refer to those whose reading and thus self-education is largely determined by themselves, those for whom reading as pleasure and understanding proceeds, not according to a prescribed and institutionalized syllabus, but associatively or randomly, according to availability and inclination, then we could well call every child who attended any of the English great public schools or grammar schools an 'autodidact'.

For the fact is that, compared with today, knowledge was often sought and gained in quite independent ways. 'A great deal of the most notable intellectual energies of the eighteenth century', to quote E. P. Thompson, 'lay outside of formal academic channelling'.[36] What the artisan William Blake has in common with the professional middle-class Wordsworth and the 'charity boy' Coleridge, the peer Lord Byron and the baronet-to-be Shelley, is that each read widely and eclectically – each under his own, often unconscious self-direction. The grammar school (and university) syllabus was so narrow that any remotely curious child was bound to go on his own search for information and any creative child, his own search for imaginative pleasure. At the vast majority of eighteenth- and early nineteenth-century English schools, if you managed to pick up what would become known as *useful* knowledge (an idea with its own chequered political and cultural history) you did it pretty much on your own. Or if you were at Christ's Hospital you switched to the Mathematical School. But the syllabus as we think of it today, the syllabus as it was being developed in the Scottish universities, the Dissenting academies, and in several enlightened private venture schools – philosophy, applied mathematics, languages, modern history, geography, *belles lettres*, what we call science – all these the grammar school boy acquired on his own if he acquired them at all. What *was* taught in the classroom, moreover, was often quite unapologetically taught as a means, not of liberating the intellect and imagination and storing the mind with useful information, but of disciplining the mind and the memory and 'enforcing social and cultural hegemonies'.[37] In a very real sense, then, all the Romantic writers were autodidacts: self-teachers. And it may be that the best thing the grammar school did for its students was to create the conditions that allowed for their intellectual and imaginative independence.

Cambridge

It was not, then, for his knowledge of Plotinus or Bacon, in other words, of *Robinson Crusoe* or the *Arabian Nights' Entertainments, Bartram's Travels* or *Purchas His Pilgrimage* – his knowledge, in short, of a vast and eclectic assortment of texts – that Coleridge the Grecian was awarded an Exhibition (scholarship) worth forty pounds a year and packed off to Cambridge just days short of his nineteenth birthday in October 1791. Boyer 'sent us to the University excellent Latin and Greek scholars, and tolerable Hebraists', Coleridge wrote in the *Biographia* (*BL* I, 11). As the son of a clergyman who had distinguished himself academically, moreover, he received on arrival an additional Rustat Scholarship worth twenty seven pounds. He had done well.

There were only the two universities in England in Coleridge's day. London University – or, strictly speaking, University College London – an extension of the Scottish educational *imperium*, would not open until 1828. Non-Anglicans (Dissenters, Catholics, Jews) were effectively barred from both universities, and where they were indulged they were unable to take out degrees. So it was that the vast majority of the teaching fellows were ordained Anglican clergymen. Of the two, Oxford was by far the more conservative politically, and had been since it had been the headquarters of the Royalist army in the seventeenth century. Cambridge in Coleridge's day also had close ties with Church and King – George III's sons went there – but was surprisingly tolerant. Until the political reaction set in during the years following the French Revolution, Cambridge produced a number of 'friends of liberty' amongst its staff – most controversially, William Frend, a Unitarian convert at Coleridge's college, Jesus, expelled from the university in 1793. Both Oxford and Cambridge were central to the Anglican establishment, however, with the sole responsibility for training the nation's Anglican clergymen who were also, like the Rev. John Coleridge, more often than not its teachers.

The quality of education and the intake at the nation's two universities had declined over the course of the eighteenth century. Contemporary accounts spoke of 'aristocratic profligacy and academic servility, of idleness on a spectacular scale, of rivalries and feuding'.[38] Most of the actual teaching was undertaken by the college tutors and the laziness of most of the permanent fellows and of the professoriate – many of whom, incidentally, held chairs in disciplines that were not formally taught at the universities – was a scandal even in the eighteenth century itself. As with the fellows, so with the students, many of them did nothing at all, with around half dropping out without taking their degrees (as Coleridge eventually would do). The few professors who did lecture seldom had an audience. 'Classical lectures', Coleridge was informed on arrival, 'are seldom given, and when given, very thinly attended' (*CL* I, 16).

There was a good deal of dissolute behaviour, being for most of the undergraduates a rite of passage. Coleridge's Christ's Hospital schoolmate Charles Valentine (Val) Le Grice had half his Exhibition withheld because of drunkenness (*CL* I, 51). The eighteenth century drank a good deal more than the nineteenth, and the students at the two universities were in training. Because of this, and because of the cloistered, all-male environment, there was also violence. In spite of decades of condemnation and controversy, duelling was still common practice amongst upper class men and not long after his arrival at Cambridge Coleridge was reporting to his brother the death of an undergraduate in a duel: 'Formerly students of Colleges were censur'd for being pedants', Coleridge was told, 'now they were too much men of the world' (*CL* I, 19). For heterosexual sex there were the college bedmakers or 'The Rookery' at Barnwell, the theatre and brothel district out past Coleridge's Jesus College along the Newmarket Road. Only the masters were allowed to marry and only half of them did. 'As with expressions of dissenting political or religious views in Cambridge, so too with sexual behaviour', writes Kenneth Johnston, 'almost anything was tolerated as long as it was kept quiet and private; only public indecorum was punished'.[39] The Cambridge prostitutes were to return to Coleridge occasionally in his dreams (*CN* 1, 1726).

There was a choice, however. It was only the 'nonreaders', as they were known, who avoided lectures and examinations. One could choose the competitive and often stressful option of becoming instead a serious 'reader', though this would be interpreted by your peers as a sign that you were poor and needed a profession. Still, no one could qualify for a church living without taking a degree and, though earlier in the century the examination system had been arbitrary and corrupt, by Coleridge's day there was an established set of academic examinations through which one could pass in order to achieve distinction, first within the college and then within the university. (Half-yearly college examinations prepared students for the university-wide examination that 'readers' would sit in their final year in competition for one of the three grades in the tripos listing.) There were, throughout, progressive and occasional awards to be won, and, ultimately, if one performed consistently well, a fellowship at one of the colleges of the university.

Coleridge had done well academically to get into Cambridge and he continued to do well for the first year and a half of his residence. Within a month – arguably prematurely, as Coleridge himself suggests – he was bragging about his industry to his brother George, an ordained clergyman and teacher like their father, who had become in turn a surrogate father to Coleridge:

> If I were to read on as I do now—there is not the least doubt, that I should be a Classical Medallist, and a very high Wrangler [the top grade]—but *Freshman* always *begin* very *furiously*. I am composing Greek verse, like a mad dog. I am very fond of Greek Verse, and shall try hard for the Brown's Prize ode.

This is perhaps the only record we have of Coleridge's projecting a work – in letters, notebooks, or table talk – that was actually and successfully completed, or completed within a time that was reasonable and remunerative. Coleridge, that is, did go on to write and submit (amongst other bids for academic distinction) a Sapphic ode on – which is to say *against* – slavery and the slave trade ('The Unhappy Fate of the Slaves in the West Indian Islands'), and did walk away with the Sir William Browne Gold Medal and the considerable acclaim that attached to it. (It required his declaiming his successful ode before the assembled Fellows at the end of the academic year.) No doubt this provided the vital momentum that he needed. After he returned from a rare tour of his brothers and mother in the west country over the summer vacation of 1792 he was selected to submit for the university's Craven Scholarship, an intensely competitive and prestigious award that involved amongst other things six days of examinations and would have guaranteed his future in the University or the Church or both. He did not get it. Although ranked in the top four, Coleridge watched the prize go to a younger scholar. He had sat examinations to renew his Rustat Scholarship and been awarded a £33 'Chapel Clerk's Place' by the Master of Jesus. But he did not win the Craven Scholarship, and with that, as Richard Holmes observes, 'his whole attitude to academic success altered'.[40]

Until his mid-thirties, Coleridge's achievements were bound up with his primary friendships: with Robert Southey in the years immediately after withdrawing from university, then, famously, with William Wordsworth. So it was in his first year at Cambridge. Thomas Middleton received the younger Coleridge quite literally into his rooms at Pembroke College (because he was low in the hierarchy, Coleridge's rooms at Jesus were damp and barely habitable), offering him as he had at Christ's Hospital praise and encouragement, as well as a model of industry and benign patriarchy. Coleridge's first extensive literary collaboration was with Middleton – on a set of Anacreon translations (*CL* I, 17). Too little is known about this particular friendship, at least compared with what is known of Coleridge's relationships with Southey and Wordsworth. No letters survive and the main tribute we have is the rather unctuous, Mr Collins-like tribute in the first chapter of the *Biographia*.[41] If we think of Middleton's intervention on Coleridge's behalf at Christ's Hospital and of Coleridge's successful first academic year at Cambridge then the debt is surely great. Coleridge's gradual abandonment of religious and political orthodoxy over his first two years at Cambridge no doubt required his abandoning the Anglican Middleton as well – unlike Coleridge, Middleton took orders and eventually became Bishop of Calcutta. But Middleton left Cambridge after Coleridge had been there only a year – abandoning Coleridge, as it were – and his absence must surely have helped to create the conditions for Coleridge's rupture with the Anglican establishment, which took place gradually over the subsequent months.

For our purposes, Middleton's exit can be seen to signal the end of Coleridge's formal education.

2

'The Progress of His Opinions in Religion and Politics': The Radical Years

To attribute the changes in Coleridge's career over the years 1792–3 to academic disappointment alone would be misleading. Other personal factors contributing to Coleridge's growing alienation from the Anglican establishment that had legally fostered him since his mother signed him over to Christ's Hospital in 1781 have already been hinted at. Besides the natural rebelliousness of youth, there were the temptations to indulgence that he encountered daily at Cambridge. At the time, Coleridge wrote with affected nonchalance of his drinking (and drunken) exploits to the Evans family in London (*CL* I, 31) – to whom, incidentally, he had become even more emotionally attached, spending his first Christmas at Cambridge there, rather than at Ottery St Mary, and falling hopelessly but silently in love with Mary Evans. There were also trips to London to catch 'the Jordan' or 'the Siddons' (*CL* I, 51) – popular actresses in a theatrical world that, for all its high cultural profile, was still morally and socially dubious enough to be fascinating. And there were the sexual delinquencies that Coleridge could hardly have been expected to confide in the Evanses. Later in life, in a letter to the scientist Humphry Davies, Coleridge had occasion to look back upon 'all the loose women I had known, from my 19th to my 22nd year, that being the period that comprizes my Unchastities' (*CL* II, 734).

Indulgence, moreover, was costly. From day one at Cambridge, having blithely invited a tradesman to furnish his unprepossessing rooms, Coleridge began accumulating debts that would require family intervention at critical moments. The first such moment was in July 1793, the end of the academic year in which he had been disappointed in the Craven Scholarship. By then his debts had reached a staggering £150 and occasioned a confession, a family conference, a family rescue, and a family reprimand (*CL* I, 59n., 68). Nor did the rescue alleviate his situation, or at least not for very long. Within four months, debts would drive Coleridge to publish professionally for the first time – 'To Fortune, On Buying a Ticket in the Irish Lottery', for which the *Morning Chronicle* paid a guinea – and then into the most desperate and sensational episode of his early life: his enlisting in His Majesty's 15th Light

Dragoons under the comic pseudonym of Silas Tomkyn Comberbache. Why he should have done this – what immediate or ultimate purpose it could serve beyond the six and a half guineas enlistment payment; whether he hoped his absence might inflict some kind of punishment upon his family – Coleridge himself could not say: 'My mind is illegible to myself', he wrote to his brother George (*CL* I, 63). This time it cost George a trip to Coleridge's regimental headquarters at Henley and quite possibly 25 guineas under the counter. And still there were the debts to pay.

Coleridge had been 'a fool even to madness': 'lost in a labyrinth, the trackless wilderness of my own bosom' (*CL* I, 63). Caught in acts that shamed and even surprised himself, Coleridge was punishing and pleading with his family at the same time. For a long time, as we saw, his sense of outrage at the death of his father and at his own abandonment by his family had been internalized and had expressed itself, first, in withdrawal, then in a more or less obsequious wooing of authority. Or in doing both at the same time. But the ambivalence felt towards and by Coleridge during a visit to his brothers James and Edward during the summer of the year prior to his enlistment, 1792, suggests a resentment that Coleridge was unable to disguise: 'both the one and the other exacted a deference', he wrote to the more sympathetic George, 'which conscious of few obligations to *them*, aware of no *real* inferiority, and laughing at the artificial claims of primogeniture, I felt myself little inclined to pay' (*CL* I, 54). The family had been proud of his achievements that summer, but had found him personally awkward (he was obviously drinking too much, for example, because his mother had to refuse him wine at the dinner table [*CL* I, 41]). They could only have been further embarrassed by the debts they would be asked to discharge in the coming years.

The pamphlets of the day

Coleridge's complaints about Edward and James during the summer of 1792 betray more than just resentment at their lack of support at crucial moments earlier in his life, however. They also betray a growing unease with the conservative values his elder brothers represented and expressed. As well as being personally awkward with his family, Coleridge no doubt was outspoken on most of the political issues occupying the nation at the time. And there were many. The 'primogeniture' that he mentions and resents – the exclusive rights to property and title of the first born son – was coming under increasing attack from radical writers like William Godwin.[1] 'If I do not visit my brother James now', Coleridge wrote to George in July 1792, 'I shall not be able to do it at any future period – on account of his Sidmouthianism' (*CL* I, 36). Coleridge's brother James had joined the army at 16 and risen to the rank of Lieutenant-Colonel in the Exmouth and Sidmouth Volunteers, marrying an heiress in 1788. Sidmouth was a fashionable provincial watering place with (like James himself) genteel pretensions.

Nine years later Coleridge would look back on these visits to his family with nothing but 'painful thoughts': 'I think of them habitually as commonplace rich men, bigots from ignorance, and ignorant from bigotry' (CL II, 756).

If there were personal reasons for the metamorphosis Coleridge would undergo in his first two years at Cambridge, in other words, there were also historical and political ones – or at least there was a vocabulary of resentment and revolt ready to hand to an eloquent undergraduate gradually losing interest in the glittering prizes offered to him by an Anglican establishment which was also, at the same time, losing interest in him.

> What evenings have I spent in those rooms! What little suppers, or *sizings*, as they were called, have I enjoyed; when Aeschylus, and Plato, and Thucydides were pushed aside, with a pile of lexicons, &c. to discuss the pamphlets of the day. Ever and anon, a pamphlet issued from the pen of Burke. There was no need of having the book before us. Coleridge had read it in the morning, and in the evening he could repeat whole pages verbatim.[2]

Val Le Grice's recollections of college nights rather neatly reflect the shift that occurred in Coleridge's priorities over the first two years of his residence in Cambridge. Coleridge was succumbing to the clamours of a political world outside the closed circuit of academic Classical studies (suggestively invoked here as 'a pile of lexicons, &c.'). His prize winning ode on 'The Unhappy Fate of the Slaves in the West Indian Islands' was perhaps an attempt to marry his political and his academic ambitions:

> O ye who will revel in the ills of Slavery, O feeders on the groans of the
>   wretched, insolent sons of Excess, shedders of our brothers' blood,
>
> does not the inescapable Eye see these things? Does not Nemesis threaten fire-
>   breathing reprisal? Do you hear? or do you not hear? how winds shake
>   the ground
>
> at its roots, and the recesses of earth groan beneath, and the depths roar terribly,
>   pledging those below to wrath against the killers![3]

Aeschylus and Thucydides (and Sappho) 'were pushed aside' and Burke (and Priestley and Frend and Tom Paine and Richard Price) rushed in to fill the vacuum.

Reflections on the revolution in France

This was, after all (as Coleridge reminded Mary Evans), what the 'Politicians' called an '*age of Revolutions*' (CL I, 51), and Coleridge 'was a sharer in the general vortex'.[4] The period from the late eighteenth to the early nineteenth century was a critical and embattled period in British and European history. Born just prior to the war with America that would lead to the colony's famous Declaration of Independence in 1776, with its insistence that 'all men are created equal', Coleridge was 16 when the Bastille was stormed on 14 July 1789, leading to the overthrow of the *ancien régime* in France – to the abolition of all hereditary titles, that is, and the formation of a bourgeois republic.[5]

In 1792 the French National Assembly voted to begin the calendar again from the year zero. Wordsworth had the privilege of travelling through France during the year immediately after the revolution and of witnessing at first hand both the inhuman privation that had led to the Revolution, and the promise of the Revolution to create heaven on earth out of the materials left behind after the destruction of the old order. In his long autobiographical poem, *The Prelude*, he records the heady days of his identification with the aims of the revolutionaries:

> 'twas a time when Europe was rejoiced,
> France standing on the top of golden hours,
> And human nature seeming born again
> *(The Prelude* [1805], VI, 352–4)

Wordsworth, and with him other young middle-class intellectuals of the 1790s like Coleridge, were convinced

> a spirit was abroad
> Which could not be withstood, that poverty,
> At least like this, would in a little time
> Be found no more, that we should see the earth
> Unthwarted in her wish to recompense
> The industrious, and the lowly child of toil,
> All institutes forever blotted out
> That legalized exclusion, empty pomp
> Abolished, sensual state and cruel power,
> Whether by edict of the one or few—
> And finally, as sum and crown of all,
> Should see the people having a strong hand
> In making their own laws, whence better days
> To all mankind.
> *(The Prelude* [1805], X, ll. 519–34)

Filled with this hope and eager to publicize it, Coleridge joined many of his university friends in a ritual endorsement of what the creators of the

American Declaration of Independence called 'certain unalienable Rights' – rights that had, to them at least as to the Americans before them, all the irrefutability of the 'self-evident'. Richard Price had spelled out some of these in *A Discourse on the Love of Our Country* (1789) delivered and published shortly after the Revolution:

> First; The right to liberty of conscience in religious matters.
> Secondly; The right to resist power when abused. And,
> Thirdly; The right to chuse our own governors; to cashier them for misconduct; and to frame a government to ourselves.[6]

Equally 'self-evident' were the arbitrariness and self-serving partiality of hereditary ruling classes. 'All hereditary government is in its nature tyranny', wrote Tom Paine in *The Rights of Man* (1791):

> It is difficult to discover what is meant by the *landed interest*, if it does not mean a combination of aristocratical land-holders, opposing their own pecuniary interest to that of the farmer, and every branch of trade, commerce, and manufacture. ... The aristocracy are not the farmers who work the land, and raise the produce, but are the mere consumers of the rent; and when compared with the active world are the drones, a seraglio of males, who neither collect the honey nor form the hive, but exist only for lazy enjoyment.[7]

After the revolution in France, it was as if a whole generation had suddenly found a common bond with the oppressed and a sense of collective purpose, and begun to see itself as uniquely privileged:

> Bliss was it in that dawn to be alive,
> But to be young was very heaven
> (*The Prelude* [1805], X, ll. 692–3)

So far so good. For a short time after the French Revolution the majority of educated Britons were prepared either to endorse this upsurge of political idealism or to look upon it with amused indifference. In so many ways, after all, the French were just catching up with the constitutional liberties afforded by the British system since the Glorious Revolution of 1688. Certainly many of the Cambridge dons, those 'friends of liberty' with leanings towards republicanism, welcomed it.[8]

'Paroxysm of alarm'

It was not long, however, before the tide began to turn against the new optimism and reforming zeal at home that accompanied the extraordinary turn of events in France. Already, in 1790, in his *Reflections on the Revolution in France*, the same Edmund Burke who had welcomed American independence 14 years earlier was writing emotively against what he saw as the contempt for tradition and hierarchy implicit in the new order of 'sophisters, œconomists, and calculators' introduced by the revolution.[9] Again, in the following year, in an *Appeal from the New to the Old Whigs*, Burke defended the consistency of his politics and denounced the wave of Francophilia following on from the revolution as dangerously naive, an encouragement to social criticism and a threat to the stability of the nation.[10] What was becoming increasingly apparent to Burke and other 'alarmists' was an unprecedented political activity amongst not just middle-class intellectuals and the provincial bourgeoisie but also the 'the lower orders', in the Constitutional and Corresponding Societies of London. Spurred on by inherited resentments about their exclusion from power – because of either class or religious nonconformity, or the accidents of history – as well as by changes in agricultural policy and deteriorating economic conditions that resulted in dispossession and migration, enlightened philosophers and self-educated artisans created a chorus of publications agitating for reform.[11]

In response to Tom Paine's popular and persuasive refutation of Burke in his bestselling *The Rights of Man*, the government introduced measures against 'seditious writings' in 1791. Societies like John Reeve's 'Society for the Preservation for the Protection of Property against Republicans and Levellers' sprang up everywhere.[12] Mobs began to rampage in the name of the 'Church and King', hounding Dissenting or freethinking intellectuals – like the mob that attacked and burnt Joseph Priestley's house in Birmingham and precipitated his exile to America. This was all part of a general reaction against 'Jacobinism', a loose term used to demonize political radicalism thought to have been inspired by the French. Like the Jews in Germany in the late 1920s and 1930s, Dissenters were becoming the scapegoats. 'Dangers which they considered as distant', alleged Charles James Fox of William Pitt and his government, 'they were not displeased that the public should suppose near, in order to excite more vigorous exertions':

> Is it nothing to give a general credit and countenance to suspicions, which every man may point as his worst passions incline him? In such a state, all political animosities are inflamed. We confound the mistaken speculatist with the desperate incendiary. We extend the prejudices which we have conceived against individuals to the political party or even to the religious sect of which they are members. ... I should not be surprised if Bishops were now to preach from the pulpit that sedition is a Presbyterian or a Unitarian vice. Those who differ from us in their ideas of the constitution, in this paroxysm of alarm we consider as confederated to destroy it.[13]

The 'paroxysm of alarm' was only exacerbated by the execution of Louis XVI of France in 1793. In 1792, three years after the storming of the Bastille, France had declared itself a republic and Louis and his queen Marie Antoinette had been imprisoned. In January 1793, the king was executed, just days before England went to war with an aggressively defensive French republic embarking on a policy of military expansion abroad and of vicious reprisal at home. The revolution then deteriorated into spiteful factionalism and official murder, particularly under the provisional government or 'Terror' of Robespierre. The ultimate result of all this would be the dictatorship of Napoleon Bonaparte and, except for a short-lived peace from 1801 to 1803, a protracted war that would end only with the Battle of Waterloo in July of 1815.

But the enthusiastic undergraduates gathering in each others' rooms during the opening years of the 1790s could not have known this. They still supported the principles of the revolution and vilified a government and a class system that exploited the exigencies of a foreign war – and, later, the threat of a foreign invasion – to deepen their hold on power. And their hold on Cambridge itself. The seat of Cambridge was in the hands of the Prime Minister, William Pitt, a one-time reformer who was himself forging a new conservative party in the wake of the revolution. 'Cambridge could appear very conservative or very radical, depending on which corners one looked into', according to Kenneth Johnston, 'but its atmosphere of political agitation was pervasive'. 'There was no single issue', Johnston continues, 'until the single issue, supporting or opposing war with France (declared in 1793), preempted all others'.[14] When that happened, Cambridge was asked to choose – as, indeed, was the rest of the nation – and it chose to support Pitt and the monarchy. Political opposition that once had been tolerated was now being openly arraigned and punished. 'To those who studied the signs of the times it was very evident that Whiggism[15] would be an unpopular profession', wrote Coleridge's contemporary Henry Gunning in his reminiscences of university life, 'and that a good opportunity now presented itself for abandoning their principles; thus their apostasy assumed the garb of patriotism, and a regard for the established religion'.[16] The Anglican establishment, in other words, was starting to think of and defend itself as such.

Coleridge, too, was making choices and forming allegiances, becoming more republican, more 'freethinking', as Cambridge became less so. The event that turned the tide in favour of the new conservatism was the trial and expulsion of Jesus College fellow, William Frend, the Unitarian convert who had already lost his teaching position in the college for writing against the Thirty-Nine Articles of the Church of England to which all university entrants were required to subscribe. The occasion of the trial was the publication of Frend's *Peace and Union* in February 1793 – 'The proper time to correct any abuse, and remedy any grievance, is the instant, they are known'[17] – and the trial took place in May, just months after the execution of Louis XVI and the declaration of war with France. Coleridge was rowdy at the trial in support of Frend, whom he had known as a fellow of his own college and would get to know better in London later, where rational Dissenters like Frend overlapped with the London Corresponding Society and the intellectual or 'philosophical' radical circle surrounding William Godwin, author the *Enquiry Concerning Political Justice* (1793). The expulsion of Frend, as the Vice-Chancellor (according to Henry Gunning) was to boast, 'was the ruin of the Jacobinical party as a *University thing*'.[18]

There are a number of versions of what actually took place at the trial of Frend, all of them suggestive of Coleridge's prominence amongst the undergraduates who did their best to express their disapproval and disrupt proceedings. Equally apparent, though, was Coleridge's unwillingness to take the risk of allying himself publicly with Frend, and the episode ended with his retreating from the public gallery in the University's Senate House unidentified and thus unpunished by the authorities. To have supported Frend publicly would have meant openly opposing the Test and Corporation Acts excluding Dissenters and, by extension, all the repressive measures – like the trial itself – introduced in response to agitation for radical reform. Coleridge was not ready yet to sacrifice a career in the Church, having '*prudence* enough', as he had told his brother George on a previous occasion, 'to *respect* that *gluttony of Faith* waggishly yclept Orthodoxy' (*CL* I, 20). Coleridge was always, as Carl Woodring says of him on another occasion, 'politically turbulent without being rash'.[19] Besides, he was emotionally incapable of the kind of open defiance it would have required and always insecure in the face of authority.

But his subterfuge in ducking out of the proceedings – if we can call it a subterfuge – was not just personal or selfish. It also reflected an acute and accommodating awareness of the many sides of the debate and of the complexity of the issues. Coleridge was ready to be radical but was uncertain as to what form, exactly, that radicalism should take. Burke's emotive conservatism exercised a powerful appeal to a young man who distrusted the chilling rationalism of the two most prominent radical authors of the 1790s, Tom Paine and William Godwin. Godwin's *Enquiry Concerning Political Justice*, an exhaustive argument for philosophical anarchy so influential on intellectual radicals like Coleridge and Wordsworth, spoke on behalf of a brave new world uninhibited by the habitual, vested interests of tradition and power (precisely those interests exalted by Burke as a set of enduring values, the more just and regulatory for being unconscious and inarguable):

> Incessant change, everlasting innovation, seem to be dictated by the true interests of mankind. But government is the perpetual enemy of change. ... Their tendency is to perpetuate abuse. Whatever was once

thought right and useful they undertake to entail to the latest posterity. They reverse the genuine propensities of man, and, instead of suffering us to proceed, teach us to look backward for perfection. They prompt us to seek the public welfare, not in alteration and improvement, but in a timid reverence for the decisions of our ancestors.

Instead, Godwin offers the dictates of enlightened reason as they occur to the individual as an individual:

It is earnestly to be desired that each man should be wise enough to govern himself, without the intervention of any compulsory restraint; and, since government, even in its best state, is an evil, the object principally to be aimed at is that we should have as little of it as the general peace of human society will permit.[20]

Godwin's conviction of the sanctity of private judgement was not just individually empowering, it was also, paradoxically, socially visionary. If each individual could be brought to act wholly motivated by reason, argued Godwin, it would necessarily secure the maximum benefit for his or her fellow human beings. His very bourgeois philosophy of individualism, in other words, is informed and driven by a millennial optimism deriving from the philosophers of the French enlightenment and from necessitarian thinkers like David Hartley, so beloved of Coleridge that he would name his first child after him.

In devising this rational alternative, however, Godwin offered an unremittingly rational solution to every moral dilemma, one that gave neither priority nor sympathy to the ties of romantic love or family or gallantry. According to his rational, utilitarian accounting, for example, 'the illustrious Bishop of Cambray' – Fénelon (1651–1715), archbishop and author of *Télemachus* (1699) – 'was of more worth than his valet, and there are few of us that would hesitate to pronounce, if his palace were in flames, and the life of only one of them could be preserved, which of the two ought to be preferred':

We are not connected with one or two percipient beings, but with a society, a nation, and in some sense the whole family of mankind. Of consequence that life ought to be preferred which will be most conducive to the general good. ...

Suppose I had been myself the valet; I ought to have chosen to die, rather than Fénelon should have died. ... understanding is the Faculty that perceives the truth of this and similar propositions; and justice is the principal that regulates my conduct accordingly. It would have been just in the valet to have preferred the archbishop to himself. To have done otherwise would have been a breach of justice.

Suppose the valet had been my brother, my father or my benefactor. This would not alter the truth of the proposition. The life of Fénelon would still be more valuable than that of the valet; and justice, pure, unadulterated justice, would still have preferred that which was most valuable. Justice would have taught me to save the life of Fénelon at the expense of the other.

Priestley and Price and Frend – the Unitarian or Dissenting intellectuals – though writing in the rationalist mode, at least offered Coleridge a form of radical protest that was informed by 'sentimental' notions like universal benevolence and tolerance and was predicated on a belief in a loving God. They offered Coleridge a form of radicalism that reached back past the secularizing Enlightenment to the seventeenth century, when the *protest*antism of the Diggers and Levellers still had access to the rhythms and rhetoric of the St James Bible and its catalogue of curses for every incarnation of the Whore of Babylon. Eventually, the Unitarians, too, would prove insufficient, but not until Coleridge had run the gamut of radical alternatives.

Pantisocracy

According to the influential periodical the *Edinburgh Review* in 1802, the revolution in France and all its repercussions derived from the 'change that had taken place in the conditions and sentiments of the people, from the progress of commercial opulence, from the diffusion of information, and the prevalence of political discussion'.[21] Wealth was the condition, opinion the force, print the means. This change invariably led to the question of authority: of who should rule over, or overrule, whom; of what entitled or empowered someone – what qualified someone – to rule at all. Coleridge's next political dream was at once more and less ambitious than the Unitarian republicanism he inherited from Priestley and Frend. More daring intellectually, more radical in its revisioning of society, it was also at the same time an effective opting out of the political battle even before he had joined it. Pantisocracy was quite literally a radical *alternative*: an egalitarian community 'on the principles of an abolition of individual property' established in pastoral seclusion away from the corruptions of the old world on the banks of the Susquehanna River in America (*CL* I, 96). Coleridge got there by way of Oxford and Robert Southey.

In the middle of June 1794, after three years on (and off) at Cambridge, Coleridge set off with a companion Joseph Hucks on a walking tour of Wales. On the way there they broke their journey at Oxford to visit his old schoolfellow, Robert Allen, and it was Allen who introduced him to the younger Balliol undergraduate, Robert Southey. 'He is truly a man of *perpendicular Virtue*', Coleridge would later tell George Dyer: 'a *down-right upright Republican!*'

(*CL* I, 152–3). The two of them, Coleridge and Southey – both radicals, both aspiring poets with heads full of heterogeneous ideas and images, and both ready to make an impression – seemed to work off the enthusiasm of each other. Southey, though younger, was strong minded enough to have taken the stand that had him expelled from Westminster and knew (or seemed to know) exactly what he wanted and what he was not prepared to tolerate: 'I am not stupid enough to be orthodox', he wrote confidently to a friend.[22] Coleridge, who didn't know what he wanted, fed off Southey's certainty. Ideas and inclinations became convictions. Coleridge, for his part, talked – and whatever he talked about, whatever ideas he promulgated, then as throughout his life, came out sounding fresher, more impressive, more enchanting.

'From this moment on', writes Rosemary Ashton, 'Cambridge would have no further hold over Coleridge'.[23] The day or two Coleridge had intended spending in Oxford became three weeks of endless talking during which, when not 'disputing on metaphysical subjects',[24] the scheme of 'pantocracy' (later 'pantisocracy') was evolved. Southey had already announced whimsical plans for a Rousseauistic escape into the wilds of America and was convinced (with Godwin) that government and private property and law were unnatural and unjust. It was a short step from here to the select community that the two of them dreamed up over these weeks, a small-scale utopia of a dozen nuclear families in which the government, property, and labour of the community were shared equally by all the adult men *and* women.

> The leading idea of Pantisocracy is to make men *necessarily* virtuous by removing all Motives to Evil—all possible Temptations.
>
> All necessary knowledge in the Branch of Ethics is comprised in the Word Justice—that the Good of the whole is the Good of the Indiv[id]ual. Of course it is each Indiv[id]ual's *duty* to be Just, *because* it is his *Interest*. To perceive this and to assent to it as an abstract proposition—is easy— but it requires the most wakeful attentions of the most reflective minds in all moments to bring it into practice—It is not enough, that we have once swallowed it—The *Heart* should have *fed* upon the *truth*, as Insects on a Leaf—till it be tinged with the colour, and shew it's food in every minutest fibre. In the book of Pantisocracy I hope to have comprised all that is good in Godwin. (*CL* I, 114–15)

In contradistinction to the rationalist Godwin, however, Coleridge comes back to the 'heart'. What most attracted him to the alternative lifestyle he and Southey proposed was its emphasis on friendship and love: 'frendotatoi meta frendous. Most friendly where all are friends' (*CL* I, 103). Coleridge's pantisocratic utopia would be an extension and elaboration of the affectionate family life he was himself denied and which he had shared momentarily in households like the Evanses':

> The ardour of private Attachments makes Philanthropy a necessary *habit* of the Soul. I love my Friend—such as he is [to me], all mankind are or *might be*! The deduction is evident—. Philanthropy (and indeed every other Virtue) is a thing of *Concretion*—Some home-born Feeling is the *center* of the Ball, that, rolling on thro' Life collects and assimilates every congenial Affection. (*CL* I, 86)

As an act of linguistic (re)creation, Coleridge's coinage – *pan-socratia*, all-governing or government by all – itself partakes of the spirit of innovation, of beginning the calendar again from the beginning, that was the legacy of the French Revolution. As Coleridge said of the word 'aspheterized' (another coinage, meaning the 'abolition of property'): 'We really *wanted* such a word—instead of travelling along the circuitous dusty, beaten high-Road of Diction, you thus cut across the soft, green pathless Field of Novelty!' (*CL* I, 84). The same can be said of Coleridge's emotional and political life. These, too, appear to begin again from the moment of his meeting Southey. 'Pantisocracy—O I shall have such a scheme of it! My head, my heart are all alive' (*CL* I, 103). Here, for the first time, are sentiments and projections in which Coleridge has himself played a direct part, and not just relayed to an eager but essentially imitative audience back in Cambridge as the latest thoughts of the polemicists. Like the poet in the telling conditional at the close of 'Kubla Khan', Coleridge has built his dome in air and tasted the pleasure of creativity.

Coleridge's excitement is captured in the letters written immediately after departing from Oxford, in which every incidental detail somehow conduces to or confirms their shared beliefs and values. With mock-indignation he mimics his companion Joseph Hucks's response to the poverty they confront on the road:

> It is *wrong*, Southey! for a little Girl with a half-famished sickly Baby in her arms to put her head in at the window of an Inn ... Why?? Because it is *impertinent* & *obtrusive*!—I am a Gentleman!—and wherefore should the clamorous Voice of Woe *intrude* upon mine Ear!?
>
> My companion is a Man of cultivated, tho' not vigorous, understanding— his feelings are all on the side of humanity—yet such are the unfeeling Remarks, which the lingering remains of Aristocracy occasionally prompt. When the pure System of Pantocracy shall have aspheterized the Bounties of Nature, these things will not be so—!(*CL* I, 83)

Most significant of all, though, was the leap this distinguished young university scholar from a recently gentrified family was able to make across the

English class barrier. Suddenly, discussing the plan with Southey in a letter, Coleridge embraces a servant of Southey's aunt, Shadrach Weeks: 'SHAD GOES WITH US. HE IS MY BROTHER!' (*CL* I, 103). It is as if the equality of human beings enshrined in the American Declaration of Independence has just struck him, like a lightning bolt.

There is no single reason why the scheme failed – if even to put it in those terms does not give unwarranted credibility to what Coleridge himself came to recognize as 'Strange fancies! and as vain as strange!'[25] Of the many reasons for its collapse, however, this one of overcoming class differences was crucial. In the end it proved impossible for Southey. Southey wanted to take servants and Coleridge thought this betrayed the very ideals of the scheme:

> my Judgement is not asleep: nor can I suffer your Reason, Southey! to be entangled in the web, which your feelings have woven. Oxen and Horses possess not intellectual Appetites—nor their powers of acquiring them. We are therefore justified in employing their Labor to our own Benefit— Mind hath a divine right of Sovereignty over Body—But who shall dare to transfer this reasoning from 'from Man to Brute' to 'from Man to Man[']! To be employed in the Toils of the Field while *We* are pursuing philosophical Studies—can Earldoms and Emperorships boast so huge an Inequality? (*CL* I, 121–2)

It is hard for us not to sympathize with Coleridge on this issue. Indeed, perhaps because it is so hard to like Southey, or to approve of the way he conducted himself throughout the whole episode, it is hard not to sympathize with Coleridge on every issue. It brought out in him a generosity of feeling towards his fellow human beings that informed his early political lectures and poetry and remained with him, only barely suppressed, for the remainder of his life. Later, in his periodical *The Friend* (1809), he would remember with justified pride the 'intense interest and impassioned zeal, which called forth and strained every faculty of my intellect for the organization and defence of the Scheme', claiming that the experience sharpened his 'insight into the nature of the individual Man' and informed his 'most comprehensive views of his social relations'.[26] However one may feel about Coleridge's later social and cultural imaginings, there is no reason to doubt this.

Sarah Fricker

The more immediate legacy of pantisocracy, however, was Sarah Fricker, designated Eve to Coleridge's Adam in the paradisal enterprise. What more than anything else made pantisocracy a curiously parochial affair was the way in which the original contributors clustered around the unremarkable Fricker family of Bristol. Coleridge had gone to Bristol after finally undertaking the pedestrian tour of Wales and exhausting his companion Hucks. A large trading port on England's west coast and like so many of the provincial cities the home of a vigorous Dissenting culture, Bristol would become the centre of gravity in Coleridge's existence over the next three years. Here he met his future friend, patron, and biographer, and the publisher of his early poetry, Joseph Cottle, a devout Dissenter willing to overlook the 'epidemic delusion' of pantisocracy and publish anything the young poets offered him.[27] Here Cottle, in turn, introduced him to Josiah Wade and other members of Dissenting intellectual and political society who became the audience and reading public for Coleridge's first efforts in the lecture hall and in print and who, over the next twenty odd years, would offer their support at vital moments, alienated only by Coleridge's increasingly vocal denunciation of Unitarianism as he grew older.

And here, too, Coleridge met Sarah Fricker. The widowed Mrs Fricker had been left with debts, five daughters, and one son. In 1794 the eldest, Sarah, was 24 years old and the youngest, George, only nine. Southey and another would-be pantisocrat, George Burnett, hoped to marry Edith and Martha Fricker respectively, and Mary Fricker was already married to willing pantisocrat Robert Lovell. That left Sarah, and Coleridge. From a complex of motives that it would be almost impossible to unravel – not least, along with 'the ebullience of *schematism*' associated with pantisocracy (*CL* I, 132), being Sarah Fricker's physical attractions – Coleridge acceded to the plan and the two of them became a couple, as Coleridge understood it for the purposes of the enterprise. When it must have been obvious to him that the enterprise was falling through, however, the expectation that he would marry Sarah pressed – and, by Southey, was pressed – upon Coleridge. Uncertain of how to act towards her, especially while trying to keep the option of a relationship with Mary Evans alive, Coleridge simply avoided the issue over the closing months of 1794.

This was easy enough to do. By September he was in London, on his way to Cambridge and physically separated from both Southey *and* Sarah. Throughout Coleridge's undergraduate years, London, within easy access of Cambridge, had offered vital freedoms – as for most people London always had and would. In September 1794 he was enjoying preaching and defending pantisocracy to old school friends in London and he returned for over a week in November after the 'Treason Trials' during which John Horne Tooke, John Thelwall, Thomas Hardy, and Thomas Holcroft were famously acquitted of high treason. And, having finally decided to abandon Cambridge without a degree, he was there again for a month during the winter. This was the period of his greatest or most exclusive intimacy with Charles Lamb. The two of them sat up nightly at the Salutation and Cat, where Coleridge was staying, consoling each other for their lost loves and swapping stories about school. But mostly, mostly Lamb listened to Coleridge recite and talk. 'I have no higher idea of heaven', he wrote to Coleridge two years later, 'Your company was the one "cordial in this melancholy vale" – the remembrance of it is a blessing partly, and partly a curse'. No doubt Coleridge's pantisocratic enthusiasms, drawing as they did on the possibility of human perfectibility assumed by Godwin and anatomized in the philosophical psychology of his latest mentor, David Hartley, had an unsettling effect on his younger and more vulnerable friend. But the real 'curse' of Coleridge's company for Lamb was its promise of heaven in the confidence and intimacy the two of them had shared. When all was said, Lamb had to return to his clerkship at East India House.

In Coleridge's case, too, reality returned with a vengeance – in the shape of Southey. Mary Evans turned Coleridge down in December and a decision about Sarah was required. Coleridge, 'resolved – but wretched' and confessing to Southey that he did not love her (*CL* I, 132), undertook to act 'honourably' towards the precariously situated Sarah: 'Mark you, Southey! – *I will do my Duty*' (*CL* I, 145). He did. Southey arrived in London on 11 January 1795 to collect him and keep him to his word. He and Sara (as he began to refer to her, dropping the 'h') would be married nine months later in October. Sadly, beyond a honeymoon period of three years, during which they appear to have been much in love, the marriage would bring only unhappiness to both of them.

Political lecturer

Though to the reader of Coleridge's and Southey's letters pantisocracy may seem doomed from the beginning, it was not in fact officially abandoned until November 1795 when Southey departed for Lisbon on his family's bidding. In the process of its deconstruction all sorts of refinements and compromises were mooted, including (besides servants) a trial run in Wales. Coleridge, however, had plenty of other political things on his mind over the course of 1795. Pantisocracy had developed his ideas into convictions and there were other, more immediate and urgent battles to be fought on the home front. With Cambridge now out of the question, moreover, he was no longer able to rely on scholarships and his family for support, turning him into a poet and polemicist in search of a livelihood. Money would have to come from the public, either through patronage or by selling his ideas in the lecture theatre or in print.

The two years between January 1795, when Southey 'rescued' Coleridge from London and escorted him back to Bristol, and the very end of 1796, when Coleridge and Sara settled at Nether Stowey, mark the period of Coleridge's greatest activity and highest profile as a political speaker and writer. During this time, his name became well enough identified with the radicalism of the mid-1790s for him to feature in Anti-Jacobin satire later in the decade. This was a radicalism besieged by the rising tide of the reaction that we have already registered, a radicalism whose purpose was no longer that of spreading the word of parliamentary and other reforms so much as of defending liberties once taken for granted but now being withdrawn by a paranoid, repressive government. Throughout 1793–5, the 'paroxysm of alarm' intensified. The celebration after the acquittals at the Treason Trial that Coleridge had rushed to join in November 1794 was a brief respite, the exception that proved reaction the rule. Other political dissidents – like the Cambridge Unitarian Thomas Fys[s]he Palmer who influenced Coleridge – were being transported to the God-forsaken penal colony in New South Wales; the Habeas Corpus Act was suspended on five occasions from 1794, permitting imprisonment without charge; Secret Service funds were being poured into a massively expanded spying and informing network. In response to a stone's being thrown at King George III in 1795, a Seditious Meetings Act prohibiting gatherings in excess of fifty people and a Treasonable Practices Act making outspoken criticism of the government a high misdemeanour were rushed through Parliament.[28] As John Thelwall complained:

> Parliamentary corruption, and an unjust and ruinous war, have reduced us to beggary and famine, and when we call for the reformation of the one, and the relinquishment of the other, Bills are brought into Parliament by Your Majesty's Ministers, which make it FELONY and HIGH TREASON to give a tongue to those miseries we cannot but feel!!![29]

It was these last, known popularly as the 'gagging acts', which brought an end to effective radical protest in the 1790s, turning Coleridge the public speaker into Coleridge the periodical writer.

By then, however, his reputation was established. It was political poetry that had originally brought him public recognition, a series of 11 very uneven 'Sonnets on Eminent Characters' published between December 1794 and January 1795 in the *Morning Chronicle*, under editor James Perry the leading Opposition newspaper until well into the nineteenth century. Poetry and commentary published in the *Morning Chronicle* – and poetry *as* commentary – thus had a cultural prominence. What Carl Woodring calls 'Coleridge's densest concentration of patriot-hymning and hero-worship'[30] – along with its obverse, disappointment and disgust – began with a paean to Thomas Erskine, the lawyer whose 'stream divine I Of unmatched eloquence' had secured the acquittal of Horne Tooke, Hardy, and Thelwall at the Treason Trials in the previous month. Coleridge then continued to publish at regular intervals sonnets on Burke ('Thou badst Oppression's hireling crew rejoice'); Priestley; the hero of the American and French revolutions, Marquis de Lafayette; the would-be liberator of Poland, Thaddeus Kosiusko; Prime Minister Pitt –

> Yon dark Scowler view
> Who with proud words of dear-lov'd Freedom came—

More blasting, than the mildew from the South!
And kiss'd his country with Iscariot mouth
(Ah! foul apostate from his Father's fame!)
Then fix'd her on the cross of deep distress,
And at safe distance marks the thirsty lance
Pierce her big side!

('Sonnet: To Pitt', ll. 4–11)

Bowles; the actress Mrs Siddons (written with Charles Lamb); William Godwin; Southey; the playwright and leading Whig politician Richard Brinsley Sheridan. The style was declamatory, the sentiments clichés, and the diction and syntax often forced and awkward. Coleridge's poetry at this time oscillated between this oratorical rant and a Bowlesian personal voice: nostalgic, sentimental, and self-pitying. Neither was distinctive or especially accomplished and Coleridge at different times expressed his reservations with both (*CL* I, 80, 116).

With the sonnets in the national press, however, Coleridge could set up in Bristol as a lecturer with a reputation for radicalism and risk taking. That reputation was only reinforced by the three or four political lectures he delivered above the Corn Market in Bristol not long after his arrival in Bristol[31] – or, at least, two of which were delivered in rooms above the Corn Market, the third had to be resituated. Coleridge charged a shilling for entry and, even though for the majority of his audience he was preaching to the converted, still the lectures were well received, drawing compliments in abundance from those willing to listen and only occasional criticisms (like that of the reporter in *The Observer* who thought his hair needed combing and that he 'would do well to appear in cleaner stockings in public'[32]). Not every member of the audience was converted, however, and the last lecture had to be moved because of the passions Coleridge had aroused. 'The opposition of the Aristocrats is so furious and determined', he wrote to George Dyer, 'that I began to fear, that the Good I do is not proportionate to the Evil I occasion – Mobs and Mayors, Blockheads and Brickbats, Placards and Press gangs have leagued in horrible conspiracy against me' (*CL* I, 152).

Reading the version published almost immediately by Coleridge as *A Moral and Political Lecture* it is hard to see why the first lecture at least should have caused such a furore. One can only assume that when Coleridge published the lecture he cut out some inflammatory passages – as he would do later in life when republishing his early political lectures in *The Friend*.[33] In spite of the support it expresses for the imprisoned radical Joseph Gerrald – 'Withering in the sickly and tainted gales of a prison, his healthful soul looks down from the citadel of his integrity on his impotent persecutors' – what remains of that first lecture is an elaborate disincentive to hasty reform, preaching the necessity of '*bottoming* on fixed principles' and of not being 'hastened into the dangerous and gigantic Error of making certain Evil the means of contingent Good' (as the French had been).[34] Coleridge's anatomization of 'the professed Friends of Liberty' in the same lecture arguably disqualifies most of the enlightened radicals of his day, and was designed to do so. Describing the various motives and mechanisms apparent amongst the reforming politicians, Coleridge distinguishes four different classes, and sanctions only the fourth:

> that small but glorious band, whom we may truly distinguish by the name of thinking and disinterested Patriots: these are the men who have encouraged the sympathetic passions until they have become irresistable habits, and made their duty a necessary part of their self interest, by the long continued cultivation of that mortal taste which derives our most exquisite pleasures from the contemplation of possible perfection, and proportionate pain from the perception of existing *depravation*.[35]

Nevertheless, one reporter at least, though writing 24 years later, recalled Coleridge as 'a favourer of revolution' and 'positively and decidedly democratic'.[36] While it is certainly true that the pantisocratic concern Coleridge expresses in the lecture to level the humble upwards and not just the aristocracy downwards is genuinely democratic, the lecture as a whole could hardly be read as a call to arms. That it could be *heard* as a call to arms suggests that Coleridge modified the content, though no doubt something can also be put down to his delivery and his impromptu asides and retorts to the audience. 'Tho' I detested revolutions in my calmer moments', Coleridge would confess eight years later to Sir George and Lady Beaumont:

> yet with an ebullient Fancy, a flowing Utterance, a light & dancing Heart, & a disposition to catch fire by the very rapidity of my own motion, & to speak vehemently from mere verbal associations ... I aided the Jacobins, by witty sarcasms & subtle reasonings & declamations full of genuine feeling against all Rulers & against all established Forms! (*CL* II, 1000–1)

Self-censorship aside, a crucial vagueness characterizes Coleridge's early political writings. This is a result in part of inconsequentiality – of Coleridge's habit of laying down an eloquent if not necessarily coherent set of methodological and intellectual conditions without ever proceeding to precise statements. The point was made by a contemporary commentator writing in the *Critical Review* of April 1795:

> This little composition is the production of a young man who possesses a poetical imagination. It is spirited, and often brilliant; and the sentiments manly and generous. Though, with one or two exceptions, we admire the style of this little work, we think it rather defective in point of precision;

and, instead of saying we have shown the necessity of forming some fixed and determinate principles of action, he should have said, we have represented certain characters. We also think our young political lecturer leaves his auditors abruptly, and that he has not stated, in a form sufficiently scientific and determinate, those principles to which, as he expresses it, he now proceeds as the most *important point*. We confess we were looking for something further, and little thought that we were actually come to the *Finis*.[37]

This will remain substantially true of Coleridge's mature prose works, which are more eloquent and ingenious in outlining what can and cannot, should and should not, be thought and said than in attempting to elaborate and defend a specific theory or position. The *Finis* then rises abruptly before us as a foregone conclusion.

But it is also true that Coleridge's political thinking simply *was* uncertain on various issues, an uncertainty that was only compounded by the pressure of censorship. Just as pantisocracy can be seen as apocalyptic and revolutionary, on the one hand, or merely as an emotionally self-serving withdrawal into domesticity, depending on which way we choose to look at it, so his lectures can be quoted or paraphrased to suit different understandings of what his political position was. On some pressing issues in 1795 Coleridge was clear. He was against the war with France, against the collusion of the various institutions of the establishment in the prosecution of the war, and against Pitt's attempts to stifle freedom of speech. This much he had in common with the Foxite Whigs and radicals of every kind. Beyond that, however, it is difficult to say. Again and again Coleridge pointed to the suffering of the poor and came down on the side of social equality and, with that, the community of property. And his version of equality and communism was God's version, he insisted, quoting the Acts of the Apostles: 'And all that believed were together, & had all things in common – and sold their possessions & goods and parted them to all men, as every man had need'.[38] In this he was more radical than many of the radicals themselves and more radical certainly than many of his supporters amongst the affluent provincial Dissenters, who wanted only an equality of opportunity, more effective representation in parliament, and the freedom to trade. But when and how for Coleridge this should be achieved remains unclear. He himself admits that the communism so central to primitive Christianity 'was soon corrupted, and that it would do so was foretold'.[39] Which leaves us waiting for a sign. To offer to 'calm and guide | The swelling democratic tide', as he does in the epigram of *A Moral and Political Lecture*, leaves his commitment to the democratic doubtful and throughout that lecture there are intimations that matters of equity might best be left to the next generation, if not to the next world.

Certainly Coleridge had no difficulty rewriting his earlier political position later, when he became personally embarrassed by his youthful radicalism and was the object of accusations of apostasy. And there were, as he protested, very real continuities between his earlier and his later thought, with their shared distrust of the commercial motive and their shared emphasis on the need for first principles and for an elite or 'elect' of some kind to speak on behalf of (rather than to) the people. The needs of the people were to be respected, in other words, but the people themselves were not to be trusted. Not, at least, until certain vital educational conditions had been met. It is also true, as he says in the *Biographia*, that his political position was 'almost equi-distant from all the three prominent parties, the Pittites, the Foxites, and the Democrats', but the proud isolation which he implies is only another way of obscuring what he did believe and what his allegiances actually were (*BL* I, 187).

Religious Musings

The same uncertainty is true of what he took to be his major work at this time: *Religious Musings*. Begun on Christmas Eve of 1794 and not completed until it was published in 1796, *Religious Musings* is a long declamatory poem in Miltonic blank verse that derives a prophetic frenzy from the Book of Revelations. What it does is to establish Coleridge's religious priorities beyond doubt. It is typical, for example, that Coleridge should have followed his political lectures with 'Six Lectures on Revealed Religion, its Corruptions, and its Political Views'. 'If it is possible to see the conservative in the early radical', writes Peter Mann, 'this is largely owing to the rôle his religious feelings and beliefs played in the formation of his political attitudes'.[40] As in his religious lectures so in his *Religious Musings*, political commentary is subsumed – and thus effectively obscured – by an apocalyptic vision of millenarian progress:

> Rest awhile,
> Children of Wretchedness! More groans must rise,
> More blood must steam, or ere your wrongs be full.
> Yet is the day of Retribution nigh:
> The Lamb of God hath open'd the fifth seal:
> And upward rush on swiftest wing of fire
> Th'Innumerable multitude of Wrongs
> By man on man inflicted! Rest awhile,
> Children of Wretchedness! The hour is nigh:
> And lo! the Great, the Rich, the Mighty Men,
> The Kings and the Chief Captains of the World,
> With all that fix'd on high like stars of Heaven
> Shot baleful influence, shall be cast to earth,

Vile and downtrodden, as the untimely fruit
Shook from the fig-tree by a sudden storm. ...
Return pure FAITH! return meek PIETY!
The kingdoms of the world are yours: each heart
Self-govern'd, the vast family of Love
Rais'd from the common earth by common toil
Enjoy the equal produce ...
And such delights, such strange beatitude
Seize on my young anticipating heart
When that blest future rushes on my view!
For in his own and in his Father's might
The SAVIOUR comes! While as to solemn strains
The THOUSAND YEARS lead up their mystic dance,
Old OCEAN claps his hands! the DESERT shouts!
And soft gales wafted from the haunts of Spring
Melt the primœval North! The mighty Dead
Rise to new life, whoe'er from earliest time
With conscious zeal had urg'd Love's wondrous plan
Coadjutors of God. To MILTON's trump
The odorous groves of earth reparadis'd
Unbosom their glad echoes ...
(*Religious Musings*, ll. 313–27, 352–6, 368–81)

And so on, and on. The millennial consolation offered here to the 'Children of Wretchedness', along with Coleridge's belief in election and Hartleian necessity, do tend to beg the question of viable political change. Again, Peter Mann: 'the pious formulas of optimism and necessity and the view of reality as "progressive" and part of a universal "process" could readily foster a lofty attitude to contemporary events'.[41] We can see why Coleridge's radical friend John Thelwall should have been so annoyed by these and similar lines: 'They are the very acme of abstruse, metaphysical, mistical rant'.[42] It was as if Thelwall glimpsed in Coleridge's 'metaphysical' propensities a perverse sublimation and tendency to mystification of which the later, conservative Coleridge would be accused by the radicals of the next generation. Certainly Thelwall was the first to sound a critical note that echoes throughout the remainder of Coleridge's career.

The Watchman

The Unitarian thinkers Priestley and Frend had offered Coleridge a form of radical protest that, unlike the republicanism of Paine and the anarchy of Godwin, was integrated with their religious beliefs. Unitarianism also, and perhaps more importantly, offered him access to an alternative culture within the official culture he had rejected. As a religion, the very word 'Unitarianism' conjured up something singular and sublime and oceanic into which Coleridge could be assimilated: 'My mind feels as if it ached to behold & know something *great* – something *one* & *indivisible*', he confessed to John Thelwall (*CL* I, 349). The Unitarian or, more broadly, Dissenting community was an earthly corollary of this celestial accommodation. Coleridge had already begun occasional preaching in Unitarian chapels and would continue to do so throughout the next three years, during which time he seriously considered becoming a Unitarian minister. By the time he came to deliver his second set of lectures, his lectures on revealed religion, he had gained the patronage of the Dissenting citizens of Bristol, including the Unitarian minister Rev. John Prior Estlin, who would become a regular correspondent; wine merchant Mr Morgan, father of the John Morgan who took Coleridge into his family after the break up with the Wordsworths and became his amanuensis; and Joseph Cottle, his generous publisher, whose occasional handouts helped sustain Coleridge throughout most of 1795. Coleridge had found a surrogate family, not exactly pantisocratic but one that would serve him generously and self-lessly well beyond his own renunciation of Unitarianism in the early nineteenth century.

This group of supporters then became the core of a new enterprise, the periodical 'miscellany' entitled *The Watchman* and published every eight days to avoid contributing 'stamp duty' – the tax imposed on daily to weekly periodicals – to the government's war effort. Coleridge, writes Cottle in his *Reminiscences*, 'convened his chief friends, with dextrous secrecy', at the Rummer Tavern in Bristol, late in December 1795, 'to determine on the size, price, and time of publishing, with all other preliminaries, essential to the launching this vessel on the mighty deep'.[43] That he was 'persuaded by sundry Philanthropists and Anti-Polemists' to set it on foot, as he claims in the *Biographia*, is doubtful (*BL* I, 179). Coleridge, like every aspiring author with an ear to the ground, had flirted with producing a periodical since his Cambridge days and had canvassed the possibility more seriously with Southey, before the two of them had fallen out. Besides, he had called the meeting and selected the first potential subscribers himself. (His describing his supporters as 'Anti-polemi[ci]sts' should alert us to the fact that Coleridge is in his apologetic, whitewashing mode.) There is, however, no reason to doubt that he had the support of those friends he did gather, or that he and these friends in turn gathered hundreds more subscribers. The Dissenting network was activated by a set of introductory letters written by Bristol supporters to their extensive business and religious connections throughout the Midlands, which Coleridge bore with him on a pilgrimage around the region. Where the account of *The Watchman* in the *Biographia* does seem entirely faithful, then, confirming as it does what we know from the narrative of Coleridge's Midlands promotion in his letters, is in the sense of communal good feeling and shared values that buoyed him throughout the opening stages of the enterprise.

With the passage of the two 'gagging' bills, Coleridge had retired from public speaking, though only after a last lecture attacking the bills which then became the basis of a pamphlet *The Plot Discovered; or An Address to the People against Ministerial Treason*, published in December 1795. The 'chief objects' of his new miscellany, according to its prospectus, were to take up where this lecture had left off: 'to co-operate (1) with the WHIG CLUB in procuring a repeal of Lord Grenville's and Mr. Pitt's bills, now passed into laws, and (2) with the PATRIOTIC SOCIETIES, for obtaining a right of suffrage general and frequent'; 'to proclaim the State of the Political Atmosphere, and preserve Freedom and her Friends from the attacks of Robbers and Assassins'.[44] It is telling that Coleridge had originally wanted James Ridgway as his publisher, but Ridgway was in Newgate for four years, having been convicted in 1794 for the publication of Tom Paine's *Rights of Man* and a scurrilous exposé of high society (*CL* I, 181 and n.).

As it turned out, the miscellaneous format made this kind of polemical concentration impossible. In aspiring 'TO SUPPLY AT ONCE THE PLACES OF A REVIEW, NEWSPAPER, AND ANNUAL REGISTER!!!' – offering foreign and domestic news, parliamentary reports, essays, and poetry 'chiefly or altogether political' – *The Watchman* was altogether too busy to make the kind of political impact to which it aspired.[45] Coleridge was often scrambling for copy, unable to rely on the 'occasional assistance from literary men of eminence' promised in the prospectus.[46] The Unitarian divine John Edwards sent two pieces, as did Dr Thomas Beddoes, and William Frend sent a letter of two or three pages, but there were thirty-two pages per eight-day issue to fill. Lamb sent nothing but the poem of a friend and Southey, a writing machine, had disappeared out of his life.

There were, moreover, other factors besides the fact of its miscellaneity and the pressure to produce that conspired to blunt the effectiveness of *The Watchman* as the organ of liberating truth it styled itself. It did offer provincial opposition to the ministry, as it said it would, attacking Pitt's and the allies' conduct of the war with a France that was still a symbol of human liberty. (Towards the end of its run, though not yet 'out of heart with the French' as he told Benjamin Flower late in 1796 [*CL* I, 268], Coleridge is beginning to remonstrate with the 'French Legislators' for betraying the ideals of the revolution.[47]) But from the first number the opposition which was the prime motive of *The Watchman* is attenuated. Coleridge's 'Introductory Essay' is philosophical on the issue of the 'gagging acts' in ways that the author of *The Plot Discovered* could never have been, arguing that, though the two acts were 'breaches of the Constitution', 'the friends of progressive Liberty may review [them] with diminished indignation'; they

> will not have been useless if they should render the language of political publications more cool and guarded, or even confine us for a while to the teaching of first principles, or the diffusion of that general knowledge which should be the basis or substratum of politics.[48]

Coleridge is here in the mode of the philosopher-critic from *A Moral and Political Lecture* (1795) to *On the Constitution of the Church and State* (1829) intent on '*bottoming* on fixed Principles'; of the poet-prophet of *Religious Musings* endeavouring to calm the democratic tide.

On top of this, Coleridge was exhausted by the time the first of what would prove only ten issues of *The Watchman* went into print on 1 March 1796. The negative aspect of having engaged his Bristol friends and extended his contacts throughout the Midlands was the sense of obligation that came with it, forcing him to labour behindhand on each number – cannibalizing the London dailies for copy and adapting whatever came to hand, while less and less frequently contributing original essays of his own. Coleridge persisted until 13 May, 'hag-ridden by the fear of being influenced by selfish motives', according to the *Biographia* (*BL* I, 184). '*O Watchman!*' he concludes the final number, '*thou hast watched in vain!*'[49] – and, it should be added, at considerable expense to the management (£35–45).[50] As so often, Coleridge's friends clubbed together to help pay off his debts to the printer, Joseph Cottle having already contributed the paper for the first six numbers (*CL* I, 208).[51]

But already, at least since his marriage to Sara Fricker in October of the previous year, he had begun the withdrawal from daily politics that was arguably implicit from the beginning of his radical engagement, as Coleridge himself suggests in the *Biographia*:

> In part from constitutional indolence, which in the very hey-day of hope had kept my enthusiasm in check, but still more from habits of classical education and academic pursuits, scarcely had a year elapsed from the commencement of my literary and political adventures before my mind sunk into a state of thorough disgust and despondency, both with regard to the disputes and the parties disputant. (*BL* I, 199)

It would not last. Within a year and a half Coleridge would be writing 'flaming' leaders in the *Morning Post* on Pitt's prosecution of the war with France and would continue to resort to journalism periodically throughout his life as a means of subsistence. For the time being, however, he would 'retire', he decided, and try his hand at poetry and philosophy exclusively.

3
'A Known and Familiar Landscape': Conversations

When he put *The Watchman* to rest and was planning his retirement from active politics in May 1796, Coleridge wrote to Poole that he was considering the options of preaching and teaching and private tutoring as sources of income for himself and the now alarmingly large group of his dependants: a pregnant Sara, her mother, her brother George, and her recently widowed sister Mary and Mary's child (Robert Lovell having died of fever) (*CL* I, 192). It is always difficult to gauge just how seriously Coleridge is weighing vocational options when he is writing to a wealthier friend in a position to alleviate his financial burdens. The next two years would find Coleridge in a state of constant if not always acute anxiety about how to bring what he called 'BREAD & CHEESE' into the family on a regular basis, and therefore would also see a number of similarly oblique cries for help (*CL* I, 222, 227). I say the next two years, because the Wedgwood annuity that would be bestowed upon him in January 1798 seemed at the time to answer this anxiety. The truth is, however, it was an anxiety that would afflict him on and off for the remainder of his life. On this occasion, Poole revealed that he and other friends and well-wishers of Coleridge had clubbed together to find Coleridge £35–40, with the promise of future installments – a 'trifling mark of their esteem, gratitude, and admiration' for the 'extraordinary marks of sublime genius' he displayed.[1] Again and again, Coleridge will be rescued by generous gifts of this kind, investments in Coleridge's future productivity largely, but also, as Poole makes plain, acts of 'gratitude' for the sheer pleasure of having listened to him talk.

The only regular jobs that Coleridge ever undertook that we would be likely to identify as such were his four months on the staff of *The Morning Post* in 1799–1800 and his secretaryship to the Governor of Malta, Sir Alexander Ball, during his sojourn there in 1804–5.[2] Otherwise there was occasional journalism and lecturing, and there was the sale of his writings. By the time he composed the *Biographia* in 1815, the sum of his practical advice to the aspiring author was 'NEVER PURSUE LITERATURE AS A TRADE', which for Coleridge was also an ethical imperative, an act of resistance to the cultural and intellectual degradation attendant upon the commercialization of the nation's imaginative and intellectual life. What he suggests an aspiring author do instead is take up a 'known trade or profession' (*BL* I, 223–4). While careful to acknowledge 'the generous and munificent patronage of Mr. JOSIAH, and Mr. THOMAS WEDGWOOD' in his own literary life (*BL* I, 205), Coleridge can hardly recommend relying on enlightened friends or an enlightened state as an alternative mode of survival. But the truth is that Coleridge himself subsisted mainly on handouts like the one from Poole and his other friends – on 'patronage', that is, after the fashion of the times.

Literary patronage

It is worth taking time out to consider the options available to Coleridge in his struggle to fund a literary life in the late-eighteenth and early-nineteenth-centuries. Officially, patronage was supposed to be dead. Samuel Johnson was said to have killed it off in a famous letter sent to the Earl of Chesterfield in 1755 in which he defines the patron as one 'who looks with unconcern on a man struggling for life in the water, and, when he has reached ground, encumbers him with help'.[3] When Alvin Kernan refers to Johnson's letter as 'the Magna Carta of the modern author',[4] spelling the death of the *ancien régime* of aristocratic patronage and the birth of the age of the bookseller and the reading public, he is only endorsing a commonplace of literary history that runs back to the eighteenth century itself through signal invocations like that of Thomas Carlyle: 'Listen, once again, to that far-famed Blast of Doom, proclaiming into the ear of Lord Chesterfield, and, through him, of the listening world, that patronage should be no more!'[5] 'Doddy, you know', wrote Johnson on another occasion (referring to his bookseller Robert Dodsley), 'is my patron'.[6]

As it happens, aristocratic patronage had never been either single or simple in its operation. The commercial publishing that replaced it, moreover, was always going to be a double-edged benefit. Having fought their way out of the frying pan, most authors found themselves in the fire – which is exactly how it appeared to Carlyle:

> At the time of Johnson's appearance on the field, Literature, in many senses, was in a transitional state; chiefly in this sense, as respects the pecuniary subsistence of its cultivators. It was in the very act of passing from the protection of Patrons into that of the Public; no longer to supply its necessities by laudatory Dedications to the Great, but by judicious Bargains with Booksellers. ... To a considerate man it might seem uncertain which method were the preferable: neither had very high attractions; the Patron's aid was now wellnigh *necessarily* polluted by sycophancy, before it could come to hand; the Bookseller's was deformed with greedy stupidity, not to say entire wooden-headedness and disgust.[7]

Reacting against what they saw as a hostile reading public which threatened to decide 'all claim to poetical honours',[8] Wordsworth and Coleridge would stigmatize the commercial ethos of professional writing as deeply inimical to the artistic temperament. Notoriously, Wordsworth would eventually go in search of precisely the kind of aristocratic patronage from which Johnson sought escape.

This was much later, however. Wordsworth's career prior to Lord Lonsdale's securing him the office of Distributor of Stamps for Westmorland (and the Penrith area of Cumberland) in 1813,[9] like Coleridge's career – and like the careers of many 'unpopular' writers from the eighteenth to our own century unable to survive by publishing alone – testifies to the operation of an *ad hoc*, decentralized system of handouts from various individuals, groups, and institutions. That there was still direct patronage during the Romantic period has been amply demonstrated, though the word is often used rather loosely by commentators. [10] When in 1816 Lord Byron sends Coleridge the substantial sum of £100 we should perhaps be careful about interpreting the gesture as an act of patronage – in a way that the Lowthers' support for Wordsworth, say, presents few difficulties. The poet and banker Samuel Rogers was undoubtedly one of the more generous patrons of the arts throughout the first half of the nineteenth century, but Rogers did not necessarily become the patron of Coleridge, Wordsworth, Walter Scott, William Godwin, Perdita Robinson, Leigh Hunt, and a host of other writers and painters, just by helping out on occasion. There was patronage, there was friendship, and there was charity, and the lines between them were not always clear. Whatever we choose to call each individual gesture, however, Coleridge benefited financially from them all.

There were a variety of alternative, more official sources of income for the writer, as it happens, some of which Coleridge utilized and others he did not. Most commonly, as we saw with *The Watchman*, there was subscription publishing. 'It is interesting to observe how the subscription method democratized literary patronage', writes Paul Korshin, making 'it possible for a community of wealthy people to contribute to the support of many authors'.[11] And there was what Korshin calls the 'job-oriented public patronage' of the Civil List.[12] A limited number of these were specifically tailored for writers, like the posts of Poet Laureate (Southey and, later, Wordsworth, would benefit from this) and the less well-known Master of the Revels, Inspector of Plays, Latin Secretary, Gazette Writer, and Embellisher of Letters to the Eastern Princes. On the other hand, any one of innumerable sinecures at the disposal of rank and office might also be granted to writers as a reward, or an encouragement, or both – like Robbie Burns's job as Exciseman or Wordsworth's post of Distributor of Stamps. Thomas Gray had received the chair in Modern History at Cambridge and George Crabbe reaped the benefit of several church livings, courtesy of the Duke of Rutland's family. These were 'gifts' in the hands of specific Cabinet members or active noblemen, but either House of Parliament could vote to approve the award of a government pension. And it is astonishing just how many writers were in receipt of a pension, amongst the better known being James Macpherson, Samuel Johnson, James Beattie, Mark Akenside, William Hayley, and William Cowper. Coleridge's estranged friend Robert Southey would end up many years later with an additional pension of £300 a year.

Finally, though less remuneratively, there was a selection of foundations, societies, academies, and amenities so characteristic of the philanthropic late eighteenth century, each one extending an occasional and limited beneficence of rarely more than two figures. From 1790, for example, there was the institution that in 1818 would receive its charter to become the Royal Literary Fund. Coleridge did comparatively well out of the Royal Literary Fund, with his first grant of ten guineas coming just as he was wrapping up *The Watchman*. He then (thanks to the intercession of William Sotheby) received another grant of £30 in 1816 – and should have been flattered, because the average grant was only £8.[13] From 1821, there was the Royal Society of Literature 'for the Encouragement of Indigent Merit, and the Promotion of General Literature', whose 'Class of Honorary Members is intended to comprise some of the most eminent literary men in the Three Kingdoms, and the most distinguished female writers of the present day'.[14] They could afford to be more generous and in 1824 Coleridge was awarded a Fellowship that paid an annuity of 100 guineas.

Coleridge the poet

Coleridge, then, availed himself of almost every variety of funding, though none of the official sources could match the generosity he and his family received throughout their lives from friends and acquaintances. In the years after he retired from lecturing and *The Watchman* in May 1796, however, most of the offers of financial assistance he received involved activities other than the philosophy and poetry he would have liked to concentrate on: 'I would write Odes & Sonnets Morning & Evening', he wrote to John Prior Estlin, '& metaphysicize at Noon' (*CL* I, 223). In July, accordingly, he turned down an invitation by editor James Perry to write for and help edit the *Morning Chronicle*: 'If I go, farewell Philosophy! Farewell, the Muse! Farewell, my literary Fame!' (*CL* I, 227). He had already begun the systematic study of philosophy and of the German language that would prove so formative in the future direction of his thinking and his life (a 'shift of interest from France to Germany' that, as Richard Holmes points out, 'marks a move away from political radicalism to more purely intellectual interests'[15]). But poetry, too, was beginning to occupy him in a way that it never had before – poetry as practice and poetry in its root sense of 'making', creating – even though, like the vast majority of his literate contemporaries, he had been writing poetry since his schooldays.

On 16 April, Joseph Cottle had brought out a collection of all the poems Coleridge was prepared to publish under his own name, under the title of *Poems on Various Subjects*. Of these, 'I pin all my poetical credit on the Religious Musings', he had written to Poole (*CL* I, 203). Part of him took great pride in that ambitious catalogue of all his religious and political beliefs, up there with Milton and St John of Revelations. Another part of him, however, felt distinctly uneasy about it and indeed about all his early poetry. There are 'instances of vicious affectation in the phraseology of that poem', he admitted to Poole; again, 'you will find much to blame in them', he wrote introducing himself and the volume to the radical John Thelwall, 'much effeminacy of sentiment, much faulty glitter of expression' (*CL* I, 207, 205). The uncertainty had to do with more than just poetic taste, it had to do with how he understood literary history, with what he perceived his own role to be and where his future might lie. What Coleridge could not have known writing to Poole was that he was about to embark upon a series of poems that would earn him a permanent place in the English canon.

There was nothing inevitable about this. Coleridge was intellectually and conversationally precocious, but there was nothing especially precocious about his youthful poetry. He had written poetry regularly and had certainly been quick on occasion to style himself a poet. By the late eighteenth century, thanks to the efforts of poets and commentators like Thomas Gray, William Collins and the Warton brothers, Thomas and Joseph, the poet had already acquired the aura that would later (thanks partly to Coleridge) be called Romantic.[16] If there were 'buds of hope, and promises of better things to come' to be found amongst his poems, however, they were few and far between (*BL* I, 6). Most of his early poetry was characterized by a determination to be poetic that expressed itself in hyperbolic language, the melodramatic overuse of apostrophe, and the frequent resort to those historical habits of style that he and Wordsworth would later condemn as 'poetic diction': periphrasis, personified abstraction, tortured syntax, archaisms, 'a general turgidness of diction and a profusion of new-coined double epithets' (*BL* I, 6). The ending of his early poem 'To a Young Lady, with a Poem on the French Revolution' – originally addressed to Ann Brunton, later to Sara Coleridge – offers a convenient catalogue of the motifs and stylistic devices from which he would struggle to extricate himself:

> With wearied thought once more I seek the shade,
> Where peaceful Virtue weaves the MYRTLE braid.
> And Ô! if Eyes, whose holy glances roll,
> Swift messengers, and eloquent of soul;
> If SMILES more winning, and a gentler MIEN
> Than the love-wilder'd Maniac's brain hath seen
> Shaping celestial forms in vacant air,
> If these demand th'empassion'd Poet's care—

> If MIRTH, and soften'd SENSE, and WIT refin'd,
> The blameless features of a lovely mind;
> Then haply shall my trembling hand assign
> No fading wreath to BEAUTY's saintly shrine.
> Nor SARA! Thou these early flowers refuse—
> Ne'er lurk'd the snake beneath their simple hues:
> No purple bloom the Child of Nature brings
> From Flatt'rys night-shade: as he feels, he sings.
>   ('To a Young Lady, with a Poem on the French
>   Revolution', ll. 29–44)

Could any poetic convention have been more strained and unnatural than the eighteenth-century 'Child of Nature'? It is not difficult to imagine what Coleridge's old schoolmaster, Jemmy Boyer, would have had to say about these lines – nor, for that matter, what Coleridge himself would have to say. 'I saw and admitted the superiority of an austerer, and more natural style', he recalls in the *Biographia*, 'But my judgment was stronger, than were my powers of realizing its dictates' (*BL* I, 8).

One of the poems not published in the 1796 edition of *Poems on Various Subjects*, 'Reflections on Having Left a Place of Retirement', rather conveniently dramatizes the struggle Coleridge was having realizing the dictates of his new critical insight. After their marriage in St Mary Redcliffe Church in Bristol on 4 October 1795, Coleridge and Sara had spent six weeks in a cottage at Clevedon, near Bristol, lovingly recalled in the opening lines:

> Low was our pretty Cot: our tallest Rose
> Peep'd at the chamber-window. We could hear
> At silent noon, and eve, and early morn,
> The sea's faint murmur. In the open air
> Our Myrtles blossom'd; and across the porch
> Thick Jasmins twin'd: the little landscape round
> Was green and woody and refresh'd the eye.
> It was a spot, which you might aptly call
> The VALLEY of SECLUSION!
>   ('Reflections on Having Left a Place of Retirement',
>   ll. 1–9)

Coleridge had hoped that pantisocracy would operate as an example for the whole human race, and here the cottage and its seclusion are said to chasten and subdue 'a wealthy son of Commerce' sauntering by:

> Methought it calm'd
> His thirst for idle gold, and made him muse
> With wiser feelings: for he paus'd, and look'd
> With a pleas'd sadness, and gaz'd all around,

> Then eyed our cottage, and gaz'd round again,
> And sigh'd, and said, *it was a blessed place.*
> And we *were* blessed.
> ('Reflections on Having Left a Place of Retirement',
> ll. 12–7)

The passage unfolds at its own leisure, taking its time as the businessman takes his time, constrained to slow down and linger, enviously. Gold itself might be idle, but its pursuit is anything but. Greed is active and insatiable. Here, however, another and altogether more relaxed pace is observed, one that is captured by the lazy verbal and syntactical repetitions (suggestive of the businessman's reluctance to renounce the vision) and a simple unambitious diction in a poem that claims in its epigraph – Horace's (misquoted) *sermoni propiora* – to be 'more appropriate for prose'.

From this Edenic retreat, however, Coleridge felt obliged to tear himself away. Not for him the self-indulgence of sentimental benevolence so characteristic of *idle* dreamers:

> The sluggard Pity's vision-weaving Tribe!
> Who sigh for Wretchedness, yet shun the Wretched,
> Nursing in some delicious solitude
> Their slothful Loves and dainty Sympathies!
> I therefore go, to fight the bloodless fight
> Of Science, Freedom, and the Truth in CHRIST.
> ('Reflections on Having Left a Place of Retirement',
> ll. 56–61)

The phrase 'delicious solitude' that with its lush sibilants would have seemed appropriate in the opening idyll is here used sarcastically and is charged with contempt. It is as if the active 'man of Commerce' has metamorphosed into a crusader and turned on the vision that, momentarily, had hoodwinked him. Fancy cannot cheat so well as he is wont to do. Again, Coleridge is on the soapbox. Accordingly, the quiet, unpretentious substantives of the opening lines give way in the end to bluster: 'a general turgidness of diction', personified abstractions, double epithets, and what we might call declamation marks (one in the opening nine lines, six in the closing nine).

Coleridge's admirable concern at the time of writing 'Reflections on Having Left a Place of Retirement' was with how he could best help the anti-war effort. What that meant from a biographical point of view was renouncing his 'delicious solitude' and returning to lecturing and campaigning for and with *The Watchman*. But in spite of the triumph of the 'heroic' motive, an unresolved tension between the private and the public voices in the poem remains, if only because the opening idyll is so much more ingenuous and convincing than what willfully supersedes it. Poetically, Coleridge had found a new voice – indeed, he had already invented what we now call the 'Conversation Poem' – but he had yet to learn to trust it.

The Conversation Poems

The short poem written two years earlier in which Coleridge first gives some intimation of the form whose finest expression would be 'This Lime-Tree Bower My Prison' and 'Frost at Midnight' is addressed and entitled, significantly, 'To a Friend' (Charles Lamb, as a matter of fact). 'To a Friend, together with an Unfinished Poem' was designed to accompany the unfinished *Religious Musings* as a sort of antidote to its mental and verbal bombast, and first appeared in a letter to Southey dated 29 December 1794:

> Thus far my scanty brain hath built the rhyme
> Elaborate and swelling: yet the heart
> Not owns it.
> ('To a Friend, together with an Unfinished Poem',
> ll. 1–3)

It was not as if the more ambitious 'rhyme' were not all about love; all the beliefs that would ultimately inform the Conversation Poems are present in abstract, declamatory form in *Religious Musings*. But 'the heart' cannot acknowledge them, choosing instead to identify with a particular friend, sharing and comparing specific sorrows:

> In fancy (well I know)
> From business wand'ring far and local cares,
> Thou creepest round a dear-lov'd Sister's bed
> With noiseless step, and watchest the faint look,
> Soothing each pang with fond solicitude,
> And tenderest tones medicinal of love.
> I too a SISTER *had*, an only Sister—
> She lov'd me dearly, and I doted on her!
> ('To a Friend, together with an Unfinished Poem',
> ll. 6–13)

Lamb's sister, Mary, was seriously ill and Coleridge shares with his friend memories of his own lost sister Nancy. The retreat from the philosophical generalizations of *Religious Musings* is not a retreat from its Priestleyan ideal of 'Universal Benevolence', but rather an endeavour to *realize* that ideal more fully, more poetically; to rediscover the universal in the particular as Coleridge's mature theory of poetry will express it. Naturally, without the manifest effort of *Religious Musings*, Coleridge's identification with Lamb enables him to feel again the presence of God and brotherly love that he invokes throughout the *Musings*:

> He knows (the SPIRIT that in secret sees,
> Of whose omniscient and all-spreading Love
> Aught to *implore* were impotence of mind)
> That my mute thoughts are sad before his throne,
> Prepar'd, when he his healing ray vouchsafes,
> Thanksgiving to pour forth with lifted heart,
> And praise Him Gracious with a BROTHER's Joy!
> ('To a Friend, together with an Unfinished Poem',
> ll. 26–32)

It is the first of many regenerating acts of sympathetic love in Coleridge's poetry. As he had written to Southey in July 1794, with his mind on the chilling rationalism of Godwin, 'Philanthropy (and indeed every other Virtue) is a thing of *Concretion* – Some home-born Feeling is the *center* of the Ball, that, rolling on thro' Life collects and assimilates every congenial Affection' (*CL* I, 84).

When in 'To a Friend' Coleridge rejects the 'elaborate and swelling' rhetoric of *Religious Musings*, he is also rejecting a way of relating to man, to nature, and to God. As with the opening of the later 'Reflections on Having Left a Place of Retirement', the conversational style and tone were essential to these new values of intimacy and 'home-born Feeling' and were as symbolic of the altered consciousness as were the new imagery and naturalistic detail – symbolic in the sense that Coleridge later defined it as both representing and partaking 'of the Reality which it renders intelligible'.[17] Before he could invent the Conversation Poem, Coleridge had to remind himself of what he already knew, which was that stressing the familiar act of love, far from trivializing his poetry, only widened its emotional and intellectual range. This act of love is the initiating step in the dissolution of the self, the caging and confining ego which is the 'problem' of these poems – as it had been of mankind generally in *Religious Musings*:

> Toy-bewitched,
> Made blind by lusts, disherited of soul,
> No common centre Man, no common sire
> Knoweth! A sordid solitary thing,
> Mid countless brethren with a lonely heart
> Through courts and cities the smooth savage roams
> Feeling himself, his own low self the whole
> (*Religious Musings*, ll. 146–52)

In *Religious Musings*, it is a more abstract recognition that the 'most holy name' of the all-pervading God is 'Love' that enables man to fly 'from his small particular orbit'

> With blest outstarting! From himself he flies,
> Stands in the sun, and with no partial gaze
> Views all creation; and he loves it all,
> And blesses it, and calls it very good!
>   (*Religious Musings*, ll. 110–3)

In the Conversation Poems, the reconciliation with creation is enacted rather than trumpeted, but it remains the ideal of the poet as it had been the ideal of the pantisocrat. The difference lies in the means by which it is to be achieved. The initiating, un*self*-conscious act of love – similar to the Ancient Mariner's unself-conscious blessing of the watersnakes – enables the poet to find within the framework of individual poems, if only momentarily, the unity with nature and God that he seeks. Failure to recognize the significance of this liberating act can lead to misinterpretation of the Conversation Poems, especially of the first and most controversial of the group, 'The Eolian Harp'.

'The Eolian Harp'

At the opening of 'The Eolian Harp: Composed at Clevedon, Somersetshire', as at the opening of the later 'Reflections on Having Left a Place of Retirement', the unity with nature, achieved through the mediation of Sara, is a *fait accompli*. As with 'Reflections' and as with all the other Conversation Poems, the compatibility of mind and nature is symbolized by the loving detail of the description:

> My pensive Sara! thy soft cheek reclined
> Thus on my arm, most soothing sweet it is
> To sit beside our Cot, our Cot o'ergrown
> With white-flower'd Jasmin, and the broad-leav'd Myrtle,
> (Meet emblems they of Innocence and Love!)
> And watch the clouds, that late were rich with light
> Slow saddening round, and mark the star of eve
> Serenely brilliant (such should Wisdom be)
> Shine opposite! How exquisite the scents
> Snatch'd from yon bean-field! and the world *so* hush'd!
> The stilly murmur of the distant Sea
> Tells us of silence.
>   ('The Eolian Harp', ll. 1–12)

The poem then proceeds to trace the wanderings of the poet's mind, instigated and informed by the interaction of the wind and the Aeolian harp, a standard household ornament set up outside the house to sound in response to the wind (like the wind chimes more common today) and a fashionable eighteenth-century symbol of (amongst other things) 'nature's music'.[18] Thoughts and 'phantasies', 'uncall'd and undetain'd', move through the poet's 'indolent and passive brain'

> As wild and various as the random gales
> That swell and flutter on this subject Lute!
> ('The Eolian Harp', ll. 39–43)

The first 'phantasy' provoked by the interaction of wind and harp is a sexual one, as explicit as any in Coleridge and a measure of the passion the two lovers shared during these months of rare intimacy:

> How by the desultory breeze caressed,
> Like some coy maid half yielding to her lover,
> It pours forth such upbraiding, as must needs
> Tempt to repeat the wrong! And now, its strings
> Boldlier swept, the long sequacious notes
> Over delicious surges sink and rise
> ('The Eolian Harp', ll. 14–9)

(The provocative 'upbraiding' of the harp/lover looks forward to the more serious upbraiding of Sara's eye at the end of the poem when the poet tries to press his intellectual intentions on her.) The sexual then dissolves into a folkloric fantasy. If we ignore for the time being the lines 26 to 33, begun in 1803 but not finally included in the poem until 1828 after an appearance in the *errata* of *Sibylline Leaves* (1817), the poem then moves with the drifting consciousness of the poet away from the present back to an earlier time and place, when 'on the midway slope | Of yonder hill I stretch my legs at noon' (ll. 34–5). Finally we have the famous pantheistic speculation for which the speaker is reproved:

> And what if all of animated nature
> Be but organic harps diversely framed,
> That tremble into thought, as o'er them sweeps
> Plastic and vast, one intellectual breeze,
> At once the Soul of each, and God of All?
> ('The Eolian Harp', ll. 44–8)

After this bold speculative pantheism, in which God is imagined as immanent in and coextensive with the physical universe, the last sixteen lines of the poem represent a sudden retreat to a fundamental, orthodox Christian attitude that has frustrated many critics. Indeed, the later addition of lines 26–33 – 'O! the one Life within us and abroad' – suggests that they frustrated the poet himself, for they invalidate the dramatic conclusion of the poem by apparently affirming the very pantheism that the poet originally renounced.

Faced with a dilemma of Coleridge's own creation, most criticism has chosen, with Coleridge, to stress the pantheistic discovery of the poem. The closing lines thus become an aberration for which the narrow-minded Sara is responsible.

> But thy more serious eye a mild reproof
> Darts, O beloved woman! nor such thoughts
> Dim and unhallowed dost thou not reject,
> And biddest me walk humbly with my God.
> ('The Eolian Harp', ll. 49–52)

However, just as Coleridge himself tended quite unfairly to hold Sara responsible for the breakdown of their marriage, so she is unfairly held responsible for what is an expression of a desperate need of Coleridge's own. A combination of our knowledge of Coleridge's and Sara's subsequently disastrous marriage and our overriding interest in Coleridge's fragmented, often derivative philosophical speculations can lead us to misplace the emphasis in the poem on what we imagine the poet would *like* to have said, had the 'governessy' Sara not been there to reprove him.[19] One thing consistently underemphasized in discussions of Coleridge's metaphysical speculation is Coleridge's pervasive ambivalence towards his own metaphysical speculation. Coleridge the intellectual could be profoundly anti-intellectual.

It is important to look at 'The Eolian Harp' as an instance or enactment of this Coleridgean ambivalence because if it is ignored there is a risk that the Conversation Poems as a group will be robbed of their formal justification. The fantasy and speculation of 'The Eolian Harp' represent not only a movement – a mental 'wandering' or 'drifting' as I have called it – but also a movement *away*. From the invocation in the opening line, the poem moves away from Sara and back into the self, into the mind of the poet. While this movement is inspired by harmony, and seeks only to find analogues for that harmony, it is also, ironically, discordant in itself as well as divisive. It is no accident that in lines 34 to 43 Coleridge describes himself as alone on a hillside, 'tranquil mus[ing] upon tranquillity'. This casual 'flashback' hints at the sundering of the two lovers that takes place in the poem, and with it the sundering of the poet and his God. The ominous 'saddening' of the clouds in the opening lines have already suggested that their paradisal unity is tenuous, the darkening of the day looking forward and backward to a state of spiritual darkness ('Wildered and dark', l. 63).

This only makes sense if we accept the poet's own interpretation that speculations of the kind he indulges in are 'shapings of the unregenerate mind' that cut him off from Sara, nature, and God, and that the search for *intellectual* enlightenment leads, paradoxically, to an emotional and spiritual darkness.

He finds himself as he was before he achieved the unity to which the domestic peace with Sara had given him access: 'Wildered' or bewildered. It is a crucial word, and is common in the spiritual autobiography represented by Coleridge's confessional letters and notebooks.

Abstruse research

Coleridge's protestations to his brother George in March 1794 that the 'dazzle of Wit' and a fondness for 'subtlety of Argument' had seduced him from the right religious path no doubt reflect a conscious or unconscious conformity to the expectations of his more orthodox brother (*CL* I, 78). But a renunciation of 'the dark & deep perplexities of metaphysic Controversy' is as recurrent a feature of Coleridge's private notebooks as it is of his often posturing correspondence (*CN* I, 27). Like the satirists before him, Coleridge sees metaphysical speculation as at best impotent to cope with the demands – specifically the emotional demands – of life:

> My philosophical refinements, & metaphysical Theories lay by me in the hour of anguish, as toys by the bedside of a Child deadly-sick. May God continue his visitations to my soul, bowing it down, till the pride & Laodicean self-confidence of human Reason be utterly done away.
> (*CL* I, 267)

At its worst, metaphysical speculation is seen by Coleridge as physically destructive and emotionally crippling. 'This perpetual Struggle, this endless *heart-wasting*', he would write to Daniel Stuart in 1806, ironically (and simplistically) blaming his marriage to Sara Coleridge for all his misfortune, 'was at the bottom of all my resolution, procrastination, languor, and former detestable habit of poison taking — : this turned me away so long from political and moral disquisition, poetry, and all the flowers & herbs that grow in the Light and Sunshine, to be meanwhile a Delver in the unwholesome quick-silver mines of abstruse Metaphysics' (*CL* II, 1178).

Throughout his life Coleridge identified in 'abstruse Metaphysics' a Circean charm which he came to associate, as he does in this letter to Stuart, with opium-taking. He even spoke of it in terms of an addiction: 'I am so *habituated* to philosophizing', he told Southey very early in December 1794, 'that I cannot divest myself of it even when my own Wretchedness is the subject' (*CL* I, 133). Like opium, metaphysics seems to have offered an initial release, an escape from the exigent demands of reality. And yet, again like opium, it is seen as having led ultimately to disaster. This, certainly, is the attitude of 'Dejection: An Ode':

> not to think of what I needs must feel,
> But to be still and patient, all I can

> And haply by abstruse research to steal
> From my own nature all the natural man —
> This was my sole resource, my only plan:
> Till that which suits a part infects the whole,
> And now is almost grown the *habit* of my soul.
> ('Dejection: An Ode', ll. 87–93 [my emphasis])

'Abstruse research', the attempt to unravel the 'perplexities of metaphysic Controversy', always had Faustian overtones for Coleridge: 'the pride & Laodicean self-confidence of human Reason'. He was never far away from the fundamentalist conviction that (as he wrote against Priestley in a letter to John Edwards in December 1796) '*Incomprehensibility* is as necessary an attribute of the First Cause as Love, or Power, or Intelligence' (CL I, 193).

'The Eolian Harp', in other words, is neither the first nor the last time that we hear him say that 'never guiltless may I speak of him, I The Incomprehensible!' (ll. 58–9). All thinking for Coleridge must be completed, if not superseded, by faith. Distinguishing between two kinds of knowledge in an early note, Coleridge asserts 'the superiority of the knowledge which we have by faith to the knowledge which we have by Natural philosophy'. Precisely where this superiority is manifested is important to the Conversation Poems as a group: 'in its dignity, in its moral effects, & lastly in the comforting of sorrow, in the giving of New Joy, & the exaltation of natural pleasures' (CN I, 6). 'Joy' would become in 'Dejection: An Ode' (1802) the powerful, creative emotion which enabled the poet to see *and* feel just how beautiful the world around him was – enabled, that is, the 'exaltation of natural pleasures'. 'In joy all individuality is lost', says Coleridge in his lectures on the history of philosophy in 1818, bringing us back to the escape from the self that is the achievement of the Conversation Poems.[20]

Coleridge consistently discovered in his own life a pattern of paradise lost through metaphysical speculation, then regained through emotional attachment. The implied action or narrative of 'The Eolian Harp' is but one example and it is with this pattern in mind that the final lines of the poem should be read:

> Well hast thou said and holily disprais'd
> These shapings of the unregenerate mind;
> Bubbles that glitter as they rise and break
> On vain Philosophy's aye-babbling spring.
> For never guiltless may I speak of him,
> The Incomprehensible! save when with awe
> I praise him and with faith that inly feels;
> Who with his saving mercies healed me,
> A sinful and most miserable Man,

Wildered and dark, and gave me to possess
Peace, and this Cot, and thee, heart-honoured Maid!
('The Eolian Harp', ll. 54–64)

Probably the best known example of Coleridge's rescue from the mires of metaphysics occurs in the first chapter of the *Biographia*, where he quotes Milton's description in *Paradise Lost* of the fallen angels confounding themselves in unresolvable philosophical issues. It is a crucial passage in Coleridge's account of his literary life that brings together, in a protracted agony of self-reflection and self-flagellation, all the issues raised by the ambivalence of 'The Eolian Harp', confirming the association of metaphysical speculation with opium and the fact that a suspicion of abstract thought accounts for the form of the Conversation Poems:

> At a very premature age, even before my fifteenth year, I had bewildered myself in metaphysicks, and in theological controversy. Nothing else pleased me. History, and particular facts, lost all interest in my mind. Poetry ... itself, yea novels and romances, became insipid to me. In my friendless wanderings on our *leave-days* ... highly was I delighted, if any passenger, especially if he were dressed in black, would enter into conversation with me. For I soon found the means of directing it to my favourite subjects
>
> > Of providence, fore-knowledge, will, and fate,
> > Fix'd fate, free will, fore-knowledge absolute,
> > And found no end in wandering mazes lost.
>
> This preposterous pursuit was, beyond doubt, injurious, both to my natural powers, and to the progress of my education. It would perhaps have been destructive, had it been continued; but from this I was auspiciously withdrawn, partly indeed by an accidental introduction to an amiable family, chiefly however, by the genial influence of a style of poetry, so tender and yet so manly, so natural and real, and yet so dignified and harmonious, as the sonnets &c. of Mr. Bowles! Well were it for me, perhaps, had I never relapsed into the same mental disease; if I had continued to pluck the flower and reap the harvest from the cultivated surface, instead of delving into the unwholesome quicksilver mines of metaphysic depths [compare *CL* II, 1178, above]. But if in time I have sought refuge from bodily pain and mismanaged sensibility in abstruse researches, which exercised the strength and subtlety of the understanding without awakening the feelings of the heart; still there was a long and blessed interval, during which my natural faculties were allowed to expand, and my original tendencies to develope themselves: my fancy, and the love of nature, and the sense of beauty in forms and sounds. (*BL* I, 16–7)

The local irony here is that chapters five to thirteen of the *Biographia*, written later than this first chapter, will be preoccupied with just such bewildering 'metaphysicks' and 'theological controversy'. But it is in the lost and regained paradise that our interest lies, and in the key word 'bewildered'. The 'amiable family' Coleridge mentions is the Evans family. It is, however, a *literary* life that Coleridge is writing and the mention of Bowles, indeed the priority given to Bowles's poetry, has far-reaching literary implications. If we go back to 1794 and Coleridge's analysis of the rescue effected by Bowles's poetry closer to the time that he first read it, we find the same story:

> when the *darker* day of life began,
> And I did roam, a thought-bewilder'd man!
> Thy kindred Lays an healing solace lent
> ('Sonnet: To Bowles', ll. 6–8)

Again, 'Wildered and dark', Coleridge finds salvation in the heart; according to the *Biographia*, Bowles was 'the first', with William Cowper, 'who combined natural thoughts with natural diction; the first who reconciled the heart with the head' (*BL* I, 25).

'I *think* too much for a *Poet*', Coleridge wrote to John Thelwall in December 1796 (*CL* I, 294). And to Southey, two years earlier: 'I cannot write without a *body* of *thought* – hence my *Poetry* is crowded and sweats beneath a heavy burthen of Ideas and Imagery! It has seldom Ease' (*CL* I, 137). Coleridge found in the blending of thought and feeling in Bowles's poetry a naturalness and an ease which his own rhetorical and philosophical style lacked. His judgement might have been 'stronger, than were [his] powers of realizing its dictates', but he was eventually able to exploit what he saw as the naturalness of Bowles's sonnets and the 'divine Chit chat' of Cowper's blank verse in *The Task* while developing the supple informal style of the Conversation Poems, capable of modulating from apparently casual anecdote or description into an unself-conscious lyric sublimity (*CL* I, 279). Behind them as a group lay this pattern of recovery from a too exclusive, too self-centred attention to abstruse theological and philosophical issues.

William and Dorothy Wordsworth

The self-centredness of 'abstruse research' will also be the theme of Wordsworth's description of Coleridge at Cambridge in the sixth book of *The Prelude* – a description no doubt deriving from Coleridge himself. There, addressing Coleridge directly, Wordsworth analyses 'the airy wretchedness | That battened on your youth':

> I have thought
> Of thee, thy learning, gorgeous eloquence,
> And all the strength and plumage of thy youth

Thy subtle speculations, toils abstruse
Among the schoolmen, and Platonic forms
Of wild ideal pageantry, shaped out
From things well-matched, or ill, and words for things —
The self-created sustenance of a mind
Debarred from Nature's living images,
Compelled to be a life unto itself.
                    (*The Prelude* [1805], VI, 305–14)

Wordsworth, typically, stresses the absence of Nature. Behind the passage lies the familiar Renaissance comparison of the vain, theological elaborations of the 'schoolmen' with the complex webs woven by spiders from their own entrails. As with corrupt poetic diction or expression, language is substituted for reality – 'words for things' – setting up an opaque medium between language and thought, on the one hand, and Nature on the other. It was a conviction that young Wordsworth and Coleridge shared and would ultimately form the fundamental premise of the controversial Preface of 1800 to their joint collection of poems, *Lyrical Ballads*.

It was, however, only one of many, many convictions that the two of them discovered they shared when, in June 1797, Coleridge leapt the fence and crossed a field to stay a fortnight with Wordsworth and his sister Dorothy at Racedown in Dorset where the pair were living rent free in a house of his friends, the Pinneys. Coleridge and Wordsworth had met briefly on a couple of occasions, the first time probably in September 1795 at John Pinney's house in Bristol. They knew each other well enough to have been mutually complimentary, though Coleridge's reference to Wordsworth in a letter to Thelwall in April of 1796 as 'a very dear friend of mine' is unlikely, more prophetic than accurate (*CL* I, 215). In the same letter he also called him the 'best poet of the age', and it is true that he was familiar enough with Wordsworth's *An Evening Walk* to have quoted from it in his 'Ode to Sara, Written at Shurton Bars' in September 1795. Coleridge was exaggerating in his letter to Thelwall, however, setting Wordsworth up as an authority in order to promote his own *Religious Musings*. What it does reveal is that the two of them had corresponded occasionally and exchanged manuscripts.

Indeed, only two months before they met at Racedown, Wordsworth had stopped in at Nether Stowey in neighbouring Somerset where the Coleridges had been living since January in a small cottage whose garden backed onto Tom Poole's tannery and large house. There, with Sara, their first child (David) Hartley, Nanny a servant girl, and twenty-year-old Charles Lloyd, a live-in pupil who had been with them since September of the previous year, Coleridge had been carrying out his plan 'to work *very hard* – as Cook, Butler, Scullion, Shoe-cleaner, occasional Nurse, Gardener, Hind, Pig-protector, Chaplain, Secretary, Poet, Reviewer, and omni-botherum shilling-scavenger' (*CL* I, 266). Lloyd's presence had been a compromise. Having seen 'that literature was not a profession by which I could expect to live' (*BL* I, 121) and spent months making tentative plans for tutoring in a wealthy home or setting up his own school, Coleridge had finally opted for accepting the unstable and epileptic Lloyd into the family as a pupil to defray costs. Now they were all crammed into the damp, pokey, mice-infested cottage where Coleridge would experience the happiest moments of his life, and it was here that Wordsworth visited them in April 1797.

At the time, as it happens, Coleridge was in low spirits and reported to Cottle that 'Wordsworth's conversation etc roused me somewhat' (*CL* I, 319). This arousal, however, was nothing compared to the way he felt after his fortnight with William and Dorothy at Racedown, when it is fair to say they got to know each other for the first time. Each one of the three reported excitedly of their discovery. Dorothy's description of Coleridge to Mary Hutchinson gives some intimation of how it was that the three of them should have created the most significant relationship in English literary history. 'You had a great loss in not seeing Coleridge', wrote Dorothy, 'He is a wonderful man' (that word again):

> His conversation teems with soul, mind, and spirit. ... At first I thought him very plain, that is, for about three minutes: he ... has a wide mouth, thick lips, and not very good teeth, longish, half-curling rough black hair. But if you hear him speak for five minutes you think no more of them. His eye is large and full, not dark but grey; such an eye as would receive from a heavy soul the dullest expression; but it speaks every emotion of his animated mind; it has more of the 'poet's eye in a fine frenzy rolling' than I ever witnessed.[21]

Coleridge, in his turn, responded with lavish praise for 'Wordsworth and his exquisite sister' (*CL* I, 330).

There can be no doubt that Dorothy, whom Coleridge met for the first time at Racedown, was a vital catalyst in all of this. Intense, spontaneous as no woman he had ever met, and acutely responsive to the sensual world in ways that Coleridge admired and to which he could relate, Dorothy possessed 'a perfect electrometer' of taste, according to Coleridge: 'it bends, it protrudes, and draws in, at subtlest beauties & most recondite faults' (*CL* I, 331). Coleridge was no more enlightened than most men of his generation when it came to women, and is on record as saying it was 'the perfection of woman to be characterless'.[22] Pantisocracy had seen women as equal, it is true, but behind the long letter Coleridge would write to his estranged wife Sara in 1802 – insisting that 'in sex, acquirements, and in the quantity and quality of natural endowments whether of Feeling, or of Intellect, you are the Inferior' (*CL* II, 888) – lay a set of entrenched patriarchal assumptions that in his personal relations with women Coleridge rarely overcame. Dorothy, however, was different; 'her eye watchful in minutest observation of nature', she engaged his attention and respect as no other woman ever had or would (*CL* I, 330–1). (The only possible exception would be Sara Hutchinson, sister of the Wordsworths' friend and later William's wife, Mary. Though for years Coleridge would be obsessed with Sara Hutchinson and would always think of her as his ideal partner, it is hard to see her as anything other than a fantasy.) Coleridge was so used to relating to people intellectually that the world of Dorothy – of both the Wordsworths – was a brave new world for him, especially coming at a time when, wearied by polemics and abstraction, he was himself beginning to seek more satisfaction in the world of nature and the senses, as we have seen in the poetry he was beginning, tentatively, to write when he met them.

But so, too, was Wordsworth on the rebound from an intense, if less histrionic and less public, relationship with contemporary history and political theory – intense enough for him to have suffered a serious depression and 'yielded up moral questions in despair'.[23] It was one of a number of uncanny symmetries that they discovered in each others' lives and ideas. Both were thinking and feeling their way out of Godwinian rationalism (no great difficulty for Coleridge, though he still planned to publish a refutation). Both were working on plays preoccupied with human freedom, culpability, and remorse: Wordsworth's *The Borderers* and Coleridge's *Osorio*. (Coleridge had his play in hand when he arrived at Racedown and much of their time was spent reading their plays to each other and projecting their London productions.) For both, poetry was beginning to focus all their revolutionary energies and both, accordingly, were striving for a more chastened idiom and for a critical language capable of defining and defending that striving. There was so much to talk about, so much to see and share.

Besides, Coleridge in 1797 was an intense friendship waiting to happen. His angry, anguished words to Southey on Southey's desertion of pantisocracy in November 1795, revealing as they are of Coleridge's emotional needs and neediness, as well as of the phenomenon of Romantic friendship, must also be seen as a prophecy determined to fulfill itself:

> You have left a large Void in my Heart—I know no man big enough to fill it. Others I may love equally & esteem equally: and some perhaps I may admire as much. But never do I expect to find another man, who will make me unite attachment for his person with reverence for his heart and admiration of his Genius! I did not only venerate you for your Virtues, I prized you as a Sheet Anchor of mine! And even [as] a Poet, my Vanity knew no keener gratification than your Praise—But these Things are past by, like as when an hungry man dreams, and lo! he feasteth—but he awakes, and his Soul is empty! (*CL* I, 173)

All these things Wordsworth would become to Coleridge: the object of his extreme, often self-abasing reverence and admiration, and the admirer and sheet anchor of his personal and intellectual and poetic strengths. More than just a bonus, however, Dorothy was the necessary condition.

Wordsworth, too, would benefit. In the first instance, Coleridge inspired and actively encouraged Wordsworth to write some of his greatest poetry, poetry that was influenced by his own Conversation Poems. Furthermore, the admiration of one so obviously intelligent and discriminating and *enthusiastic* as Coleridge helped Wordsworth – for good *and* ill, it has to be said – to an unparallelled confidence in his own abilities.

The greatest beneficiary in all this, however, was poetry. Meeting the Wordsworths, Coleridge rediscovered poetry for the first time, as it were, not just in the commonplace sense of 'finding a voice' – which they both did, several in fact – but also in the sense of finding in poetry a personal, cultural, and spiritual significance that, outside a handful of quite extraordinary poems, was Coleridge's greatest legacy to English-speaking culture. Poetry was never a substitute religion for Coleridge. We have already seen the importance of God and Christian revelation in his life, and the bulk of his writings serve this interest. But it is equally true to say that Coleridge's work to define poetry and the creative faculty – 'What is poetry? is so nearly the same question with, what is a poet? that the answer to the one is involved in the solution of the other' (*BL* II, 15) – made it so *vital* to our psychological and cultural lives that it became possible for the post-Romantic world to see creative literature as an alternative salvation.

And it was, according to the arguably oversimplified account in the *Biographia*, Wordsworth's genius – its 'union of deep feeling with profound thought; the fine balance of truth in observing with the imaginative faculty in modifying the object sought' – that inspired Coleridge's search: 'This excellence, which in all Mr. Wordsworth's writings is more or less predominant, and which constitutes the character of his mind, I no sooner felt than I sought to understand' (*BL* I, 80, 82). If his need to undertake a major reevaluation of human creativity did not occur to Coleridge instantaneously, as he suggests here – what he felt at the time, next to Wordsworth, was his own comparative insignificance as a poet: 'a *little man by his* side' (*CL* I, 325) – still his poetry and letters testify to the importance the whole issue of creative genius assumed. Already in his political writings the imagination had been exerting an obvious fascination – as in his speculations on Robespierre, for example, who

possessed a glowing ardor that still remembered the *end*, and a cool ferocity that never either overlooked, or scrupled, the *means*. What that *end* was, is not known: that it was a wicked one, has by no means been proved. I rather think, that the distant prospect, to which he was travelling, appeared to him grand and beautiful; but that he fixed his eyes on it with such intense eagerness as to neglect the foulness of the road. If however his intentions were pure, his subsequent enormities yield us a melancholy proof, that it is not the character of the possessor which directs the power, but the power which shapes and depraves the character of the possessor.[24]

Now his thoughts were focused more intensively on poetry, though Robespierre and all the other world-gardeners and dreamers of power would turn up again before very long in the shape of Kubla Khan.

'This Lime-Tree Bower My Prison'

'This Lime-Tree Bower My Prison' is a typical product of the honeymoon period of Coleridge's relationship with the Wordsworths. No sooner had the three met than they determined to live within creative proximity to each other and the Wordsworths had the good fortune to secure a large house, Alfoxden, not more than four miles from Nether Stowey. For the pedestrian enthusiasts that the three of them were – walking and pedestrian tours had become an expression of freedom and of solidarity with the people for many middle and upper class intellectuals – four miles was nothing. (Long enough, though, for Coleridge to use it as an excuse to stay over on many occasions, leaving Sara at home with baby Hartley.) Coleridge returned from Racedown in late June and Alfoxden was leased in mid July. For the moment, however, the Wordsworths were only part of a more ambitious project. Coleridge had set about orchestrating an alternative to pantisocracy, gathering together a close-knit circle of what he took to be kindred spirits (with Sara, it should be said, very much on the periphery). Charles and Mary Lamb had been exhorted to join him, consistently, ever since the tragedy of September 1796 in which Mary had killed their mother in a fit of insanity. They arrived on 7 July, only a week before the Wordsworths settled into Alfoxden and ten days before the arrival of another keenly sought after guest, the radical London lecturer John Thelwall.

Coleridge always claimed that love was 'the vital air of [his] Genius' (CL I, 471). Now he had it in abundance. Here was Tom Poole, patron, friend, and father figure whose house (and extensive library) could be reached through the back yard. Here was Charles Lamb, whom he had got to know intimately during his London retreat at the Salutation and Cat in the winter of 1794, and to whom he had been writing long letters of comfort and consolation. Thelwall was expected and here, preeminently, were the Wordsworths. Coleridge immediately embarked on a virtuoso piece, 'This Lime-Tree Bower My Prison', addressed explicitly to Lamb but implicitly to the Wordsworths – in the original version, the poet addresses Sara and, collectively, 'my Friends'[25] – celebrating their new, shared values and instigating between himself and Wordsworth a poetry of allusion and counterpoint that would continue into the early nineteenth century.[26]

Fittingly, then, 'This Lime-Tree Bower My Prison' offers the clearest example of all the Conversation Poems of the redeeming power of love, emphasizing the point that an escape from the self is both a poetic technique and a moral and spiritual imperative. The poem begins on a note of petulant self-preoccupation and complaint – Coleridge was prevented by a scalded foot from accompanying his friends on a walk – with the casual particularity of the poet's imprisonment within the lime-tree bower subtly suggesting his imprisonment within the self:

> Well, they are gone, and here must I remain
> This lime-tree bower my prison! I have lost
> Beauties and feelings, such as would have been
> Most sweet to my remembrance.
> ('This Lime-Tree Bower My Prison', ll. 1–4)

Pricked by envy, the poet pursues his friends in his imagination, first, down 'the still roaring dell', and then out under 'the wide wide heaven'. By the time the poet feels specifically for, and with, the 'gladness' of his friend – 'My gentle-hearted Charles' (l. 28) – all thought of his own discomfort has been lost in sympathy for the 'evil and pain | And strange calamity' from which Lamb is imagined to emerge.

'Love', Coleridge wrote in an early note, 'transforms the soul into the object loved' (*CN* I, 189). Lamb's journey has become his own, in more ways than one. The naturalistic detail of the poet's imaginative descent into the purgatorial 'roaring dell' reveals an absorption in the natural world that, because it has replaced his initial absorption in himself, testifies to his spiritual liberation:

> The roaring dell, o'erwooded, narrow, deep,
> And only speckled by the mid-day sun;
> Where its slim trunk the ash from rock to rock
> Flings arching like a bridge;—that branchless ash,
> Unsunned and damp, whose few poor yellow leaves
> Ne'er tremble in the gale, yet tremble still,
> Fanned by the water-fall! and there my friends
> Behold the dark green file of long lank weeds,
> That all at once (a most fantastic sight!)
> Still nod and drip beneath the dripping edge
> Of the blue clay-stone.
> ('This Lime-Tree Bower My Prison', ll. 10–20)

This loving attention to detail, moreover, is all vicarious, all on behalf of Charles. His anticipation of Charles's aesthetic gratification in a rush of sympathetic identification becomes in turn the poet's imaginative gift or offering, inspired by the unconscious act of love which is his point of departure from an isolated (incarcerated) self.

There are in fact four journeys alluded to here. Firstly, there is the literal journey undertaken by Charles Lamb, Sara, and William and Dorothy Wordsworth that occurred outside the poem and the poet's imagination. Secondly, there is the poet's imaginative recreation of that journey, undertaken on their behalf. Thirdly, there is Charles's symbolic journey from pain to gladness, from the city (darkness, imprisonment) to nature (freedom and light). Last but not least, there is the poet's own, *spiritual* journey – *via* the journey he imagines for Charles – from self-centred isolation (darkness, imprisonment) to selfless participation in nature and God (freedom and light).

Much of the 'argument' of the poem is carried on by what might otherwise appear only realistic or incidental imagery, especially by the compound image of the sun and sunlight. Just as the poet begins isolated and cut off, so the 'roaring dell' in the passage above is 'only speckled by the mid-day sun', while the 'branchless ash' is, in turn, *'Unsunn'd'* (ll. 11, 13–14). Once under 'the wide wide heaven', however, everything is said to live 'in yellow light' – or, rather, everything is *commanded* to live 'in yellow light', according to the poet's quasi-divine fiat. The landscape, streaming with sunlit glory, automatically invokes the 'Almighty Spirit' (ll. 21, 36, 42):

> Shine in the slant beams of the sinking orb,
> Ye purple heath-flowers! richlier burn, ye clouds!
> Live in the yellow light, ye distant groves!
> And kindle, thou blue ocean! So my Friend
> Struck with deep joy may stand, as I have stood,
> Silent with swimming sense; yea, gazing round
> On the wide landscape, gaze till all doth seem
> Less gross than bodily; and of such hues
> As veil the Almighty Spirit, when yet he makes
> Spirits perceive his presence.
> ('This Lime-Tree Bower My Prison', ll. 34–43)

'Let there be light', said Coleridge, 'and there was light'. And *'it was* good'.

Not only is the landscape that Coleridge conjures in this passage transformed by the sunlight, but the very bower which had once been a prison becomes a witness of this translucence of God in his creation: 'Pale beneath the blaze | Hung the transparent foliage' (ll. 47–8). This access of sunlight through the 'transparent foliage' spells the dissolution of the imprisoning bower and the release of the prisoner. The movement outwards of the poet's mind and spirit in an act of sympathetic identification has enabled the movement inwards of the sun. The poet's act of love for Charles and for the natural world participates in the Divine love which creates and sustains all existence, as the sun sustains the natural world. 'Man knows God only by revelation from God', remarked Coleridge in his notebooks in the same year, 'as we see the sun by his own light' (*CN* I, 209).[27]

'This Lime-Tree Bower My Prison' expresses Coleridge's sense of 'the one Life, within us and abroad' that he meditates in 'The Eolian Harp', a sense which he also discovered in Hebrew poetry: 'In the Hebrew Poets each Thing has a Life of it's own, & yet they are all one Life. In God they move, & live, & *have* their Being' (*CL* II, 866). In a final, brilliant image (both inspired and shining), a lone rook – a black, traditionally raucous and ugly bird, symbolizing death – is momentarily swallowed up by the sun, gathered into the 'one Life':

> when the last rook
> Beat its straight path along the dusky air
> Homewards, I blest it! deeming its black wing
> (Now a dim speck, now vanishing in light)
> Had cross'd the mighty Orb's dilated glory
> While thou stood'st gazing
> ('This Lime-Tree Bower My Prison',
> ll. 68–73)

The poet, Charles, and the rook, all with a life of their own, establish covenant or community in this last gesture and become one life. The creaking of the bird's wing, once 'dissonant' like the opening mood of the lonely and resentful poet, is now subsumed into a larger harmony: 'No sound is dissonant which tells of Life' (l. 76).

But the significance of the sunlit landscape of 'This Lime-Tree Bower My Prison' does not end here. In the same letter to William Sotheby of 1802 in which Coleridge records his discovery of the Hebrew poets' sense of unity, he also related it to the faculty which, as poets, they appeared to him to possess 'beyond all others': the imagination. It was not the first occasion. He had suggested an association between the 'one Life' and the poetic imagination earlier, in *Religious Musings*, when addressing 'the Elect' under a different name:

> Contemplant Spirits! ye that hover o'er
> With untired gaze the immeasurable fount
> Ebullient with creative Deity!
> And ye of plastic power, that interfused
> Roll through the grosser and material mass
> In organizing surge! Holies of God!
> (*Religious Musings*, ll. 402–7)

Continuing this association between the 'plastic', modifying power of creative genius and the creative and sustaining power of God, the sunlit landscape of 'This Lime-Tree Bower My Prison' – the 'deep radiance' tingeing the walnut tree and 'full on the ancient ivy'; the 'dilated glory' of the setting sun (ll. 51–3, 72) – represents, as well as Divine unity, a world transformed by the poet's imagination. Coleridge uses precisely this analogy for the effects of imagination at the opening of the fourteenth chapter of the *Biographia*:

> During the first year that Mr. Wordsworth and I were neighbours, our conversations turned frequently on the two cardinal points of poetry, the power of exciting the sympathy of the reader by a faithful adherence to the truth of nature, and the power of giving the interest of novelty by the modifying colors of imagination. The sudden charm, which accidents of light and shade, which moonlight or sunset diffused over a known and familiar landscape, appeared to represent the practicability of combining both. (*BL* II, 5)

Conversations

'This Lime-Tree Bower My Prison' confirms that it was indeed on the cardinal points of poetry that their conversations turned during the first year they were neighbours. Coleridge had written a great poem on the need for 'home-born Feeling' – for unself-conscious love – to liberate the imagination and reconnect with nature and God. He had written it, moreover, in a form he had himself developed: 'A Poem which affects not to be Poetry' as he sub-titled 'Reflections on Having Left a Place of Retirement'; a poem intimate and familiar and yet capable of profundities the heart could own. At the time of its composition, 'The Eolian Harp' had been a favourite of his – *the* favourite, according to a letter to Thelwall on December 1796 (*CL* I, 295); by next year, it was 'the most perfect Poem, I ever wrote'.[28] It was only many years later, however, that Coleridge would recognize that his new priorities and his experiments had helped him to an original and influential formula:

> Let me be excused, if it should seem to others too mere a trifle to justify my noticing it—but I have some claim to the thanks of no small numbers of readers of poetry in having first introduced this species of short blank verse poems—of which Southey, Lamb, Wordsworth, and others have since produced so many exquisite specimens.[29]

The Conversation Poems as a 'species' record the apparently casual rhythm of the mind, expanding and contracting, as it observes, experiences, *muses* – sharing its musings either throughout or intermittently with a friend or loved one, while at the same time making an intimate out of the reader. Yet, like 'This Lime-Tree Bower My Prison', each of the Conversation Poems is organized in a way that turns out to be far from casual, implicitly and explicitly using its immediate personal experience to dramatize issues of vital 'metaphysical' import.

It was to a later poem, 'The Nightingale', that Coleridge gave the subtitle eventually adopted by twentieth-century criticism to stand for the whole group: 'A Conversation Poem'. As well as meaning an 'interchange of thoughts and words; familiar discourse and talk', *conversation* means (quoting the *Oxford English Dictionary*) 'the act of living or having one's being *in* or *among*', 'the action of consorting with others; living together; commerce, society, intimacy'. Coleridge had found all of this in July 1797 and would next year, his *annus mirabilis*, go on to create his greatest poetry, not just in the conversational mode but also in an astonishing new 'supernatural' mode that seemed to come out of nowhere.

4
'The Poet, Described in *Ideal* Perfection': *Annus Mirabilis*

Charlotte Poole, who had disapproved of Coleridge from the beginning and been horrified at the thought of his living so close to her cousin Tom, was 'shocked to hear that Mr Thelwall has spent some time at Stowey this week with Mr Coleridge, and consequently with Tom Poole'. 'Alfoxden house', she heard, 'is taken by another of the fraternity': 'To what are we coming?'[1] To what indeed. Coleridge, Wordsworth, and Thelwall might have thought of themselves as disaffected with politics in their different ways, but the report of the special agent, James Walsh, dispatched by the Home Office in August 1797 to investigate their activities saw them as 'a mischiefuous gang of disaffected Englishmen' and a 'Sett of violent Democrats'.[2] Anxiety about a French invasion along the west coast was high after French ships landed 1200–1400 soldiers at Fishguard in Wales earlier in the year and rumours about the seditious activities of Poole's friends' were rife in the district.[3] Thelwall, after all, had been arrested for treason and spent time in the Tower. In a largely comic account in the *Biographia* of the suspicions they aroused, Coleridge recalls that his topographical jottings for a long poem to be entitled 'The Brook' were misinterpreted as laying plans for an enemy invasion and that the 'government spy' misheard a reference to Spinoza in their conversation as 'Spy nosey' and took it as a reference to himself. If the paranoia they generated was more serious than Coleridge later allowed, it was certainly ironic, given that the three of them were seeking asylum in what Thelwall described to his wife as an 'enchanting retreat (the Academus of Stowey)'.[4]

So suspicious did their neighbours become that Coleridge was obliged to put Thelwall off later when he wrote seeking Coleridge's assistance in finding somewhere local for himself and his family. 'You cannot conceive the tumult, calumnies, & apparatus of threatened persecutions which this event has occasioned round about us', Coleridge wrote to Thelwall by way of apology: 'If *you* too should come, I am afraid, that even riots & dangerous riots might be the consequence' (*CL* I, 343–4). We have to allow for an element of exaggeration in this, given that it cannot have been easy refusing Thelwall and Coleridge at the best of times was inclined to overdramatize. To give him his due, however, Coleridge had indeed tried hard to help settle Thelwall nearby, harder than one might have expected given their 'disagreeing' – or so Coleridge wrote to Josiah Wade – 'on almost every point of religion, of morals, of politics, and of philosophy' (*CL* I, 339). But not only did the two of them like each other 'uncommonly well', Thelwall also represented for Coleridge a challenge to his powers of religious persuasion – or was it religious enchantment? He had hoped to convert London's leading radical as he would later convert the atheistical William Godwin.[5]

Caverns measureless to man

The Lambs and Thelwall were gone by the end of July, leaving Coleridge and the Wordsworths to their new friendship and to frequent daytime and nightime rambles around the countryside of Nether Stowey. And to their poetry. It is probably to 'the fall of the year, 1797' that we owe one of the best known, if not necessarily the best understood of all the poems in the English canon: 'Kubla Khan'. Its fame or notoriety lies in part at least in the circumstances of its creation, as recorded by Coleridge in an apologetic preface when he finally agreed to publish the poem – 'or, Vision in a Dream', or 'Fragment', or 'psychological curiosity', as he preferred to think of it – many years later in 1816. It is in the 1816 preface that Coleridge tells his story of having 'retired to a lonely farm-house between Porlock and Linton':

> In consequence of a slight indisposition, an anodyne had been prescribed, from the effects of which he fell asleep in his chair at the moment that he was reading the following sentence, or words of the same substance, 'Purchas's Pilgrimage:' 'Here the Khan Kubla commanded a palace to be built, and a stately garden thereunto. And thus ten miles of fertile ground were enclosed by a wall.' The author continued for about three hours in a profound sleep, at least of the external senses, during which time he has the most vivid confidence, that he could not have composed less than from two to three hundred lines; if that indeed can be called composition in which all the images rose up before him as *things*, with a parallel production of the correspondent expressions, without any sensation or consciousness of effort. On awaking he appeared to himself to have a distinct recollection of the whole, and taking his pen, ink, and paper, instantly and eagerly wrote down the lines that are here preserved. At this moment he was unfortunately called out by a person on business from Porlock, and detained by him above an hour, and on his return to his room, found to his surprise and no small mortification, that though he still retained some vague and dim recollection of the general purpose of the vision, yet, with the exception of some eight or ten scattered lines and images, all the rest had passed away like the images on the surface of

a stream into which a stone has been cast, but, alas! without the after restoration of the latter.

Only popular culture credits Coleridge's account of the poem's genesis, probably because, like the poem itself only in a different way, the account simplifies and sensationalizes the process of creation. There is a general feeling amongst scholars that it does contain some truth, however, especially that part of the story which coincides with the much shorter explanation that came to light in 1934 in the earlier, though undated, Crewe manuscript: 'This fragment with a good deal more, not recoverable, composed in a sort of Reverie brought on by two grains of Opium, taken to check a dysentery, at a Farm House between Porlock & Linton, a quarter of a mile from Culborne Church, in the fall of the year, 1797'. The 'person on business from Porlock' makes no appearance – what would he or she have been doing wandering around knocking on the doors of lonely farmhouses anyway? – nor does the poet in this earlier version seem so well equipped in his makeshift retreat. That the poem should have originated in an opium trance, however, and have appeared in a moment of inspiration to have unfolded, as a totality, before the poet's mind, only to have ultimately eluded him, does not seem especially fantastic.

Only a sense that the poem remained incommensurate with its original inspiration would explain why Coleridge never credited himself with the masterpiece, or why he should have insisted on the fragmentariness of a poem that most readers are content to read as complete. If it remains a mystery – and I mean the poem itself, now, not its composition – it is a mystery because of what is there, not because of what is missing. We must remember that Coleridge was born and educated in the eighteenth century, which (like his old schoolmaster James Boyer) privileged good sense and intelligibility. He may ultimately have come to believe that poetry may keep better faith with human experience by remaining suggestive and mysterious, but what he had created in 'Kubla Khan' still seemed to him unrealized, a 'psychological curiosity' that never metamorphosed into a poem. (The meaning of *The Rime of the Ancient Mariner* may be no clearer, but that, arguably, is the point.)

The fact remains that, on paper at least, Coleridge took less interest in 'Kubla Khan' than in any of his other major poems. We have already seen that he came to recognize in his Conversation Poems an influential formal innovation. Collectively and individually, Coleridge took pride in them, and left notes as to how they should be interpreted and valued. The same is true of his *Rime of the Ancient Mariner* and *Christabel* amongst what we call (after the *Biographia*) his 'supernatural' poems (*BL* II, 6). We can date most of his poetry fairly accurately from versions sent to sympathetic friends. Not so with 'Kubla Khan'. And yet ... why is it that so many of his friends and contemporaries recalled hearing him recite it? Byron urged him to publish it, surely because Byron recognized it as paradigmatic of the kind of exotic orientalism for which he was himself celebrated. But Byron had heard Coleridge recite it at what must have been a large gathering at his house in Piccadilly early in April 1816.[6] Rosemary Ashton has suggested that it may be 'the first great non-discursive poem'.[7] Perhaps it was also the first great performance poem since the decay of oral culture?

That the poem should be all about inspiration and creativity only adds another layer of complexity. Without trying to unravel them all, it may be worth rehearsing what appears to be going on in the poem. There are, we note, four sections or movements, each with a distinct focus and demarcated by more or less abrupt transitions. The precise structural and 'argumentative' relations between these sections is uncertain, though the fact that they *are* related in some significant way is clear from cross references, shared imagery, and grammatical connectives.

It is best to take them in the order we come across them during reading. We know that Kubla Khan was a great oriental despot, and that oriental despotism was renowned in the Western imagination for its extreme authoritarianism and its luxury. It is hardly surprising, then, that Kubla's originary gesture should partake of both:

> In Xanadu did KUBLA KHAN
> A stately pleasure-dome decree:
> Where ALPH, the sacred river, ran
> Through caverns measureless to man
> > Down to a sunless sea.
> So twice five miles of fertile ground
> With walls and towers were girdled round;
> And here were gardens bright with sinuous rills
> Where blossom'd many an incense-bearing tree;
> And here were forests ancient as the hills,
> Enfolding sunny spots of greenery.
> > ('Kubla Khan', ll. 1–11)

('Khan', incidentally, often spelt 'Can' in the period, should rhyme with 'ran' and 'man'.) Kubla has decreed a paradise, girdling (containing, constraining) the sacred river Alph (the suggestion here is of something divine and original, as in alpha, the first letter of the Greek alphabet) in order to reduce fertile, untamed vegetation to ordered gardens and realize his vision of endless, uninterrupted pleasure. And vision here is the operative word, a vision realized in and as command.

Marvellous as Kubla's creation is – its romantic strangeness and beauty matched by the magic the poet's own prosodic art(ifice) – the God-like absoluteness of the despot's power should surely, with our long tradition of tragic overreachers, give us pause. The second section of the poem, accordingly, appears to offer what the first cannot contain, what has been left out of account, signalling opposition to Kubla's vision with its opening conjunction:

> But oh that deep romantic chasm which slanted
> Down the green hill athwart a cedarn cover!
> A savage place! as holy and enchanted
> As e'er beneath the waning moon was haunted
> By woman wailing for her demon-lover!
> And from this chasm, with ceaseless turmoil seething,
> As if the earth in fast thick pants were breathing,
> A mighty fountain momently was forced:
> Amid whose swift half-intermitted Burst
> Huge fragments vaulted like rebounding hail,
> Or chaffy grain beneath the thresher's flail:
> And mid these dancing rocks at once and ever
> It flung up momently the sacred river.
> Five miles meandering with a mazy motion
> Through wood and dale the sacred river ran,
> Then reached the caverns measureless to man,
> And sank in tumult to a lifeless ocean:
> And mid this tumult Kubla heard from far
> Ancestral voices prophesying war!
>
> ('Kubla Khan', ll. 12–30)

What Kubla's act of colonizing and beautifying leaves out of account is the mystery of origins and destinations, the sheer amoral power of the creative impulse, captured in the unmistakably sexual description of the deep romantic chasm and of the orgasmic origin of the river itself – the river as life and, concomitantly, as time. It is a very pagan 'holiness' and 'sacredness' Coleridge is dealing with here, something primitive or 'savage' behind and beyond the tenuous civilization of Kubla's fantasy. Kubla's authoritarian gesture in realizing his dream and building his 'stately pleasure-dome' brings into play forces that threaten the dream itself: 'Ancestral voices prophesying war!'

Like the eighteenth century, the Romantic period was obsessed with the dream of power and what Dr Johnson called 'that hunger of imagination which preys incessantly upon life'.[8] The difference is that, unlike the eighteenth century, which looked to the ancient world, to Russia and the East for its exemplary despotisms, the Romantic period saw in the French Revolution and its successive 'directories', and later in Napoleonic imperialism, that dream imposed by the powerful on a global scale for the first time in the modern era. Coleridge, as we saw, was fascinated by the arrogant, uncompromising idealism of Robespierre, by 'the power which shapes and depraves the character of the possessor'.[9] Later, in 1803, Coleridge would refer cryptically in his notebooks to the 'Poet Bonaparte – Layer of a World-garden' (*CN* I, 1166), surely thinking of his own Kubla Khan and of the double-edged nature of the human imagination. Kubla is a version of the '*commanding* genius' described in the second chapter of the *Biographia* as impressing 'their preconceptions on the world without, in order to present them back to their own view with the satisfying degree of clearness, distinctness, and individuality'. Such a man is transformed in 'times of tumult' from a Prospero-like figure 'formed to exhibit a perfect poem in palace, or temple, or landscape-garden' into 'the shaping spirit of Ruin' (*BL* I, 32–3).

Though arguably corrupt, then, and transitory, Kubla's dream is nonetheless 'a miracle of rare device' – or so we are told in the next section, which returns, topographically and thematically, to Kubla's creation:

> The shadow of the dome of pleasure
> Floated midway on the waves;
> Where was heard the mingled measure
> From the fountain and the caves.
> It was a miracle of rare device,
> A sunny pleasure-dome with caves of ice!
> ('Kubla Khan', ll. 31–6)

The elaborate balancing act that was art for Coleridge seems to be celebrated in these lines, bringing together as they do light and dark, fire and ice (the sunny dome and the caves of ice) and orchestrating the distant sounds of both the originary fountain and the caves of dissolution and death. The dome itself, reflected on the moving, changing waters of the river captures this seemingly miraculous (though surely tenuous) equipoise: vitality arrested; death forestalled; time standing still.

The final section introduces two new players into this 'mingled measure': an Abyssinian maid who functions as Muse for the other character, the poet, now suddenly writing in the first person and self-dramatizing:

> A damsel with a dulcimer
> In a vision once I saw:
> It was an Abyssinian maid
> And on her dulcimer she play'd,
> Singing of Mount Abora.
> Could I revive within me
> Her symphony and song,
> To such a deep delight 'twould win me,
> That with music loud and long,
> I would build that dome in air,
> That sunny dome! those caves of ice!
> And all who heard should see them there,

And all should cry, Beware! Beware!
His flashing eyes, his floating hair!
Weave a circle round him thrice,
And close your eyes for holy dread:
For he on honey-dew hath fed,
And drank the milk of Paradise.
('Kubla Khan', ll. 37–54)

That the poet represents a reprise of the ambitious Kubla in some way, creating a comparably miraculous 'dome', but creating it 'in air' this time – and creating it under the inspiration of a visionary maid who sings of what is taken to be a reference to *false* paradise ('Mount Abora' was 'Mount Amora/Amara' in the manuscript, suggesting the false Abyssinian paradise of Milton's *Paradise Lost*, IV, 280–7) – all this seems certain. What kind of a reprise, exactly, is less certain. What is the tonal and grammatical strength of 'Could I revive within me I That symphony and song'? 'If only I could'? The dream of the artist is not liable to the corruption that seems endemic in the dream of the warlord and despot, but are domes in air to be preferred to tremulous domes reflected midway on the waves? Is the poet not, like the despot, locked into a mysterious cycle of creativity and destruction, as his audience in these final lines seems to recognize by distancing themselves from him? Are poetic ambitions less arrogant, less selfish than political ones? How are we to read this final (self-)image – as a celebration of Romantic genius, isolated from ordinary humanity by its inspiration, or as an implicit criticism of its anti-social posturing?

'Kubla Khan' raises many such questions, too many for Coleridge himself, perhaps. Was it because he felt no confidence in what it meant that he discounted, even distrusted the universally acknowledged charm of the poem? Was the poet, as Camille Paglia suggests, censuring his own insight into the 'sexually dual daemonic powers' haunting his dream life?[10] The only thing we can point to with any certainty is the irony of the poem itself as an enchanting artefact. A poet – Coleridge, this time – *has* built a stately pleasure-dome in air, as it happens, and unlike the dreams of civilization realized on earth by the powerful, from 'Ozymandias' to Napoleon, it has lasted and in doing so caught the rapt attention of generations of poets and generations of readers.

The Wedgwood bequest

It was also in the fall of the year 1797 that Coleridge first met Thomas Wedgwood, a meeting whose impact on his life was comparable with Wordsworth's own, though for different reasons. Tom and John Wedgwood – with their brother Josiah, wealthy legatees of their recently dead father (also

Josiah), whose famous neoClassical designs for his pottery are still reproduced today – stayed with the Wordsworths for six days at Alfoxden in the middle of September. There, inevitably, they met Coleridge. The chronically ill and manic-depressive Tom Wedgwood was an amateur everything: amateur philosopher, amateur scientist, amateur educationalist. He was a child of the English Enlightenment's most prominent group of thinkers and experimental scientists, the Lunar Society, comprising, along with potter Josiah Wedgwood Senior, Erasmus Darwin (Charles's grandfather), steam engine inventor James Watt, educationalist Richard Edgeworth (novelist Maria's father), Joseph Priestley, the painter Joseph Wright of Derby, the physician and scientist Thomas Beddoes, and many more. Tom Wedgwood's wide-ranging interests appealed to Coleridge and made Coleridge's own vast store of knowledge and endless, speculative talk irresistible to him.

In November, Coleridge reaped the first benefit of the association: an offer of a guinea a week for contributions in verse and prose to Daniel Stuart's *Morning Post*. The offer was brokered by Stuart's brother-in-law and another beneficiary of the Wedgwood patronage, James Mackintosh, on the prompting of the Wedgwoods themselves. It was a start. Then, in early December 1797, Coleridge visited the Wedgwoods at their residence, Cote House, near Bristol, and on Christmas day received from Tom and Josiah an offer of one hundred pounds to enable him 'to defer entering into an engagement, we understand you are about to form from the most urgent of motives' (*CL* I, 363). Coleridge, in short, was broke. No doubt during the visit to Cote House he had been vocal about his financial embarrassment on the failure of his play *Osorio* to impress the management of Drury Lane. Coleridge had hoped for a return of £500–600 to set up a regular income for his wife and fund a trip to Germany to continue his studies in German literature and philosophy, but when that proved out of the question had taken to rehearsing schemes for preaching, teaching, and journalism again, in search of the elusive 'Bread & Cheese'. The specific 'engagement' mentioned in the Wedgwoods' letter was almost certainly the Unitarian church living at Shrewsbury which John Prior Estlin had arranged for Coleridge. (Again, we are reminded of the extensive system of unofficial patronage on offer in a society priding itself on its philanthropy.) Though the living was not officially offered to Coleridge until 28 December he was aware of the vacancy and that attempts were being made on his behalf.

Coleridge in the first instance accepted the Wedgwoods' offer of £100. Then, on learning that the Shrewsbury living was his if he and the congregation approved of each other, he turned it down. Though immensely grateful, he explained to Josiah, what was necessary at this stage was 'a regular income sufficient to free me from all anxiety respecting my absolute wants', and the move to Shrewsbury would mean £120 in salary and a house worth £30 (*CL* I, 366). The Wedgwoods took the hint and in an act of disinterested munificence offered him 'an annuity for life of £150 to be regularly paid by us, no condition whatsoever attached to it' (*CL* I, 373–4n.). Coleridge was staying with the family of young William Hazlitt near Shrewsbury at the time, where he had gone to acquaint himself with the congregation, and in a famous essay written 25 years later Hazlitt recalls Coleridge's receiving the offer:

> When I came down to breakfast, I found that he had just received a letter from his friend T. Wedgwood, making him an offer of 150*l*. a-year if he chose to wave his present pursuit, and devote himself entirely to the study of poetry and philosophy. Coleridge seemed to make up his mind to close with this proposal in the act of tying one of his shoes.[11]

Coleridge had recently turned 25 and was being offered security for himself and his family for the rest of his life, with no obligation to produce a word, let alone a word on a topic of the Wedgwoods' choosing. Wings on his back, or an albatross around his neck?

The Rime of the Ancyent Marinere

Coleridge allowed none of this anxiety and networking about a livelihood to dampen his enthusiasm for his new and effectively daily communion with the Wordsworths, or to affect his productivity. If he was right about the date of 'Kubla Khan', the *annus mirabilis* from mid-1797 to mid-1798 saw complete versions, not only of 'Kubla Khan' and of 'This Lime-Tree Bower My Prison', but also of the other Conversation Poems 'Frost at Midnight' and 'The Nightingale', and of the first part of *Christabel*. There were other, less well-known poems throughout the year as well, each significant in its own way and formally distinct. There was, for example, his political allegory against Pitt adapting the witches' speeches from *Macbeth*, 'Fire, Famine, and Slaughter: A War Eclogue'; there was his formal recantation of support for the French after they invaded Switzerland in 'France: An Ode' and there was the long blank verse meditation on his feelings for his country, 'Fears in Solitude: Written in April 1798, during an Alarm of an Invasion'. Most importantly of all, though, the year saw the writing and revision of the first version of *The Rime of the Ancient Mariner* (the version without the marginal gloss that has become such a familiar part of the poem). It would appear as the first poem in his and Wordsworth's celebrated volume, *Lyrical Ballads*, published in September 1798.

The first indication we have both of *The Rime of the Ancient Mariner* and of the *Lyrical Ballads* is in a letter Dorothy wrote to Mary Hutchinson on 20 November 1797 saying that, on a recent ramble to the coast, Wordsworth and Coleridge had 'employed themselves in laying the plan of a ballad, to be published with some pieces of William's'.[12] Not until March 1798 would 'the ballad' be complete. The title of their collaborative, experimental volume when it appeared six months later was paradoxical; lyrics are conventionally short, meditative or mood poems in the first person that can take many forms, regular and irregular, while ballads are third person narrative poems with a very regular stanzaic pattern (quatrains, say, with alternating four and three stress lines rhymed ABCB). The interest of the title for our purposes is as an indication of their fascination with what was considered to be a primitive or folk form. Begun as an oral form, popular ballads had been around since the late Middle Ages and sensational 'broadside ballads' were still being sold by itinerant hawkers to the labouring classes to be read out as group entertainment. For Coleridge and Wordsworth it was part of a more general search for elemental, unsophisticated *demotic* forms capable of articulating emotions and values that were not exclusive to an élite culture, but were shared across different classes. Thomas Percy's *Reliques of Ancient English Poetry* (1765), an anthology of ballads from the Middle Ages and after, reproduced for a modern audience (with unacknowledged refinements), was then enjoying considerable favour.

Equally fascinating for Coleridge was the Gothic mode. Indeed, many of the older and more of the recent (especially German) ballads dealt with the bizarre, the marvellous, and the macabre in a way that we loosely identify as Gothic. The Gothic was also popular at the time – popular enough to have made a small fortune for 'The Great Enchantress', Mrs (Ann) Radcliffe, which no doubt appealed to two impoverished poets hoping to finance a trip to Germany. Many years later, Coleridge recalled how his and Wordsworth's endeavours to collaborate on one Gothic project, 'The Wanderings of Cain', broke down good humouredly when it was realized that Wordsworth's sensibility would not bend that way.[13] Coleridge's, on the other hand, did. Spectacularly. His response to Gothic sensationalism – in Schiller's *The Robbers*, for example – was as primitive and visceral as any popular hair-raiser could ask (*CL* I, 122). The more imitative and impressionable of the two poets, Coleridge could write like Wordsworth – was even, in 'Frost at Midnight', writing in meditative, Wordsworthian blank verse before Wordsworth himself. Wordsworth, however, could not turn his hand to the Gothic.

It was when their literal collaboration broke down – their attempts to co-write individual poems, that is – that the two of them started to think of their respective offerings as antithetical in positive and complementary ways:

> During the first year that Mr Wordsworth and I were neighbours, our conversations turned frequently on the two cardinal points of poetry: the power of exciting the sympathy of the reader by a faithful adherence to the truth of nature, and the power of giving the interest of novelty by the modifying colours of the imagination. The sudden charm which accidents of light and shade, which moonlight or sunset diffused over a known or familiar landscape, appeared to represent the practicability of combining both. These are the poetry of nature.

The thought suggested itself (to which of us I do not recollect) that a species of poems might be composed of two sorts. In the one, the incidents and agents were to be (in part at least) supernatural—and the excellence aimed at was to consist in the interesting of the affections by the dramatic truth of such emotions as would naturally accompany such situations, supposing them real. And real in this sense they have been to every human being who, from whatever source of delusion, has at any time believed himself under supernatural agency. For the second class, subjects were to be chosen from ordinary life. The characters and incidents were to be such as would be found in every village and its vicinity, where there is a meditative and a feeling mind to seek after them or notice them when they present themselves.

In this idea originated the plan of the *Lyrical Ballads*, in which it was agreed that my endeavours were to be directed to persons and characters supernatural, or at least romantic; yet so far as to transfer from our inward nature a human interest and semblance of truth sufficient to procure for these shadows of imagination that willing suspension of disbelief for the moment, which constitutes poetic faith. (*BL* II, 5–6)

Coleridge's contribution to the volume was not made to order in this way, but the distinction is valid enough. Both Wordsworth and Coleridge shared with each other and with the Gothic tradition an obsession with 'guilt and sorrow' (to borrow the title of an early Wordsworth poem), indeed the basic plot of *The Rime of the Ancient Mariner* came from Wordsworth, not Coleridge: 'I had been reading in Shelvocke's Voyages, a day or two before, that, while doubling Cape Horn, they frequently saw albatrosses in that latitude', Wordsworth recalled in 1843, ' "Suppose", said I, "you represent him as having killed one of these birds on entering the South Sea, and that the tutelary spirits of these regions take upon them to avenge the crime" '.[14] To explore and express that guilt and its attendant psychological agonies in *The Rime of the Ancient Mariner*, Coleridge slid effortlessly into the bizarre and threatening world of nightmare in a way that Wordsworth could not do, creating an allegory of alienation and isolation of uniquely compelling power.

Wilfully strange rather than conversational and familiar, then, *The Rime* is an archetypal 'romantic' poem in the sense that Coleridge's contemporaries used that word: exotic; remote in time or place; otherworldly. The antiquarian impulse that made Percy's *Reliques* such a favourite was particularly apparent in the first version, which in occasional spelling and locution imitated Percy's rendering of medieval poetry. Compare the anonymous 'The Marriage of Gawaine' from Percy's collection with the 1798 version of Coleridge's *The Rime*:

> King Arthur lives in Merry Carleile,
> And seemely is to see;

And there with him queene Guenever,
    That bride soe bright of blee.

And there with him queene Guenever,
    That bride so bright in bowre:
And all his barons about him stoode,
    That were both stiffe and stowre.

The king a royale Christmasse kept,
    With mirth and princelye cheare;
To him repaired many a knighte,
    That came both farre and neare.

And when they were to dinner sette,
    And cups went freely round:
Before them came a faire damsèlle,
    And knelt upon the ground.
          ('The Marriage of Sir Gawaine',
                ll. 1–16)[15]

It is an ancyent Marinere,
    And he stoppeth one of three:
"By thy long grey beard and thy glittering eye
    "Now wherefore stoppest me?

"The Bridegoom's doors are open'd wide
    "And I am next of kin;
"The Guests are met, the Feast is set, —
    "May'st hear the merry din.["]

But still he holds the wedding-guest—
    There was a Ship, quoth he—
"Nay, if thou'st got a laughsome tale,
    "Marinere! come with me."

He holds him with his skinny hand,
    Quoth he, there was a Ship—
"Now get thee hence, thou grey-beard Loon!
    "Or my Staff shall make thee skip.["]

He holds him with his glittering eye—
    The wedding-guest stood still
And listens like a three year's child;
    The Marinere hath his will.
        (*The Rime of the Ancyent Marinere*, ll. 1–20)

The rhythm is more varied in the Coleridge poem, which escapes the plod-
ding iambics of the older poem, but otherwise both have simple, sometimes

forced rhymes, innocent padding, a high level of repetition (though Coleridge repeats, and varies his repetition, to greater effect), and, by manipulating the tense of the action, a narrative immediacy – as one would expect of a primitive, oral tradition. The same antiquarian impulse is still manifest in the final version of *The Rime of the Ancient Mariner* (which I will use from here on), and indeed is highlighted rather than disguised by the epigraph Coleridge adapted from the superstitious Thomas Burnet's *Archeologiæ Philosophicæ* (1692) and the antiquarian gloss that Coleridge added in 1817. *The Rime of the Ancient Mariner* is old-fashioned in the sense of 'fashioned to look old' – not a hoax, like Thomas Chatterton's *Rowley Poems* or James Macpherson's *Ossian*, but a fashionable anachronism. It was 'antiqued', as we say of furniture.

The difference in taste and talent between Coleridge and Wordsworth manifest in the impasse over 'The Wanderings of Cain' would ultimately prove divisive. Within a year of publication, Wordsworth can be found complaining to their publisher Joseph Cottle that 'the old words and the strangeness' of *The Rime* 'have deterred readers from going on',[16] and later, more publicly, that 'the imagery is somewhat too laboriously accumulated'.[17] What was elaborate in *The Rime*, Wordsworth found laboured, overwrought. Nor was it just occasional antiquated spellings and locutions ('ancyent', 'quoth he', 'I wist', 'eftsones') that Wordsworth had in mind. These were easy enough to deal with and Coleridge removed many of the more obstructive ones for the next edition. Wordsworth's real discomfort with the poem was with the fact that, instead of being drawn only from nature as he would advocate in the 1800 Preface to *Lyrical Ballads*, its images and incidents were drawn from exotic travel literature and fairy and folk tale, not to mention dream and nightmare.[18]

The result was a setting and a journey that were patently fantastic – a setting and a journey inside the mind:

> We were the first that ever burst
> Into that silent sea.
> (*The Rime of the Ancient Mariner*,
> ll. 105–6)

In this, *The Rime* resembles Bruno Bettelheim's fairy tale:

> The strange, most ancient, most distant, and at the same time the most familiar locations which a fairy tale speaks about suggest a voyage into the interior of our minds into the realms of unawareness and the unconscious.
>
> The fairy tale, from its mundane and simple beginning, launches into fantastic events. But however big the detours—unlike ... a dream—the process of the story does not get lost.[19]

What *The Rime* and the fairy or folk tale also have in common (besides inte-
riority and the fantastic) is the fact that both, at some symbolic level, touch
on human anxieties usually censored by the rational mind. If it is difficult to
determine the exact significance of the recurrent images in Coleridge's
extreme, elemental seascape – sun and moon; heat and cold; movement and
stasis (or paralysis); drought and rain – it is not difficult to accept that they
do indeed signify. And it is the same with the supernatural or demonic
elements, so figurative of the mental state Coleridge portrays. For Coleridge,
the Gothic always was a psychology:

> A lady once asked me if I believed in ghosts and apparitions. I answered
> with truth and simplicity: *No, madam! I have seen far too many myself.*
> I have indeed a whole memorandum book filled with records of these
> phænomena, many of them interesting as facts and data for psychology,
> and affording some valuable materials for a theory of perception and its
> dependence on the memory and imagination.[20]

Again, in one of his notebooks: 'The best service which the Mesmerism or
Zoomagnetism has yet done is that [of] reducing the whole of Dæmonology
and Diabolography to Neuropathology'.[21]

The effect of this fantastic, nightmare imagery and these fabulous events
in *The Rime*, aided and abetted by the romantic *defamiliarization* of the
archaic language and by the primitive ballad form and its sensational immediacy, is to recapture some of the naivety [cp. p 205] and enigma – as well as
the sheer terror – of the folk narrative, with its simple, insistent repetitions
and rhyme:

> All in a hot and copper sky,
> The bloody Sun, at noon,
> Right up above the mast did stand,
> No bigger than the Moon.
>
> Day after day, day after day,
> We stuck, nor breath nor motion;
> As idle as a painted ship
> Upon a painted ocean.
>
> Water, water, everywhere,
> And all the boards did shrink;
> Water, water, everywhere,
> Nor any drop to drink.
>
> The very deep did rot: O Christ!
> That ever this should be!
> Yea, slimy things did crawl with legs
> Upon the slimy sea.

About, about, in reel and rout
The death-fires danced at night;
The water, like a witch's oils,
Burnt green, and blue and white.

And some in dreams assurèd were
Of the Spirit that plagued us so;
Nine fathom deep he had followed us
From the land of mist and snow.

And every tongue, through utter drought,
Was withered at the root;
We could not speak, no more than if
We had been choked with soot.

Ah! well-a-day! what evil looks
Had I from old and young!
Instead of the cross, the Albatross
About my neck was hung.
(*The Rime of the Ancient Mariner*,
ll. 111–42)

The art of Coleridge's *Rime*, however, is not, finally, of the naive kind at all. Rather it is what we call a *literary* ballad through and through. So obsessively crafted is it, even or especially in its affected naiveties, that it would be possible to produce a catalogue of all the available rhetorical devices – and some that have yet to be classified – based on *The Rime of the Ancient Mariner* alone:

The fair breeze blew, the white foam flew,
The furrow followed free;
We were the first, that ever burst
Into that silent sea.

Down dropped the breeze, the sails dropped down,
'Twas sad as sad could be;
And we did speak only to break
The silence of the sea.
(*The Rime of the Ancient Mariner*,
ll. 103–10)

I hardly need to demonstrate the familiar sound effects of assonance, alliteration, internal rhyme and half-rhyme ('first'/'burst'; 'speak'/'break'), and onomatopœia, but it might be worth drawing attention to some of the less well-known rhetorical devices organizing the poetry here, in order to give some intimation of just how elaborate an artifice the whole poem is. Note, for example, the *polyptoton* (the repetition of a word with a variation of form) –

> Into that **silent** sea.
>
> The **silence** of the sea.

– and the *antimetabole* or syntactic reversal used to sharpen the sense or contrast the ideas conveyed: '**Down dropped** the breeze, the sails **dropped down**'. Note the forging repetition achieved by the *isocolon* 'The fair breeze blew, the white foam flew', a figure exploiting phrases of approximately equal length and similar syntactical structure (here identical: article + adjective + noun + verb). The movement of the line (and of the ship) is strengthened in this case, as so often in the poem, by the internal rhyme, the equal quantity of the vowels, and the alliterative coupling: 'breeze blew'/'foam flew'.

So, throughout the poem, the reader is driven onwards by one prosodic or rhetorical flourish interlinked with and following another, no less than she or he is drawn onwards by the haunting narrative itself – prosodic and rhetorical flourishes that become the origin of some of the poem's subtlest and most sophisticated effects and make the poem the most brilliantly orchestrated in our literature. *Epizeuxis* (the emphatic consecutive repetition of a single word); *anaphora* (the repetition of one word or phrase at the beginning of successive clauses or verses); *analepsis* (the repetition of the same word at the beginning and end of the same clause or verse):

> Alone, alone, all all alone,
> Alone on a wide wide sea!
> (ll. 232–3)[22]

These virtuoso flourishes conspire with the stark imagery and bizarre, yet curiously inevitable events (like those of nightmare) to embroil Coleridge's readers in an experience not unlike the Mariner's own – an experience close to their hearts and beyond their complete understanding.

Interpretation

But not, tellingly, beyond their *conjecture*. Interpretations of *The Rime* abound and spawn like creatures of the Coleridgean deep. Like dream, the visionary, allegorical form of the poem seems to demand interpretation – and, arguably also like dream, frustrates it. This frustration is only compounded by the fact that we know only too well what it is all about – it is all about transgression, punishment, appeasement, redemption, guilt, and the Mariner himself is busy identifying the significance of his own experience. Unthinkingly, the Mariner kills the albatross that appeared to save his beleaguered ship under duress and, as a result, it seems all hell has broken loose.

The Mariner is then subject to some exquisite torture until he blesses the slimy watersnakes – and the blessing proves to be the kind of liberating, unself-conscious act of love that occasions redemption and recovery in the Conversation Poems. Through it, the Mariner finds the reconciliation with Nature and God for which he yearns:

> O happy living things! no tongue
> Their beauty might declare:
> A spring of love gushed from my heart,
> And I blessed them unaware:
> Sure my kind saint took pity on me,
> And I blessed them unaware.
>
> The selfsame moment I could pray;
> And from my neck so free
> The Albatross fell off, and sank
> Like lead into the sea.
> (*The Rime of the Ancient Mariner*,
> ll. 282–91)

It is the gesture's very unconsciousness – its spontaneity – that seems to underwrite its authenticity, as the unconsciousness of his identifications with Charles had unleashed their healing powers in 'This Lime-Tree Bower My Prison'.

But the Mariner's suffering does not end there:

> The other was a softer voice,
> As soft as honey-dew:
> Quoth he, "The man hath penance done,
> And penance more will do."
> (*The Rime of the Ancient Mariner*,
> ll. 408–9)

Nor, indeed, are we ever allowed to imagine him absolved of his sin, if it is a sin (the jury is out on that one). Whatever we call it, however, no amount of confession or expiation will ever relieve the Mariner, other than momentarily, of the burden of what he's done and what he knows:

> "O shrieve me, shrieve me, holy man!"
> The hermit crossed his brow.
> "Say quick," quoth he, "I bid thee say —
> What manner of man art thou?"
>
> Forthwith this frame of mine was wrenched
> With a woful agony,

> Which forced me to begin my tale;
> And then it left me free.
>
> Since then, at an uncertain hour,
> That agony returns:
> And till my ghastly tale is told,
> This heart within me burns.
>   (*The Rime of the Ancient Mariner*,
>   ll. 574–85)

A prisoner of his own past actions, the Mariner is condemned to 'pass, like night, from land to land' (l. 586) and compelled to repeat his tale to those who, for good or ill, *must* hear it: 'To him my tale I teach' (l. 590).

What it is exactly that the tale teaches, however, remains a mystery, and this in spite of the fact that *The Rime* is one of the most extensively interpreted and famously interpretable poems in the language. Richard Holmes offers an abbreviated critical anthology:

> The ballad has been variously interpreted as a Christian allegory of fall and redemption; a moral study of the origins of Evil; a symbolic account of the *poète maudit* figure; an autobiographical vision of opium addiction; a 'Green parable' of man's destruction of nature and Nature's revenge; and a psychological investigation of post-traumatic stress syndrome with its well established features of obsessive recall and compulsive guilt.[23]

Even the most superficial investigation into the poem's critical history will tell you how radically oversimplified Holmes's list remains, for all that it can be said to represent the most common readings of the poem. David Beres, for example – and admittedly the example is an extreme one – believes the albatross that the Mariner destroys is a symbol of Coleridge's wife and mother, and that the Mariner's suffering is to be interpreted as 'pregenital punishment for a preoedipal crime'. The 'silly buckets on the deck' that the Mariner dreams are filled with dew (ll. 297–9) are said to symbolize 'the mother's breasts, previously empty and cruel, now full and forgiving'. The otherwise awkward fact that the Albatross is male (l. 40) inspires Beres to conclude that 'the mother was a masculine, rejecting female'.[24]

Strained Freudian and Jungian readings like this one of Beres' abound, as I said, revealing some of the fallacies and hinting at the ultimate arbitrariness of critical interpretation generally and of psychoanalytic interpretation in particular. If nothing else, however, the number and extremity of these kinds of readings of *The Rime* tell us something about the poem's form and style – and, I would argue (risking yet another interpretation), something about what is happening in the poem, what it is about. The irrepressible desire to understand the significance of the narrative – to make sense of it, as we say – readers and critics of *The Rime* share with the unlikely characters that feature in the tale itself: the Mariner, the Wedding-Guest and (later and most obviously) the marginal glossarist. For this, ultimately, is the temptation of the enterprise of interpretation and whatever else *The Rime* might be about, it is about interpretation – about the need to reduce the mysterious and irrational and arbitrary in our experience to something manageable and ordered, in a kind of moral mathematics or bookkeeping.

Here every interpreter has a problem, however. The disparaging comments of Wordsworth that I quoted earlier reflect a difficulty, not just with the poem's expressive mode, but also with the status and meaning of individual actions and incidents and with the ultimate incoherence of the narrative as a symbolic allegory. The details simply do not 'add up'.

The problem, moreover, is further complicated by uncertainty as to just how far the Mariner and the glossarist – and indeed the poet himself – are to be trusted. In the light of what it all might mean, for example, it is interesting to observe the change the 'Argument' of the poem underwent between 1798 and 1800, as the various critical apparatuses introduced by Coleridge conspired to constrain a heavily moral and theological reading of the poem:

ARGUMENT (1798)

How a Ship having passed the Line was driven by Storms to the cold Country towards the South Pole; and how from thence she made her course to the tropical Latitude of the Great Pacific Ocean; and of the strange things that befell; and in what manner the Ancyent Marinere came back to his own Country.

ARGUMENT (1800)

How a Ship, having first sailed to the Equator, was driven by Storms, to the cold Country towards the South Pole; how the Ancient Mariner cruelly, and in contempt of the laws of hospitality, killed the Sea-bird; and how he was followed by many and strange Judgements; and in what manner he came back to his own Country.[25]

The marginal gloss that we find in most modern editions of the poem (1817, revised 1828) is entirely in keeping with this pious adjudication:

> The ancient Mariner inhospitably killeth
> the pious bird of good omen.

> ... the Albatross begins to be avenged

> His shipmates cry out against the ancient
> Mariner, for killing the bird of good luck.

> But when the fog cleared off, they justify
> the same, and thus make themselves
> accomplices in the crime.
>
> The curse is finally expiated.
>
> And ever and anon throughout his future
> life an agony constraineth him to travel
> from land to land;
>
> And to teach, by his own example, love
> and reverence to all things that God
> made and loveth.

How far the gloss is to be relied upon for its interpretation is something else again, however, and something readers must decide for themselves. What is certain, as I suggested earlier, is that the gloss offers an often stylized reading of an antiquarian narrative by an equally antiquated editor – not Coleridge himself, but an at times credulous, always judgemental Coleridgean *persona* modelled on Coleridge's reading of sixteenth- and seventeenth-century prose and part of the antiquarian affectation:

> A Spirit had followed them; one of the invis-
> ible inhabitants of the planet, neither
> departed souls nor angels; concerning whom
> the learned Jew, Josephus, and the Platonic
> Constantinopolitan, Michael Psellus, may
> be consulted. They are very numerous, and
> there is no climate or element without one
> or more.

As it is with the glossarist, so is it with the Mariner himself as an exemplary interpreter of his own tale and the authority for the poem's most common reading:

> 'He prayeth best, who loveth best
> All things both great and small;
> For the dear God who loveth us,
> He made and loveth all.'
> (*The Rime of the Ancient Mariner*,
> ll. 614–17)

The only certainty about the 'moral' of the poem, however, is that there is a deeply human compulsion to find a moral in what ultimately resists moralization, just as it resists other kinds of explanation and resolution. Coleridge's greatest debt to his reading of exotic literature like primitive ballads and folk and fairy tales is a sense of the disproportion and illogic in the relations between things:

Mrs Barbauld once told me that the only faults she found with the Ancient Mariner were—that it was improbable, and had no moral. As for the probability—to be sure that might admit some question—but I told her that in my own judgment the chief fault of the poem was that it had too much moral, and that too openly obtruded on the reader. It ought to have had no more moral than the story [in the *Arabian Nights*] of the merchant sitting down to eat dates by the side of a well and throwing the shells aside, and the Genii starting up and saying he must kill the merchant, because a date shell had put out the eye of the Genii's son.[26]

Two years earlier, in a conversation that became conflated with this one, Coleridge again criticized himself for having made 'the moral sentiment too apparent', and also for having brought 'it in too much as a principle or cause in a work of such pure Imagination'.[27] This was not so much to absolve the Mariner as to take an ironic perspective on his and other attempts to rationalize human action and suffering. For however we choose to interpret the Mariner's actions, two things remain inexplicable or mysterious: human motive (or the lack of it) – the Mariner's spontaneous violence against the bird – and the operation of human conscience. To quote the character Rivers from Wordsworth's *The Borderers*:

> Action is transitory—a step, a blow,
> The motion of a muscle, this way or that,
> 'Tis done—and in the after-vacancy
> We wonder at ourselves like men betrayed:
> Suffering is permanent, obscure and dark,
> And hath the nature of infinity.
> (*The Borderers*, III, v, 60–5)

For an accurate or adequate reading, therefore, we need not take the Mariner, *or* the wedding guest, *or* the glossarist, *or* the fictional 'editor', *or* anyone else at their word. Through this search for meaning and authority Coleridge is able to explore the whole nature of *and need for* authority – critical; moral; religious.[28] *The Rime* is, as I said, about interpretation, but interpretation not just in the sense of *finding* or *discovering* meaning and value in the face of meaninglessness and arbitrariness, but also in the sense of *making* meaning and value.

What remains irrefutable in all this is the fact of human suffering – specifically, the Mariner's guilt and melancholy isolation:

> The many men, so beautiful!
> And they all dead did lie:
> And a thousand, thousand slimy things
> Lived on; and so did I.
> (*The Rime of the Ancient Mariner,*
> ll. 236–9)

Nor, at the end, in spite of his wishful fantasy of Christian community –

> To walk together to the kirk
> With a goodly company!—
>
> To walk together to the kirk,
> And all together pray
> (*The Rime of the Ancient
> Mariner,* ll. 603–6)

– is the Mariner ever welcomed back into either the congregation or society. His compulsion to repeat and retreat tragically alienates him from his dream community. The narrative is framed by a marriage feast, conventionally symbolic of social and divine harmony. Not only does the Mariner *interrupt* the marriage feast at the beginning, however, but the wedding-guest, too, is obliged to turn his back upon its potentially comic resolution at the very end, dividing from the community in a way that echoes the Mariner's isolation from the community of sailors:

> now the Wedding-Guest
> Turned from the bridegroom's door.
>
> He went like one that hath been stunned,
> And is of sense forlorn:
> A sadder and a wiser man,
> He rose the morrow morn.
> (*The Rime of the Ancient Mariner,*
> ll. 620–5)

We are back in what the poet W. B. Yeats called the 'foul rag-and-bone shop of the heart',[29] back with a Coleridgean isolation that was at once immediate and personal – not to say psychopathological – and yet at the same time profoundly representative. As well as expressing Coleridge's own sense (and dread) of emotional and existential isolation, in other words, the guilt and alienation so exhaustively traced in *The Rime* can also be read as an account of what it means to be human. Perhaps because the last two centuries have seen so much existentialist angst we are in danger of becoming immune to figurations of 'the horror' at the heart of darkness. What is certainly true is that our coming so much later than Coleridge and being the inheritors of a Romanticism indebted to Coleridge make it difficult to appreciate the fact that *The Rime of the Ancient Mariner* was an unprecedented expression of spiritual and existential solitude.

There is, in all this bleakness, one significant consolation, both for Coleridge and for the reader. There is the poetry. Coleridge has succeeded in recapturing from the ballad tradition a dramatic immediacy which, aided by the incantation of its prosody and its prosodic and rhetorical virtuosity, is entrancing in ways that, as all readers have noticed, resemble the Mariner's own. We are 'dragged ... along like Tom Piper's magic whistle', as Charles Lamb said, defending the poem against Wordsworth's obtuseness.[30] Listening 'like a three years' child' to the Mariner (l. 15), the wedding-guest embarks upon what is admittedly an agonizing journey, one as far removed experientially and emotionally from the joy and celebration of the wedding feast as the tale is removed from the familiar world. The reader, too, is constrained to hear and to relive the tale. Their consolation is the captivating richness of the Mariner's storytelling – a richness that one recognizes not only as 'poetic', but as in some sense representative of the poetic, of poetry itself. This magic may make the poetry especially resistant to 'translation' into explanatory paraphrase and moral generalization, yet this pleasurable magic also insists on the uniqueness of poetry as a way of understanding and articulating and shaping experience. This would be the object of Coleridge's literary criticism in the coming years.

Coleridge was haunted by *The Rime of the Ancient Mariner* throughout the remainder of his life, in a number of ways. The poem itself he would rework for *Sibylline Leaves* (1817) and the collections of his poems of 1828 and 1834: adding, refining, clarifying, and complicating at the same time. More uncannily than this, however, its imagery and incident returned to him on occasion. During the first extended sea voyage of his life, his passage to Malta, for example, he saw the ship's boy shimmying up the main mast 'with a large Leg of Mutton swung, Albatross-fashion about his neck' (*CN* II, 1997)[31] and remarked, *déjà vu*, precisely the phenomenon of mindless cruelty that had triggered the action of his poem:

Hawk with ruffled Feathers resting on the Bowsprit—Now shot at & yet did not move—how fatigued—a third time it made a gyre, a short circuit, & returned again/5 times it was thus shot at/left the Vessel/flew to another/& I heard firing, now here, now there/& nobody shot it/but probably it

perished from fatigue, & the attempt to rest upon the wave!—Poor Hawk!
O Strange Lust of Murder in Man!—It is not cruelty/it is mere non-feeling
from non-thinking. (*CN* II, 2090)

The analogy between himself and the Mariner is recognized again and again
in his private notebooks.

But what really haunted Coleridge about *The Rime* was its success –
though not in the worldly sense, for the anonymous *Lyrical Ballads* was
little noticed in the Reviews and *The Rime* 'uniformly abused' (notably by
Southey, who dismissed it as 'a Dutch attempt at German sublimity').[32]
Its success in Coleridge's eyes amounted to a recognition that he had created something that was astonishing and unique, not just among his own
varied output but in all literature – something with a claim far beyond its
pretence at being a humble ballad and something that had required, along
with his peculiar genius, both intense and protracted labour. Ironically, in
achieving this, Coleridge had only added to the burden of expectation
under which he had laboured since infancy. Now there could be no
question of his capability, and it returned to humiliate him for the remainder of his career, for he would never again be capable of the kind of sustained creativity that went into his masterpiece. Try as he might, he could
never conclude his other major excursion into the land of faery, *Christabel*,
in which, as he says in the *Biographia*, he 'should have more nearly realized
my ideal, than I had' in *The Rime* (*BL* II, 7). Begun in the *annus mirabilis* of
1797–8, it could not be finished in time for the first edition of *Lyrical
Ballads*, then, two years later, even after he had managed a second part, he
failed again for the second edition of 1800. It was not until 1816 that it was
finally published, as a fragment, at the behest of Byron – a 'wild, and sin-
gularly original and beautiful poem', Byron called it in a note in his *The
Siege of Corinth* (1816). But unfinished.

'Frost at Midnight'

Another thing for which the years 1797–8 were distinguished in Coleridge's
career was autobiography. After the turbulent political years, Coleridge was
taking stock for the first time, composing himself as he would do again in
1815 and as Wordsworth would do in Goslar in Germany in 1799. This time,
however, Coleridge wrote privately, for himself and for Tom Poole, in a series
of letters from which I have had occasion to quote. With his having stirred
up past memories in this way, it was hardly surprising that some of his
poetry should share with the letters their incidents and images and emotions. Tentative explorations of his past and what it meant had been made in
his dedication to his *Poems on Various Subjects* (1797), a short lyric 'To the
Rev. George Coleridge of Ottery St Mary, Devon, with Some Poems' sometimes included amongst the Conversation Poems. It was not until Coleridge

wrote out of contentment and hope, however, as he did in February 1798, that he could effectively assimilate and imaginatively recast the past. The result was the finest of his Conversation Poems, 'Frost at Midnight'.

'Frost at Midnight' has the same pattern of redemption from self-centred 'solitude' (l. 5) that has been traced in 'This Lime-Tree Bower My Prison', the same reconciliation of apparent informality with tight formal organization and of minute natural detail with philosophical significance that are universally identified as the achievement of the Conversation Poems. There are, however, none of the occasional infelicities that marred 'This Lime-Tree Bower My Prison'. The earlier poem's explicit moral, for example, has a self-consciousness – even self-righteousness – that strains against the attitude of humility so crucial to its argument:

> sometimes
> 'Tis well to be bereft of promis'd good
> That we may lift the soul, and contemplate
> With lively joy the joys we cannot share.
> ('This Lime-Tree Bower My Prison',
> ll. 64–7)

In a letter to William Sotheby in September 1802, Coleridge would attribute his beloved Bowles's decline as a poet to his 'perpetual trick of *moralizing* everything':

> never to see or describe any interesting appearance in nature, without connecting it by dim analogies with the moral world, proves faintness of Impression. Nature has her proper interest; & he will know what it is, who believes & feels, that every Thing has a Life of it's own, & that we are all *one Life*. A Poet's *Heart* & *Intellect* should be *combined, intimately* combined & *unified* with the great appearances in Nature. (*CL* II, 864)

The 'trick' of moralizing, in short, betrays the kind of alienation of mind from nature that the poet in the Conversation Poems endeavours to overcome.

'Frost at Midnight' begins with the landscape in the grip of a frozen calmness that, for the poet, is almost preternatural, Gothic. Far from pacifying the poet, as we might expect, it only disturbs and agitates him:

> The Frost performs its secret ministry,
> Unhelped by any wind. The owlet's cry
> Came loud – and hark, again! loud as before.
> The inmates of my cottage, all at rest,
> Have left me to this solitude, which suits
> Abstruser musings: save that at my side

> My cradled infant slumbers peacefully.
> 'Tis calm indeed! so calm, that it disturbs
> And vexes meditation with its strange
> And extreme silentness.
> ('Frost at Midnight', ll. 1–10)

The poet's restlessness betrays the extent to which he is out of phase with the natural world. His child, on the other hand, slumbering 'peacefully', is identified with a universal calm that suggests not death, but hibernation, a slumbering latency. 'If winter comes', asks Shelley at the end of the 'Ode to the West Wind', 'Can Spring be far behind?'

Contrary to what the poet says in a classic instance of the 'pathetic fallacy' – a term coined by the Victorian critic John Ruskin for the projection of human emotions onto nature – the 'sole unquiet thing' is *not* the film or thin flake of soot 'which fluttered on the grate' (l. 15), but the poet himself. An 'idling Spirit' (l. 20), he projects his dissonant mood onto the film, as the artificial poet projects his melancholy onto the nightingale in Coleridge's poem of the same name. The poet alone is 'unquiet', ill at ease. All the while, however, 'The frost performs its secret ministry'. What this mysterious 'ministry' might be is only revealed – and then obliquely – in the final image or images of the poem. It is enough at this stage to know that some beneficial change is being secretly wrought.

Then, in the subtlest transition of all in the Conversation Poems, the second verse paragraph moves to memories of the poet's schooldays:

> But O! how oft,
> How oft, at school, with most believing mind,
> Presageful, have I gazed upon the bars,
> To watch that fluttering *stranger!* and as oft
> With unclosed lids, already had I dreamt
> Of my sweet birth-place, and the old church-tower,
> Whose bells, the poor man's only music, rang
> From morn to evening, all the hot Fair-day,
> So sweetly, that they stirred and haunted me
> With a wild pleasure, falling on mine ear
> Most like articulate sounds of things to come!
> So gazed I, till the soothing things, I dreamt,
> Lulled me to sleep, and sleep prolonged my dreams!
> And so I brooded all the following morn,
> Awed by the stern preceptor's face, mine eye
> Fixed with mock study on my swimming book:
> Save if the door half opened, and I snatched
> A hasty glance, and still my heart leaped up,
> For still I hoped to see the *stranger's* face,

Townsman, or aunt, or sister more beloved,
My play-mate when we both were clothed alike!
('Frost at Midnight', ll. 23–43)

In one sense, the connection is obvious enough: watching the film, the poet recalls the superstition that 'the films were called *strangers* and supposed to portend the arrival of some absent friend' and this, in turn, reminds him of the number of anxious hours he spent as a schoolboy hoping for the arrival of a loved one. From the dream-like inaudibility of the world outside the mature poet, we have moved to dreams of his 'sweet birth-place' and voluntary dreams of 'soothing things'.

But the associative, seemingly accidental nature of the connection should not obscure the complex and suggestive relationship between the state of the poet *now*, as expressed in the opening 23 lines, and the state of the poet *then*, as a child. From his isolation as a meditative adult we have moved to his isolation as a child. The memory is both evocative and explanatory, establishing the continuity of human life and personality while at the same time suggesting the way in which (in Wordsworth's fine phrase) 'the child is father to the man'[33] – the way in which the poet Coleridge has been 'fathered' by the child Coleridge. The experience of the fatherless schoolboy, dispatched and signed over to Christ's Hospital, informs and constrains the lonely, alienated adult of the poem's opening. In the Wordsworthian terms of the poem, it is an alienation from love and nature.

There is, however, another and more vital transition taking place in this movement between the two verse paragraphs. From the slumbering baby (his child Hartley) we have moved to Coleridge the child. We are being prepared for the elaborate *chiasmus* or crossover that will take place in the poem, the reversal and substitution of one generation for and by another that is the poem's recognition and its triumph. What links the two verse paragraphs more than anything else is the film dancing on the grate – not just because it prompts the recollection, but because it expresses in a paradox the movement in the poem from estrangement to love and reconciliation. The film, though called a *stranger*, is believed to usher in familiar love.

Accordingly, the poem returns to the present – to his 'Dear Babe, that sleepest cradled by my side' (l. 44) – and the poet begins the familiar movement out of the self. A preoccupation with his own isolation, present and past, changes into a promise to his child that he will not suffer as the poet himself has suffered. 'I was reared', says the poet, deprived of love and Nature:

In the great city, pent 'mid cloisters dim,
And saw nought lovely but the sky and stars.

> But *thou*, my babe! shalt wander like the breeze
> By lakes and sandy shores, beneath the crags
> Of ancient mountain, and beneath the clouds,
> Which image in their bulk both lakes and shores
> And mountain crags
> ('Frost at Midnight', ll. 51–8)

The reflexivity of lake and sky (the one the 'image' of the other) suggests the more complex reflexivity (the inverted image) of poet and child, subject and object. Coleridge describes himself as a youth with eyes 'Fixed with mock study on a swimming book' (l. 38), unable in his anxiety to focus on the language of men. His son, Hartley, on the other hand, shall 'see and hear'

> The lovely shapes and sounds intelligible
> Of that eternal language, which thy God
> Utters.
> ('Frost at Midnight', ll. 58–61)

This transition from one language to another also takes place in the present, however, and for the benefit of the poet himself. Although the poem opened with his musing on some abstruse point of metaphysics – the language of humanity, note – he now finds himself, in his imaginative anticipation of Hartley's youth, reading and recreating nature as the language of God. Through his child, he has rediscovered a home in the world beyond the confines of the 'thirsty Cares' and 'dim regards' that in *Religious Musings* are said to 'Self-center' (l. 89–91) – as he had through Charles in 'This Lime-Tree Bower My Prison'. The personal pronouns say it all. After the reference to 'my babe' in line 54, the first person pronoun disappears altogether, an extraordinary thing in a lyric poem and an index of the success of the poet's self-effacing act of love.

The best index of all, however, is the beautiful and moving combination of prayer and benediction with which the poem closes:

> Therefore all seasons shall be sweet to thee,
> Whether the summer clothe the general earth
> With greenness, or the redbreast sit and sing
> Betwixt the tufts of snow on the bare branch
> Of mossy apple-tree, while the nigh thatch
> Smokes in the sun-thaw; whether the eave-drops fall
> Heard only in the trances of the blast,
> Or if the secret ministry of frost

Shall hang them up in silent icicles,
Quietly shining to the quiet Moon.
('Frost at Midnight', ll. 65–74)

Coleridge, in his wisdom, removed six anecdotal lines from the end of the first version because 'they destroy the rondo, and return upon itself of the Poem', which 'ought to lie coiled with its' tail round its' head'.[34] Looking out of and beyond his own isolation in the present and the past and into his child's future, the poet is at last able to see *and* feel the beauty of the world. The frost, like the sunlit landscape of 'This Lime-Tree Bower My Prison', has transformed the landscape – as has Coleridge's imagination, regenerated by love and faith. Coleridge has become part of the landscape. No longer the 'stranger' – the outsider and the 'sole unquiet thing' – he has now been assimilated into Nature, and the contrasting quietude is stressed: '*Quietly* shining to the *quiet* Moon'.

But if the poet has been assimilated into the landscape, so, too, has the landscape been assimilated by the poet. After all, the landscape with which 'Frost at Midnight' closes is not a perceived landscape but an imagined landscape. Coleridge has unified present and future, summer and winter, man and child, God and Nature. No better instance exists in all of Coleridge's poetry of 'the Poet's *Heart & Intellect ... combined, intimately* combined & *unified* with the great appearances in Nature'.

All which then we were

For all the occasional structural similarities between *The Rime* and the Conversation poems – and I am thinking here of the basic 'plot' of transgression, isolation, and redemption that I have referred to – they remain as emotionally as they are formally and generically distinct. Coleridge's Conversation Poems take isolation to be a kind of psycho-spiritual dis-ease ('unquiet') to be overcome by a mind working in concert with God and nature. They enact and celebrate their own triumph over alienation and loneliness. In a more sceptical, more critical age like our own, conditioned as we are by psychoanalysis and various forms of ideological critique to prefer latent before manifest content, we have become suspicious of the conscious affirmations and willed transcendence of poems like 'This Lime-Tree Bower My Prison' and 'Frost at Midnight'. Not surprisingly, then, it is for us the spiritual and psychological condition of alienation and loneliness that Coleridge's poetry expresses most powerfully, most convincingly - that, and his own raw need for affection and community:

To be beloved is all I need,
And whom I love, I love indeed.
('The Pains of Sleep', ll. 51–2)

Of this kind of despair and isolation – and despair and isolation would become, after the Romantics, commonplaces of our cultural and existential imagining – *The Rime of the Ancient Mariner* is surely the consummate poetic expression.

If it was also intended as a pre-emptive strike, however, an attempt to forestall the condition by enacting it, it was not successful. Coleridge had struggled with dissolution, debt, dereliction, and depression during the Cambridge years, and the years of high political profile and his early marriage had brought their share of personal and financial problems. For all that, it is fair to say that in September 1798, when the *Lyrical Ballads* was published by Cottle, his problems had yet to begin. He had two children, two-year-old Hartley and baby Berkeley, a marriage in which he had frankly invested little but which was relatively untroubled, and he had two friends in William and Dorothy whose company was so stimulating that after over a year together they were still planning future movements with each other in mind. Indeed, on 14 September 1798 the three of them would embark for Cuxhaven in Westphalia, Germany, for the next stage of their literary lives together. Coleridge had everything to look forward to and the promise of a regular income to help him achieve it.

It would be wrong to suggest it was down hill all the way from this point in his career, if only because that would underestimate Coleridge's extraordinary powers of recovery. 'Coleridge was a man who could confess spiritual despair at midday', as Richard Holmes reminds us, 'and dine out brilliantly at midnight'.[35] And according to the way these things work, we may not have had some of Coleridge's searching reflections on creativity had the creative impulse itself survived. But the fact is it did not survive, as Coleridge was the first to point out, at least not in the form of poetry. We are left with what amounts to an elegy in Wordsworth's *The Prelude*, commemorating Coleridge's and poetry's *annus mirabilis* as one blooming summer

> when on Quantock's grassy hills
> Far ranging, and among the sylvan coombs,
> Thou in delicious words, with happy heart,
> Didst speak the vision of that ancient man,
> The bright-eyed Mariner, and rueful woes
> Didst utter of the Lady Christabel;
> And I, associate in such labour, walked
> Murmuring of him, who—joyous hap—was found,
> After the perils of his moonlight ride,
> Near the loud waterfall, or her who sate
> In misery near the miserable thorn;[36]
> When thou dost to that summer turn thy thoughts,
> And hast before thee all which then we were,

To thee, in memory of that happiness,
It will be known—by thee at least my friend,
Felt—that the history of a poet's mind
Is labour not unworthy of regard
                    (*The Prelude* [1805], XIII, 393–410)

5
'The Toil of Thinking': Private Notes and Public Newspapers

'Frost at Midnight' was published along with 'Fears in Solitude' and 'France: An Ode' in a small quarto of 23 pages by the famous radical publisher Joseph Johnson, friend of William Godwin and Mary Wollstonecraft and founder of the *Analytical Review*, whom Coleridge met a number of times during his stay in London before embarking for Germany. Johnson, in turn, gave Coleridge a letter of credit for £25 to be cashed by an English bookseller in Hamburg, though Coleridge protested to his wife that the money was for work to come, not for work completed (*CL* I, 417–18, 417n.). It is just possible that Johnson paid for the volume itself in cash at the time and invested a little more in Coleridge's future, having received him 'civilly the first time', according to Coleridge, 'cordially the second, affectionately the third', before finally taking leave of him 'with tears in his eyes' (*CL* I, 420). Once again, Coleridge's 'one-versation' had endeared him to a willing patron.

The brief association with the high profile Johnson is telling. Coleridge might have become less radical and progressively less interested in politics over the previous two years, but that had not stopped his name from becoming a byword in the conservative press for hysterical Jacobinism. This pamphlet of poems was his considered riposte to his critics, published (as the *Lyrical Ballads* was not) under his own name, with the name of Joseph Johnson of St Paul's Churchyard equally apparent. (As J. C. C. Mays points out, 'the names of the publisher and the author claimed an interest in advance of what the pamphlet contained'.[1]) If Johnson was keen to be associated with poems of 'recantation' by a former firebrand now openly suspicious of French imperial intentions and feeling for his country in its hour of need, it did not work. Johnson would soon be in the King's Bench prison serving six months for sedition for another publication. Coleridge, however, had other seas to sail.

Travelling north: Germany

'On Sunday morning, September 16, 1798, the Hamburg Pacquet set sail from Yarmouth: and I, for the first time in my life, beheld my native land

116

retiring from me' (*BL* II, 160). So Coleridge opens his 'Satyrane's Letters' on his experience in Germany, reflections and opinions that began their life as letters to his wife, Sara, and Tom Poole in Nether Stowey and were later adapted for his periodical *The Friend* (1809), before finally becoming part of the miscellaneous material imported into the *Biographia* to pad out its second volume (*BL* II, 160–206). That it was not the first indication Coleridge had had of his feeling for England is apparent from 'Fears in Solitude', but its depth surprised him and nationalism would become a frequent characteristic of his political and cultural commentary from this time onwards. It is perhaps fitting that the feeling should have been roused by a visit to the font of Romantic nationalism, Germany, but Coleridge did not go to Germany in search of England. He went in search of the German language and German literature. Though he originally planned a tour of only three months, he would stay for ten, learning basic German and practising translating at the house of a widowed Lutheran pastor and five of his children in Ratzeburg until February 1799, before proceeding to the University of Göttingen where until May he attended various lectures in natural history, physiology, anatomy, and theology. He eventually returned home in late July 1799 after a tour of the Hartz mountains and some inconclusive research in Wolfenbuttel and Helmstedt.

For travelling companions he had William and Dorothy Wordsworth and a recent acolyte, John Chester, the last 'attracted to Coleridge's discourse as flies are to honey', according to Hazlitt.[2] It had been decided that Sara would not accompany them, that she should be spared the travelling and domestic disruption, though it is obvious that Coleridge also saw it as another opportunity for temporary independence. He was not the first man to begin fatherhood with a fascinated attention to every aspect of his child's life, only to lose a daily interest in his child's routine. Nor was he the first father filled with uncontrollable emotion at the thought of his absent children who nonetheless absented himself whenever possible, which he had taken to doing long before the trip to Germany with the Wordsworths. Coleridge loved his children dearly and certainly had a father's vanity when it came to any signs of distinction, but he could never look after them and never successfully dissociate them from Sara in order to see them as individuals. As Lamb confided in Crabb Robinson many years later, Coleridge 'ought not to have a wife or children; he should have a sort of diocesan care of the world, no parish duty'.[3]

The Coleridge family did not survive the trip to Germany: it did not survive Coleridge's dilatory selfishness nor did it survive the death of baby Berkeley from a smallpox inoculation in February 1799, the agonizing knowledge of which Sara was prevailed upon by Tom Poole to keep from Coleridge for fear of his being overwhelmed and abandoning his trip. If we did not know Poole to have been a caring and generous friend, determined to protect Coleridge from himself, it would be hard to forgive the calculated insensitivity of his assuring Coleridge that in all her sufferings Sara '*never forgot herself*' and, even now (one month later), 'does not make herself miserable by recalling the engaging, though, remember, mere instinctive attractions of an infant a few months old. Heaven and Earth! I have myself within the last month experienced disappointments more weighty than the death of ten infants'.[4] Sara's suffering during Berkeley's illness and after his death, and her subsequent sense of abandonment, cry out from the letters she was allowed to write to Coleridge at this time: 'oh! I am tired of this cruel absence – my dear, dear Samuel, do not lose a moment of time in finishing your book – for I feel like a poor deserted thing'.[5] In future, whenever she nagged Coleridge about his obligations or accused him of neglecting them, it would be charged with the resentment she must have felt at his being absent when their child died and (though she was not allowed to ask it of him) his not returning when it was finally revealed to him – not only not returning, but wilfully protracting his stay, in the last instance for a holiday tour with some new found young friends.

Poole's well meaning insensitivities were a measure of his anxious determination that Coleridge should fulfil the destiny for which God and the Wedgwoods had chosen him. For this was to be a new phase in Coleridge's literary life. We might regret the fact that Coleridge did not go on to write more than the occasional distinguished poem, but unlike Wordsworth he had never for a moment seen himself only as a poet. The bequest he had been offered was to free him up for 'poetry and philosophy'. Both. His poetry had gone well enough, in spite of his protesting (as he would do more and more frequently, to the frustration of his other friends) that he was but a little man next to Wordsworth, who, he would later insist, made him see his own verse writing as empty pretension.[6] What he had yet seriously to venture and to risk was his reputation *as a thinker* – a reputation that, we note, Wordsworth never coveted. Coleridge's ambition was now to become a scholar and a philosopher (an 'intellectual' as we would say). Here was an area where he had excited expectations ever since he had begun to talk and it was now incumbent upon him to stop talking for a while and attempt to research and write a major work. '*Begin* no poetry – no original composition', Poole enjoined.[7]

The major work Coleridge had chosen (along with a history of the German peasants for Josiah Wedgwood) was to be an unconscious rehearsal for the *Biographia Literaria*: a literary life of the scholar, poet, and theologian Gotthold Lessing, into which Coleridge would interweave (so he eventually decided) a critical history of German literature from its origins (*CL* I, 454–5). 'So large a work with so great a variety of information from sources so scattered', he told Sara, '& so little known even in Germany, will, of course, establish my character for industry & erudition, certainly; & I would fain hope, for reflection & genius' (*CL* I, 484). No less. To do this, he needed to familiarize himself with the best that was known and thought in Germany because it was in Germany, he had believed since 1796, that it was all happening. And that meant learning the German language, the primary object of his travels.

To the surprise and relief of Coleridge's family and friends in England jealous of his obsession with the Wordsworths, Coleridge split up with William and Dorothy after only two weeks: 'The Wordsworths have left you', wrote Poole bluntly, 'so there is an end of our fears about amalgamation, etc.'.[8] The split was motivated partly by money: Wordsworth and Dorothy were perpetually horrified at what appear to have been inflated prices, making it difficult for the better funded Coleridge to relax. But the real reason, surely, is that Coleridge realized too late that they should never have been there in the first place – as fruitful as the wrong choice ultimately proved in sending Wordsworth, holed up with his sister during a freezing winter in Goslar, in search of his lyrical and autobiographical origins and leaving us with an extraordinary collection of verse. There was nothing in Germany to attract the poet or his sister and Coleridge was selfish and shrewd enough to have recognized that the Wordsworths' sense of cultural dislocation would only weigh upon and divert his own ambitions. Coleridge talked of Wordsworth's 'unseeking manners', knowing his own to be the very reverse (CL I, 459). Certainly his first ambition to learn the language would have proved impossible with the perpetual temptation to share observations and insights in English that the Wordsworths' company offered.

What Poole knew in congratulating Coleridge on his independence from the Wordsworths was that Coleridge was on a mission, and for various personality reasons needed to be kept to his task.

Speak nothing but German. Live with the Germans. Read in German. Think in German. Make a strict arrangement of your time and chain yourself down to it. This may not be advisable for the generality, but I am persuaded it would counteract a disease of your mind—which is an active subtilty of imagination ever suggesting reasons to push off whatever excites a moment of languor or ennui. This many of your friends call irresolution. No one has more resolution than you; no one sooner sees the side of a question on which the balance of argument turns. But then that same habit of giving free scope to the activity of your imagination, makes it death to you to chain the mind long to any particular object.[9]

Poole was right, but Coleridge did manage to chain his mind to a strict set of objects during his time in Germany. 'What have I done in Germany?', he would ask his patron Josiah Wedgwood on the eve of his departure:

I have learnt the language, both high & low German / I can read both, & speak the former so fluently, that it must be a *torture* for a German to be in my company—that is, I have words and phrases enough, & I arrange them tolerably; but my pronunciation is hideous.—2ndly, I can read the oldest German, the Frankish and the Swabian. 3rdly—I have attended lectures on Physiology, Anatomy, & Natural History with regularity, & have endeavoured to understand these subjects.—4th—I have read and made collections for an history of the Belles Lettres in Germany before the time of Lessing—& 5thly—very large collections for a Life of Lessing ... my main business at Göttingen has been to read all the numerous Controversies in which L[essing] was engaged / & the works of all those German Poets before the time of Lessing, which I *could not*, or could not *afford* to buy—. For these last 4 months, with the exception of last week in which I visited the Harz I have worked harder than, I trust in God Almighty, I shall ever have occasion to work again—this endless transcription is such a body-and-soul-wearying Purgatory! (*CL* I, 518–19)

Coleridge, free from the responsibility of his young family, had led the life of a university student again – there is evidence of the same rowdy drinking parties, the same intense argument well into the night: 'roaring, kissing, embracing, fighting, smashing bottles & glasses against the wall, singing – in short, such a scene of uproar I never witnessed before, no, not even at Cambridge' (*CL* I, 476). As was his wont, he had made friends very quickly. His willingness to make a fool of himself, to join in discussion and to take linguistic and conceptual risks, while all the while betraying obvious critical intelligence and an earnest commitment to the life of the mind, appealed to his German peers, reinforcing the 'ridiculous partiality or rather madness for the English' Coleridge remarked soon after his arrival (*CL* I, 429). He had made friends, too, amongst the expatriate Englishmen completing their studies abroad. Charles and Frederick Parry, Anthony Hamilton, Clement Carlyon, and George Greenough (the last two would later in life write generous reflections on their experience with Coleridge) – all joined Coleridge and Chester later on his tour of the Hartz mountains and they even plotted a further trip to Sweden together.

There was, however, a vital difference between Cambridge and Göttingen that Coleridge registered at the time: the syllabus at Göttingen more closely resembled that of the progressive Dissenting Academies and the Scottish universities in its breadth and intellectual currency. (Many of the English students he befriended were studying medicine, not available at Oxford and Cambridge.) Coleridge, moreover – partly by virtue of his age, of course, and of his being an Englishman – enjoyed close intellectual (argumentative) relations with the German scholars who taught him and was even granted borrowing rights from the library in common with the academic staff (*CL* I, 494). While at Cambridge Coleridge had swept aside his studies to discuss the latest pamphlet, at Göttingen the topic of the lecture room became part of the lively intellectual debate of the evening.[10] It is hard to avoid the impression reading Coleridge's letters during his time at Göttingen that he belonged in a university, especially where that university (as in Scotland or in Germany) aspired to being at the centre of the intellectual life of the nation: 'My God! a miserable Poet must he be, & a despicable Metaphysician [whose] requirements have not cost more trouble & reflection than all the lea[rning of] Tooke, Porson & Parr united' (CL I, 494).

What was surely most depressing for Coleridge was not that he had failed to exploit the opportunity offered by his German visit. Quite the reverse, as we saw: he had learned German well enough to discourse with ease with university professors, attended lectures, made notes on his university studies and even more copious notes towards his projected work on Lessing and the history of German poetry. Yet still he had nothing concrete to show for it, no substantial work of 'reflection & genius' as a fitting monument to these uncharacteristically focussed and sustained exertions. He did, later, publish translations of Schiller's plays Wallenstein and Die Piccolomini (and, less nobly, an unacknowledged translation of Friederike Brun's poem 'Chamonix beym Sonnenaufgange' as 'Hymn before Sun-rise, in the Vale of Chamouny').[11] But no Life of Lessing ever appeared in the years following his visit and he would never again have the opportunity for such untrammelled research.

Coleridge and German thought

The limitations imposed on European touring by the war with France meant that, simply by process of elimination, in the late 1790s more Britons were travelling to the German provinces than ever before. Not everybody in Britain was as convinced as Coleridge of Germany's cultural and intellectual distinction, however. Indeed, for most Britons in the 1790s and especially for conservative writers in journals like the Anti-Jacobin, German literature meant the literature of the Sturm und Drang ('storm and stress'), readily available in English translation: Goethe's Sorrows of Young Werther, Schiller's The Robbers, Bürger's ballads. These melodramatic texts, preaching the values of spontaneity, sexual passion, and individuality – Werther was thought to have instigated a cult of suicide – had become associated with the English Jacobin novel and had thus become part of the culture wars of the 1790s.[12] It was with this association in mind that Coleridge wrote soon after his arrival defending the German literati (and himself): 'It is absolutely false that the literary Men are Democrats in Germany – Many were; but like me, have published Abjurations of the French – among which number are Klopstock, Goethe (the author of the "Sorrows of Werter") Wieland, Schiller & Kotzebu' (CL I, 435).

Until the early nineteenth century, knowledge of German literature and culture was dependent on energetic, isolated figures like Southey's friend William Taylor of Norwich, who published translations of Goethe and Bürger and Lessing and contributed scores of articles on German topics to the Monthly Review and the Monthly Magazine, many of them later collected and published as *Historic Survey of German Poetry* (1828–30) – the survey that Coleridge planned but did not get around to writing. But in spite of Taylor's efforts little German literature was familiar to the British reading public when Coleridge embarked in September 1798, and even less was known about German philosophy. Few people had ever heard of Immanuel Kant's self-declared 'Copernican revolution', for example, and those who had heard of it, knew it (as Coleridge himself knew it) only as something grand and unintelligible. As early as May 1796, Coleridge was designing a sophisticated school syllabus that included the study of 'Man as an *Intellectual* Being: including the ancient Metaphysics, the systems of Locke & Hartley, – of the Scotch Philosophers – & the new Kantian S[ystem]' (*CL* I, 209). But Coleridge had yet to read Kant and, more surprisingly, his sojourn in Germany in 1798–9 was not to be the occasion of his initiation into the transcendental idealism of the Kantian tradition that he would ultimately adopt and develop. It was not until around 1801 and after that Kant, as Coleridge says in the *Biographia*, 'took possession of me as with a giant's hand' (*BL* I, 153). Nor did he become familiar with the work of the early German Romantics during his stay, in spite of the fact that he had originally planned to study at the University of Jena (*CL* I, 209–10), where the Schlegel brothers – Friedrich and August Wilhelm – Ludwig Tieck and Novalis were all writing in and around their short-lived but influential journal the *Athenaeum* (1798–1800). As with Kant and the post-Kantians, it would take some time before the work of these early German Romantics would find its way through to England.

In spite of these time lapses, however, we can still date the honeymoon of Coleridge's long and complicated marriage to German thought to this trip of 1798–9, when for the first time he embraced an intellectual culture that he found immediately compatible: erudite, syncretizing, speculative, idealist. It would be hard to overestimate the influence of German philosophy and literary theory on Coleridge's ideas, an influence manifest in every area of his mature thinking. Eventually, he would become the chief mediator of German philosophical idealism in England, 'Explaining metaphysics to the nation', as Byron put it in the Dedication to his *Don Juan* – before going on to complain: 'I wish he would explain his Explanation' (ll. 15–16).[13] (For the second generation of liberal-radical Romantics, like the Whig satirists Byron and Thomas Love Peacock, Coleridge's Teutonic unintelligibility was part of a strategy of mystification, symptomatic of his growing political conservatism.[14]) And he is arguably the only literary *theorist* amongst the English Romantics – the only writer, that is, attempting a systematic account of 'literature' as a mode of creative apprehension and reception explained in psychological and philosophical terms.

Having said that, Coleridge's indebtedness to the Germans has proved, at best, a mixed blessing, though the fault lies entirely with Coleridge himself. Already during his own lifetime he was being accused of plagiarism – of relying word for word on August Wilhelm Schlegel in his literary lectures of 1811, for example, when distinguishing between mechanical and organic form and between classical and romantic drama, and word for word on Schelling when defining and defending the dynamic philosophy in the *Biographia*. And it was true. How far Coleridge can be said to have found in German writers the expression of ideas he had himself been struggling to articulate since the mid-1790s is another question, however, and the answer depends upon how generously we choose to interpret the occasional, casual speculation of his letters and notebooks and poems, and the frustration he discovers with the home-grown materialism of Locke and Hume (and Hartley and Priestley) before Kant took possession of him 'as with a giant's hand'.[15]

Travelling north: The Lake District

When Coleridge returned from Germany in July 1799, however, these literary transgressions were all in the future. There were other problems, problems closer to home. He had delayed his return to Sara as long as he could which served only to widen the rift that, in spite of long letters full of homesickness and protesting his love for her, was beginning to open up between them. By October he was complaining to Southey that 'the wife of a man of Genius who sympathizes effectively with her Husband is a rara avis [i.e., rare bird] with me' (*CL* I, 540). And he had overspent. He wrote to Josiah Wedgwood of his needing 'to *anticipate* for 40 or 50 pound' his allowance for the following year, though 'before Christmas I shall have repayed myself' (*CL* I, 519). Whatever 'money-book' he may have had in mind when he assured Wedgwood that he would make good the advance (*CL* I, 540), the way he finally chose to straighten out his finances was to go to London and write for the *Morning Post*. But that decision, in response to an offer from the editor and proprietor Daniel Stuart, would not come until later in the year. Until the offer was made, Coleridge remained domestically and emotionally unsettled, living largely in the West country at Nether Stowey with Poole or at Bristol, but torn between there and London and the Wordsworths' Lake District. It was during this time, in September 1799, that Coleridge wrote to Wordsworth soliciting the poem that, out of the autobiographical blank verse fragments Wordsworth had begun in Goslar in Germany, would become Wordsworth's greatest poem, the 'poem to Coleridge' that we know by the name of *The Prelude*:

> I wish you would write a poem, in blank verse, addressed to those, who, in consequence of the complete failure of the French Revolution, have thrown up all hopes of the amelioration of mankind, and are sinking into an almost epicurean selfishness, disguising the same under the soft titles of domestic attachment and contempt for visionary *philosophes*. It would do great good, and might form part of 'The Recluse'. (*CL* I, 527)

The very fact that it was Wordsworth who was being asked to undertake the poem and to incorporate it into his projected *magnum opus* 'On Man, on Nature, and on Human Life', *The Recluse*,[16] betrays Coleridge's lack of confidence in his own powers no less than his related conviction of Wordsworth's genius. The letter also reveals Coleridge's own political disillusionment, his need for the kind of therapy he hoped Wordsworth's poem would bring, and his understanding of his new role as a 'visionary *philosophe*'.

With Coleridge's mind and heart in the Lake District, it is perhaps not surprising that nothing was being done on his German materials beyond visiting the Wedgwoods at Upton in Wiltshire with assurances. Then, during a sudden trip to Bristol in late October when he had been introduced to the young scientist Humphry Davy, news of Wordsworth's illness reached him. He prevailed upon Joseph Cottle and the two of them made a sudden departure in Cottle's carriage, arriving in Sockburn-on-Tees in County Durham four days later, at the farm of Tom and George Hutchinson, brothers of Wordsworth's future wife, Mary, of Sara, and of Joanna. (Wordsworth was not ill, as it happened.) Coleridge was on the threshold of his first visit to the place with which, rightly or wrongly, his name would be forever associated, thanks largely to Francis Jeffrey, editor of the leading quarterly periodical the *Edinburgh Review*. Jeffrey began in the first number of the *Edinburgh Review* in October 1802 to write of Wordsworth, Southey, and Coleridge as belonging to a school or 'sect' that he would later characterize as having 'haunted for some years about the lakes of Cumberland' – thence, 'lake poets' and 'lakish'.[17] For Jeffrey, the title carried the charge of narrow regionalism or provinciality – even escapism – and was implicitly opposed to his own version of Enlightenment cosmopolitanism. What the more worldly and party political Jeffrey saw in the three writers' identification with the Lake District was, ironically, a withdrawal from the liberal, reforming ideals of the French Revolution into a kind of 'epicurean selfishness'.

In the *Biographia* and elsewhere, Coleridge dismissed the association of his, Southey's, and Wordsworth's names as mere journalistic adventitiousness, given 'how utterly unfounded was the supposition, that we considered ourselves, as belonging to any common school' (*BL* I, 51n.). But it had, if nothing else, geography and ideology on its side. Coleridge would gravitate towards the Lakes from this day in October 1799 until the rupture with Wordsworth in 1810 eleven years later, and from 1799 and 1803 respectively Wordsworth and Southey would settle there for the remainder of their lives. And all three of them, having begun their literary careers as radicals, supporting the French Revolution across the channel and more democratic reform at home, would become conservative apologists and theorists in middle age. Coleridge, moreover, when Wordsworth whisked him off the day he arrived in late 1799 to meet up with his brother John Wordsworth and undertake a lightning, fortnight tour of the whole Lake District – Windermere, Grasmere, Ullswater, Ennerdale Water, Buttermere – Coleridge responded to his new environment with the enthusiasm of a religious convert. 'You can feel what I cannot express for myself', he wrote to Dorothy, 'how deeply I have been impressed by a world of scenery absolutely new to me' (*CL* I, 544). A series of painterly sketches begins, at times obsessively minute in detail and, as in 'This Lime-Tree Bower My Prison', fascinated throughout by chiaroscuro effects:

> What a scene! Where I stand, on the shore is a triangular Bay, taking in the whole of the water view—on the other shore ... now it is all one deep wall of white vapour, save that black streaks shaped like strange creatures, seem to move in it & down it, in opposite direction to the motion of the great Body!—& over the forks of the Cliff behind, in shape so like a cloud, the Sun sent cutting it his thousand silky Hairs of amber & green Light— I step two paces, and have lost the glory, but the edge has exactly the soft richness of the silver edge of a cloud behind which the Sun is travelling!— The fog has now closed over the Lake, & we wander in darkness. (N91)

Once Coleridge settled at Greta Hall in 1800 these sketches would only become longer and more detailed – more absorbed – as if straining to assimilate the sky-, water- and landscape into the language of his private notebooks.

Coleridge's Notebooks

It is from this time that we notice a significant shift in Coleridge's notebook writing habits, with necessary ramifications for his writing habits more generally. When Coleridge began using notebooks in the mid-1790s, they were a resource for his future writing, especially for his poetry. Single ideas or expressions or project titles were listed as discrete entries to be followed up, or not, depending on whether or not the idea or expression or project still seemed valid and generative when consulted again at some time in the future.

> When lulled Reason sleeps on the stormy Bosom of Transport, as a ship boy in the Shrouds—

> Love, that soothes misfortune and buoys up Virtue—the pillow of Sorrows, the wings of Virtue.

> Optimist—by having no will but the will of Heaven, we call in Omnipotence to fight our battles!—

> This is the true Sublime of Man! this the Meridian Majesty of our Nature!

> What (Burke's book) repugnant feelings did it excite? I shuddered while I praised it—a web wrought with admirable beauty from a black bag of Poison!

> The helmet of Virtue needs not the plume of Praise!—

Strikes me blind by lightning flashes of Wit!—

The deep & dark perplexities of metaphysic Controversy!—

Real Pain can alone cure us of imaginary ills! We feel a thousand miseries till we are lucky enough to feel Misery:

Turbid Joy ending in Sorrow—dissipation.

Dwarfing Earth's giant Ills.

What we must do, let us love to do. It is a noble Chemistry, that turns Necessity to Pleasure!

Jonas—a monodrama—

Vide Hunter's Anatomy of a Whale—

and so on (*CN* I, 20–32). Anyone familiar with Coleridge's writings will identify later incarnations of a number of these ideas and expressions (in letters and lectures, for example, in the 'Ode to Sara, Written at Shurton Bars' and *Religious Musings*). Otherwise, as in the projected monodrama, nothing would come of them. But they remained in service to a more public literary life. On his own in Germany, Coleridge began to make more copious notes for his own future reference – most obviously for his study of Lessing, but also for planned studies of past and present German culture as well as detailed topographical notes during his tour of the Hartz mountains. But still there is a sense in which these notes from Germany were directed towards some act of publication (making public).

At a certain point towards the end of the decade, however, his resort to his notebooks for descriptive and speculative purposes picks up momentum and becomes habitual, as Coleridge moves without thinking to record an impression or idea that might have no immediate reality for him otherwise. In a notebook entry of May 1808 addressing his notebook itself, Coleridge would recognize this:

> Ah! dear Book! Sole Confidant of a breaking Heart, whose social nature compels *some* Outlet. I write more unconscious that I am writing, than in my most earnest modes I *talk*— ... every generous mind ... feels its *Halfness* — it cannot *think* without a symbol — neither can it *live* without something that is to be at once its Symbol, & its *Other half* — (That phrase now so vulgar by the profane Use of it was most beautiful in its origin-) — Hence I deduce the habit, I have most unconsciously formed, of *writing* my inmost thoughts — I have not a soul on earth to whom I can reveal them — and yet
>
> 'I am not a God, that I should stand alone'
>
> and therefore to you, my passive, yet sole true & kind, friends I reveal them. *Burn you I certainly shall, when I feel myself dying*; but in the Faith, that as the Contents of my mortal frame will rise again, so that your contents will rise with me, as a Phoenix from its pyre of Spice & Perfume. (N463, ll. 1–3, 37–48)

As Coleridge's ideas become more prolific and more various, and as his research becomes less and less focussed, the notebook entries increase and, like sorcerer's apprentices, begin to dominate his mental and his writing life. No longer servicing published works and public genres, 'the notebook' or 'notebooks' become a working habit and a genre in their own right.

Always self-contained and more often than not discontinuous, the notebook entries show a mind ever alert and ever responsive – responding sometimes with a Shandean alacrity to every passing idea and image that occurs to him, no matter how trivial or whimsical, as if every observation (physical and intellectual) must have its moment in writing: 'What a beautiful Thing urine is, in a Pot, brown yellow, transpicuous, the Image, diamond shaped of the Candle in it' (N292). In their very spontaneity and frequency and variety, however, Coleridge's notebook outpourings lack the '*progressive transition*' of organizational method that he was himself to define so eloquently in *The Friend*: 'without continuous transition, there can be no Method, so without a pre-conception there can be no transition with continuity. The term, Method, cannot therefore, otherwise than by abuse, be applied to a mere dead arrangement, containing in itself no principle of progression'. Mind in the notebooks – Coleridge's mind – is taken hostage by the rich and endless diversity of its own experience and, for all Coleridge's aspiration towards intelligible relationship and ultimate unity, will not be disciplined (or reduced) to manageable order. Even individual entries are overtaken by the sheer chaotic fertility of human thought:

Now how to get back, having thus belabyrinthed myself in these most parenthetical parentheses? Cut thro' at once, & now say in half a dozen Lines what a half a dozen Lines would have enabled me to say at the very beginning / but my Thoughts, my Pocket-book Thoughts at least, move like a pregnant Polypus in sprouting Time, clung all over with young Polypi each of which is to be a thing of itself — and every motion out springs a new Twig of Jelly-Life/ (N385, ll. 64–70)

The fleeting and the fragmentary overwhelm and mock the more sustained and systematic works that Coleridge is persistently and fantastically projecting in the notebooks themselves.

The notebooks are, in this sense, if not Coleridge's greatest, certainly his most characteristic work: they reflect a mind unwilling to exclude, folding every vista, every vision, every dream, every passing thought, and the acts of seeing and dreaming and thinking themselves, into the relentless wakefulness of its hyperactive and often artificially stimulated imagination:

Wednesday Morning, 20 minutes past 2 o'clock. November 2nd. 1803. The Voice of the Greta, and the Cock-crowing: the Voice seems to grow, like a flower on or about the water beyond the Bridge, while the Cock crowing is nowhere particular, it is at any place I imagine & do not distinctly [?see]. A most remarkable Sky! The Moon, now waned to a perfect Ostrich's Egg, hangs over our House almost — only so much beyond it, garden-ward, that I can see it, holding my Head out of the smaller Study window. The Sky is covered with whitish, & with dingy *Cloudage*, thin dingiest Scud close under the moon & one side of it moving, all else moveless: but there are two great Breaks of Blue Sky — the one stretching over our House, & away toward Castlerigg, & this is speckled & blotched with white Cloud — the other hangs over the road, in the line of the Road in the shape of a I do not know what to call [it]: but this is the Figure — this is unspeckled, all blue — 3 Stars in it / more than in the former Break — all unmoving. The water leaden white, even as the grey Gleam of Water is in latest Twilight. — Now while I have been writing this & gazing between whiles (it is 40 M[inutes] past Two) the Break over the Road is swallowed up, & the Stars gone, the Break over the House is narrowed into a rude Circle, & on the edge of its circumference one very bright Star — see! already the white mass thinning at its edge fights with its Brilliance — see! it has bedimmed it — & now it is gone — & the Moon is gone. The Cock crowing too has ceased. The Greta sounds on, for ever. But I hear only the Ticking of my Watch, in the Pen-place of my Writing Desk, & the far lower note of the noise of the Fire — perpetual, yet seeming uncertain / it is the low voice of quiet Change, of Destruction doing its work by little & little. (N266)

Asra

The tendency to privacy marked by Coleridge's increasing intellectual and emotional investment in his notebooks was only compounded by the need for secrecy that his affair with Sara Hutchinson occasioned. This, too, began on this brief visit north in late October and November of 1799. Immediately on his completing his tour of the Lakes with Wordsworth, Coleridge returned to the farm at Sockburn-on-Tees to see Dorothy and the Hutchinson sisters, falling in love with the plain but independent and personable Sara. It was an affair that commentators, then and since, have found both puzzling – there is nothing physically or intellectually striking about Sara, whose 'features were plain and contracted, her figure dumpy, and devoid of grace and dignity'[18] – and yet somehow inevitable, given Coleridge's idolization of Wordsworth and all things Wordsworthian. Sara was part of a new family whose intimacy and contentment the unsympathetically married Coleridge envied, just as he envied them their poetry and (now) their lakes. It was also an affair that the conservative Christian in Coleridge could only ever see as 'illicit' and one that had to be conducted largely, if not quite exclusively, in his own imagination. Most of the fleeting physical contact that the two of them would enjoy occurred during this brief week on the farm at Sockburn. Coleridge in a notebook entry records – or does he imagine? – 'The long entrancement of a True-love's Kiss' (*CN* I, 578). Three years later he would recall (in Latin) that on the 24 November 1799 he had 'pressed Sara's hand a long time behind her back, and then, then for the first time, love pricked me with its light arrow, poisoned alas! and hopeless' (*CN* I, 1575). Sara – or Asra as she was anagrammatically renamed to distinguish her from Sara his wife – was the ideal lover whom fate and his own folly had conspired to deny him. He would address her mute and idealized projection in his notebooks as he would address the notebooks themselves on occasion. Because she would listen and sympathize as the other Sara would not, she became the object of his intense adoration and frustrated importunities and the repository of his superabundant woes. Coleridge's last great poem, his 'Dejection: An Ode' of 1802, in which he recounts his losses and measures his impotence and desperation against the hope that had buoyed his youth, began its life as a much longer verse letter addressed to Sara Hutchinson.

Fleet Street

It was at the end of their tour of the Lake District that Daniel Stuart's letter offering Coleridge work on the staff of the *Morning Post* arrived. From the very centre of what would become his imaginative retreat he was being called into the very centre of the metropolis. It had been two years now since the professional writer and lecturer James Mackintosh had brokered work for Coleridge with his brother-in-law Stuart. Until six months before he left for Germany, Coleridge regularly contributed political poetry and occasionally contributed prose commentary characterized by the Jacobin fervour of his Bristol lectures. Both had helped raise the paper's profile and popularity. (Coleridge had also agreed to send copy from Germany, but there is no record of his having done so and every indication of Stuart's despairing of it. 'Do you think I have any reason to hope for Communications from him?', Stuart enquired of Sara Coleridge in February 1799, when Coleridge would have been en route to Göttingen.[19]) But this occasional contributing was a long way from installing himself and his family in 21 Buckingham Street, the Strand, near the offices of the *Morning Post* and working on the next day's copy 'from I-rise to I-set – i.e. from 9 in the morning to 12 at night – a pure Scribbler' (*CL* I, 552). In all, between his arrival at the end of November 1799 and his departure a little over four months later on 2 April 1800, Coleridge would contribute more than seventy articles or 'leaders', some (like a famous article on William Pitt) as long as 3000 words. Until December 1799, in other words, Coleridge had sold his poems to the newspaper and written the occasional article; now he was a journalist.

The rise of the periodical press in the eighteenth century was as spectacular a rise as any in modern Britain, the surest sign that a publishing revolution had taken place since 1695, when the Licensing Act limiting the number of printing presses was suspended. The newspaper had evolved to meet a new demand for information ('intelligence') and, later, for a critical position or *opinion* on most aspects of communal life, joining magazines and Reviews and a steady stream of pamphlets and encyclopædias in offering information and argument in a condensed and readily accessible form. Ephemeral publications discussing contemporary events had been around since the Elizabethan period, and newspapers or newsbooks (called 'corantos') had begun to appear in numbered sequences as early as the 1620s.[20] It was not until 1702, however, that the first successful London daily paper commenced publication. 'The public may, in time', wrote Britain's best-known journalist William Cobbett in 1811, 'see how *they* will be affected by the *freedom* or *slavery* of this great and moral engine'.[21] The government, however, had seen it much, much earlier. The number of newspapers that started up in the early eighteenth century became so alarming that in 1712 the government had introduced a stamp duty to keep up their price and restrict their readership. (Coleridge, you will recall, had issued *The Watchman* every eighth day to avoid stamp duty.[22]) In spite of stamp duty, however, which had been regularly increased throughout the century and would last until 1855, the number of newspapers carrying the most recent commercial, political, and social information relevant to the life of the community it serviced had grown steadily throughout the eighteenth century.

By the end of the eighteenth century, when Stuart conscripted Coleridge onto the staff of the *Morning Post*, there were over 250 newspapers in Britain issued 'periodically' (usually from daily to weekly). Most offered only limited information about trade or commerce, as they had from the beginning, but more and more of them had started featuring the foreign and domestic news that was once the exclusive province of the élite, while at the same time offering some interpretative commentary. In London alone there were more than fifteen dailies, including amongst the more influential *The Morning Chronicle*, *The Morning Herald*, *The Times*, and Stuart's *Morning Post*. The circulation of these would reach as many as 6000 during the Napoleonic period, and in times of scandal or controversy (like the Queen Caroline affair, in which the Prince of Wales tried to divorce his wife on receiving the kingship) could reach as high as 14–16,000.

It was not until 1814, when *The Times* newspaper finally installed a steam press, that newspaper production became capable of meeting any demand the public might make of it. And it was not until 1816, when William Cobbett began issuing his *Political Register* for twopence, that a radical, unstamped ('pauper') press began to develop, opening up for the first time the possibility of mass circulation that frightened the more conservative Coleridge and provoked from him dire warnings about the vulgarization consequent upon the expansion of an indiscriminate reading public. It would be wrong, therefore, to imagine that in the early nineteenth century newspapers had anything like the habitual and universal appeal they have today. Like the books and magazines with which they shared the market, they remained the preserve largely of the middle and upper classes. But already by the end of the eighteenth century the press had become the ubiquitous presence we recognize it as today. With the political and cultural consciousness of the nation having quickened in the 1790s under the impetus of the war with France and its effect on trade and prices, the newspaper had made itself indispensable. The letters of contemporary politicians are full of marvelling over events first brought to their attention by the newspapers and the government began intercepting 'packets' sent by journalists from the battlefields of Europe to keep itself up to date.

Because of the presence and influence of the press, senior government ministers and members of the opposition invested heavily in newspapers as an effective form of party propaganda. Ministerial payments to the press had become so well established by the 1790s that Pitt was paying editors of newspapers from the Civil List secret service money. Even when subsidized, however, the press had to rely on sales and advertisements to survive. Polemic might have been house-trained by political pay-offs and the perennial threat of arrest for 'seditious libel', but information was still at a premium and competition fierce. Like so many other aspects of British culture in the Romantic period, the world of newspapers was a world of supply and demand, driven more by commercial than by political interests. The periodical press would not have expanded as it did, nor as many periodicals been launched during the Romantic period (over 4000 between 1790 and 1832, according to Jon Klancher[23]), had it not been potentially lucrative. Having bought the *Morning Post* in 1795 for only £600, Stuart was able to sell it in 1803 for £25,000 and with his other successful ventures would later purchase a 'pleasure dome' and live in semi-retirement at Wykeham Park, a 300-acre estate near Banbury.

This is not to say that individual newspapers were politically disinterested or indifferent. Far from it. The *Morning Post* under Stuart, for example, was an identifiably Opposition paper and, for all its prevarication on certain issues, remained trenchantly anti-ministerial and anti-war (at least until Coleridge turned it around in 1802 and it became trenchantly anti-Napoleon and pro-war). During the early 1790s, Stuart himself had been deputy secretary of the Society of the Friends of the People, a group campaigning for parliamentary reform with which Coleridge had flirted, though never joined. In a pamphlet of 1794 entitled *Peace and Reform, Against War and Corruption*, Stuart had openly promoted reform and defended the French Revolution. But still, to quote David Erdman, 'the virtues of the *Morning Post* in its best years were elasticity and variety, not consistency'.[24] It had this in common with all the other major papers, written with what Coleridge called 'the tastes of [Lon]don Coffee house men & breakfast-table People of Quality' in mind (*CL* I, 627). In most cases, that is, not only did opinion have to adjust to changing circumstances but commercial interests also encouraged a kind of diplomacy – or hedging of bets – in which a variety of interests and opinions would be represented within the pages of one newspaper. In the *Biographia* Coleridge would take pride in the political position of the *Morning Post* as heterogeneous: '*anti-ministerial* indeed, yet with a very qualified approbation of the opposition, and with far greater earnestness and zeal both anti-jacobin and anti-gallican' (*BL* I, 212). The newspaper, in other words, fulfilled its obligations to its readers and even to the government itself by adopting a uniformly critical position. Again, Coleridge is being less than honest, figuring elasticity and expediency as noble impartiality, playing up the continuities and playing down the shift of allegiance the *Morning Post* underwent. If it was all these at different times, it was far more consistently radical in the early years.

Coleridge and journalism

Most writers and thinkers during the Romantic period involved themselves in the periodical press in some form or other, writing for magazines and reviews, certainly, to supplement whatever income from book publishing they could manage. (The single-minded Wordsworth was an exception, as was the aristocratic Byron.) Indeed, Southey's writing career is exemplary in this way. Even after he became Poet Laureate in 1813, Southey was obliged to be as much of a professional as any writer of his generation, supplementing the income he received from his oriental and Gothic epics, and his many anthologies, biographies, histories, translations, and literary editions by publishing poetry in magazines, almanacs, and annuals, writing for the *Morning Post* and the *Courier*, and reviewing for the *Quarterly Review* from its inception in 1809.[25] Few could stand comparison with Southey for the sheer, not to say promiscuous variety and extent of his output, but the pattern and the spread of publications is typical.

At different times, Coleridge, Southey, Godwin, Lamb, and Thelwell all contributed to the *Morning Post*. To say that most writers published in the periodical press, however, is not to say that they were all journalists. For one thing, newspapers were not exclusively interested in what we think of as 'news' (trade, commerce, politics). Like magazines, newspapers often published poetry and songs and anecdotes and book extracts and reviews of books as well – as they still do. To write for a newspaper, then, could mean any one of a number of things. Of all the 'literary' writers of the Romantic period, only very few were engaged for any length of time, as Coleridge was, in daily and weekly journalism, with its direct and sometimes causal connection to daily and weekly politics. Certainly few would have sat up all night reporting on sittings in the House of Commons as Coleridge did on three occasions (*CL* I, 568–9). (Parliamentary sittings began in the late afternoon, after the working day.) While the bulk of his journalistic output falls into separate, intensive periods, like this first four months in London at the turn of the century, Coleridge's confirmed and conjectural contributions to newspapers over twenty odd years were extensive enough nearly to have filled three volumes of his *Collected Works* – four if we include *The Watchman*, five if we include *The Friend* (1809–10). Newspapers do not usually feature prominently in literary histories and literary lives, and the oscillation in Coleridge's literary life between the immediate, public world of newspaper journalism at one extreme and the intensely private world of the observations and ruminations in his notebooks at the other is remarkable. Indeed it was unique.

Having said that, it is also true that Coleridge's best journalism, like his best literary criticism, shares with the intensely introverted self- and dream analysis a fascination with the motives of human character and action:

> William Pitt was the younger son of Lord Chatham; a fact of no ordinary importance in the solution of his character, of no mean significance in the heraldry of morals and intellect. His father's rank, fame, political connections, and parental ambition were his mould:—he was cast, rather than grew. A palpable election, a conscious predestination controlled the free agency, and transfigured the individuality of his mind; and that, which he *might have been*, was compelled into that, which he *was to be*. ...
>
> The influencer of his country and his species was a young man, the creature of another's determination, sheltered and weather-fended from all the elements of experience; a young man, whose feet had never wandered; whose very eye had never turned to the right or to the left; whose whole track had been as curveless as the motion of a fascinated reptile! It was a young man, whose heart was solitary. ... A plant sown and reared in a hot-house, for whom the very air, that surrounded him, had been regulated by the thermometer of previous purpose; to whom the light of nature had penetrated only through glass and covers; who had had the sun without the breeze; whom no storm had shaken; on whom no rain had pattered; on whom the dews of Heaven had not fallen!

And so on, preternaturally adult child with a fatal gift for public speaking which has emptied his words of passion and authenticity to render him an automaton who (it comes as no surprise) ultimately proves incapable of an original, liberating idea: 'never controlling, never creating events, but always yielding to them with rapid change, and sheltering himself from inconsistency by perpetual indefiniteness'.[26] Pitt, in Coleridge's construction, is a professional politician who has never been allowed the freedom to become a human being. As fascinated as its author may seem with psychology, however, analysis and speculation is always at the service of a polemic in which Pitt is not so much psychologically analysed, as psychologically disqualified. The cumulative repetition of Pitt's effective dehumanization as a child moves way beyond disinterested analysis into a ritual, often poetic reinforcement of Coleridge's theme.

What is also worth noting here is the way in which Coleridge portrays Pitt as a version of himself: the precocious mastery of language; the deprivation of nature in childhood; the ultimate isolation. It will be the same eight years later when Coleridge offers his brilliant analysis of a character on another stage: Shakespeare's Hamlet. Reshaping himself as his character, Coleridge – a veritable Proteus – is able to achieve subtle and compelling insights. Of course, for Coleridge, the similarity with Pitt is implicitly self-justifying rather than self-damning, highlighting the difference between the two of them as he would have seen it. The talented Pitt is educated 'in the science and management of *words*'[27]; Coleridge, a genius, is truly eloquent. (Though one wonders with what degree of self-consciousness Coleridge described Pitt as 'sheltering himself from inconsistency by perpetual indefiniteness'!) The article on Pitt was to form part of a diptych with another on Napoleon, in which Pitt and Napoleon were to reflect 'similar situations, with the greatest dissimilitude of character'.[28] The article on Napoleon, however, though long promised and eagerly anticipated, was never written – because he did not want to flatter Napoleon's vanity with the attention, Coleridge later disingenuously claimed.[29] Coleridge's own biographical investment may to some extent have pre-empted Napoleon's role in the contrast.

The same tendency to oscillate that we witness in Coleridge's generic output also marked his attitude to journalism itself. He was often embarrassed by his connection with the newspapers, inclined to see it at best as 'Bread & Cheese'. 'By *Press as a Trade*', he wrote to John Prior Estlin, 'I wish you to understand, reviewing, newspaper-writing, and all those things in which I proposed no fame to myself or permanent good to society – but only to gain that bread which might empower me to do both the one and the other on my vacant days' (*CL* I, 372). At worst, it was as a form of prostitution, 'in which a delicacy of moral feeling & moral perception would with the greatest difficulty be preserved' (*CL* I, 376). The newspaper only achieved a secure social status and authority when in 1817 Thomas Barnes took over the editorship of *The Times* and it became at once more independent and more effectual. Besides relying on a network of foreign correspondents – including Coleridge's and Wordsworth's friend, the diarist Henry Crabb Robinson – Barnes used copy from prominent political insiders like Henry Brougham, the KC and Whig politician (later Lord Chancellor) who was also the mainstay of the *Edinburgh Review*. Even with the rise of *The Times*, however, the world of Fleet Street was still a morally and socially ambiguous one. In 1796, for example, Stuart had been found guilty of manufacturing copy to exploit the stockmarket ('stockjobbing') and was widely suspected of making a habit of it.[30] 'Dan's a Scotchman', Coleridge reluctantly confided to Henry Crabb Robinson, 'who is content to get rid of the itch when he can afford to wear clean linen'.[31] The kinds of often clandestine pay-offs newspapers were receiving at the turn of the century also cast a permanent shadow over their collective reputation and were especially complicated by the multiple ownership of sometimes rival newspapers. Again, Stuart is typical, absorbing the dying *Telegraph* and *Gazeteer* and buying into the *Courier* while still running the *Morning Post*.

Like most journalists, however, Coleridge took pride in the fact that newspapers circulated his opinions to a wide audience, wider certainly than that enjoyed by his political pamphlets and *The Watchman*:

> Yet it is not unflattering to a man's Vanity to reflect that what he writes at 12 at night will before 12 hours is over have perhaps 5 or 6000 Readers! To trace a happy phrase, good image, or new argument running thro' the Town, & sliding into all the papers! Few Wine merchants can boast of creating more sensation. Then to hear a favorite & often urged argument repeated almost in your own particular phrases in the House of Commons—& quietly in the silent self-complacence of your own Heart chuckle over the plagiarism, as if your were grand Monopolist of all good Reasons!—But seriously, considering that I have Newspapered it merely as means of subsistence while I was doing other things, I have been very lucky—the New Constitution, the Proposals for Peace, the Irish Union—; &c &c—they are important in themselves, & excellent Vehicles for general Truths. I am not ashamed of what I have written. (*CL* I, 569)

When not on the defensive, Coleridge would brag that he had single-handedly raised the profile of newspaper journalism. According to the *Biographia*, he had only 'acceded to the proposal on the condition, that the paper should thenceforwards be conducted on certain fixed and announced principles, and that I should be neither obliged nor requested to deviate from them in favor of any party or any event' (*BL* I, 212). If no coherent set of principles would ever emerge, other than as assurances – and Stuart, incidentally, was doubtful about having made such a promise[32] – there was certainly an impressively detached authority that Coleridge brought to his journalistic commentary. It derived partly from the implication of a wide and intimate knowledge of the world and its history, partly from an implied – and resigned – knowledge of human nature. In his first article on arrival in London at the end of 1799, the new French Constitution drawn up on Bonaparte's arrival in Paris is given a magisterial analysis in the context of what is historically and humanly possible:

> The prejudices of superstition, birth, and hereditary right, have been gradually declining during the last four centuries, and the empire of property as gradually establishing itself in their stead. Whether or no this too will not in a distant age submit to some more powerful principle, is, indeed, a subject fruitful in dreams to poetic philosophers, who amuse

themselves with reasonings on unknown quantities; but to all present purposes it is a useless and impertinent speculation. For the present race of men Governments must be founded on property. ... In America where the great mass of people possess property, and where, by the exertion of industry, any man may possess it in its most permanent form, this principle may, perhaps, co-exist with universal suffrage; but not so in old and populous countries, in which the land is of high value, and where the produce of individual labour can hardly be large enough to admit of considerable accumulation.

This is the classic attitude of the journalistic feature writer, the writer who has seen it all before, or seen it all coming, and knows where it fits into the scheme of things ('for the present race of men'). Trust him, he knows what is worth troubling our thoughts about and what is unprofitable speculation. And it was resolute in a way that Coleridge otherwise was not, resolute in the way that Poole had observed when advising him on his German studies: 'no one sooner sees the side of a question on which the balance of argument turns'.[33] Stuart remarked on this and compared it favourably with Coleridge's more ambitious literary and philosophical writings in a late letter to Coleridge's nephew and son-in-law, H. N. Coleridge:

> To write the leading paragraph of a newspaper I would prefer him to Mackintosh, Burke, or any man I ever heard of. His observations were not only confirmed by good sense, but displayed extensive knowledge, deep thought and well-grounded foresight; they were so brilliantly ornamented, so classically delightful. They were the writings of a Scholar, a Gentleman and a Statesman, without personal sarcasm or illiberality of any kind. But when Coleridge wrote in his study without being pressed, he wandered and lost himself.[34]

What is extraordinary in his article on the French constitution is that Coleridge achieves his authority at the expense of his own youthful idealism, when he amused himself with reasonings on the 'unknown quantities' of aspheterism and pantisocracy. Somehow Coleridge manages both nostalgia and self-irony, manages to keep open the option of a new and improved future in a proto-Marxist analysis of historical development (feudalism, bourgeois capitalism, socialism) while at the same time dismissing such dreams as irrelevant 'to all present purposes'. The beliefs and desires of the writer on this, as on the issue at hand, remain suggestive but indeterminate. Aloof. The new French constitution is criticized in a way that draws on and indicts Britain's own electoral practices and Coleridge manages at the same time to condemn human venality generally (and any attempt at fair representation) and both the British and the French electoral systems in particular, insofar as they will not admit the corruption that this journalist knows to be endemic in the system. As a practical interpretation of what the constitution entails it is forceful and convincing, though what is right or desirable, and what inevitable, remains unclear.

Whether or not Coleridge can be said to have raised the standard of journalism, his other claim that the articles he wrote for Stuart's *Morning Post* and, later, for his *Courier* contributed substantially to the papers' success – Stuart, Coleridge told his brother in 1809, owes 'a very large fortune not indeed *exclusively* to my efforts but so far that without them he could have done nothing' (*CL* III, 238) – seems to be true. Stuart certainly was successful, as I said. When he bought the *Morning Post* in 1795, its circulation had fallen to about 350 copies per day. It flourished under his editorship and half-proprietorship, with sales increasing to 2000 by the time that Coleridge joined the staff and to more than 4500 by 1803, when it was sold. Stuart himself, though resentful about what he saw as Coleridge's arrogant claims in the *Biographia*, admitted as much to Coleridge on 29 September 1802 when, after a hiatus of six months, Coleridge sent him a set of lively epigrams and a series of articles comparing France with the Roman Empire:

I have received the last of your Comparison. The whole forms an excellent Article & I really assure you it is much admired. Peltier is translating it for his [French language] Journal. I am afraid to give Lot II of Epigrams as I fear I may be under the necessity of dealing them out at one a time for want of other poetry; though I must say you have most liberally supplied me and I am astonished & delighted.—The best of all is the sale of the Paper which has been drooping since May as it always does, is now lively & recovering though the season for that is not till November.[35]

And it was the second of Stuart's and Coleridge's newspapers, the *Courier* (edited by T. G. Street), that would later achieve record sales figures of 16,000. The choice of Coleridge, allowing him his head in editorial matters, is a tribute to Stuart's discrimination. Coleridge's staying as long as he did and returning as often as he did is a tribute to Stuart's ability to apply the right kind and degree of pressure on someone so labile. 'Stuart was from first to last the great link between my father and all newspaper employment', wrote Coleridge's daughter and editor Sara, 'the Proximate Cause of all he performed in that way'.[36] That so successful a manager of people and money as Stuart should have striven so hard to keep Coleridge on confirms that he understood and greatly valued his contribution.

Just how wide Coleridge's readership was remains subject to debate. The issue of the extent and strength of his journalistic influence was another one on which he was prone at times to exaggerate – in a way that, especially after meeting Wordsworth, he never exaggerated the value and accomplishment of his poetry. Quite the reverse, as we have seen. It is no doubt a measure of his insecurity about the respectability of journalism '*as a Trade*' that he should have overreacted and made self-aggrandizing claims about his role. Coleridge arrived on the scene at the same time as Napoleon Bonaparte, for example, monitoring and (after 1802) deploring the rise and rise of the French emperor's career, ultimately reversing his policy on France to urge a return to war during the Peace of Amiens. In the *Biographia* he makes the bizarre claim that he was 'a specified object of Buonaparte's resentment during my residence in Italy in consequence of those essays in the Morning Post' and in fear of his life from the occupying French troops (*BL* I, 216).

If nothing else, however, Coleridge's conspiracy theory reflects the centrality of the daily press to the political life of the nation at the turn of the nineteenth century – and, we must grudgingly concede, Coleridge's occasional centrality to the daily press. Given the kind of forceful – and felicitously quotable – generalization of which he was capable as the omniscient and anonymous leader writer of one of the city's most popular newspapers it is hardly surprising that he should have found his own phrases on the lips of MPs in the House of Commons that evening. Flattering as this was, however, it was not flattering enough to tempt him to accept Stuart's offer of a proprietary interest when he reminded his employer that he had only ever intended to stay in London for a few months. By 21 March 1800 he was writing to Poole:

> If I had the least love of money, I could make almost sure of 2000£ a year / for Stuart has offered me half shares in the two papers, the M.P. & Courier, if I would devote myself to them with him—but I told him, that I would not give up the Country, & the lazy reading of Old Folios for two Thousand Times two thousand Pound—in short, that beyond 250£ a year, I considered money as a real Evil—at which he stared; for such Ideas are not animals indigenous in the Longitudes & Latitudes of a Scotchman's Soul. ... You, of course, will not hint a word to any [one] of Stuart's offer to me.—He has behaved with th[e] most abundant honor & generosity. (*CL* I, 582)

No doubt Poole was meant to feel gratified by Coleridge's choice of the country, but Coleridge was careful not to specify *which* country he would be returning to. Since Germany he had been protesting in letters his love for Poole and his determination to remain within proximity to the most supportive of his friends since his Bristol days. Whenever he did protest, however, he protested too much, and Wordsworth's name and the Wordsworths' endeavours to lure him to the Lake District were never far away when he ruminated on where to settle – and it had to be somewhere and soon, for Sara Coleridge was pregnant again. The first thing he did on quitting London on 2 April 1800 was to travel north again, joining the Wordsworths and the Hutchinsons at the house in Grasmere that would later be named Dove Cottage. Immediately he set about finding a place for himself and Sara, Hartley, and the unborn Derwent.

6

'To Rust Away': The Lost Years 1800–6

The residence negotiated by the Wordsworths for the Coleridge family was the front half of a substantial place called Greta Hall, whose owner occupied the rear. Atop a small hill that nestled in a moat-like horse-shoe curve of the River Greta, it looked out over Lake Keswick and Bassenthwaite Water and up into 'the most fantastic mountains, that ever Earthquakes made in sport' (*CL* I, 615). Behind it, '& entering into all our views', rose the mountain known as Skiddaw (*CL* I, 610). 'I question if there be a room in England which commands a view of Mountains & Lakes & Woods & Vales superior to that, in which I am now sitting', Coleridge wrote to Godwin from his study in Greta Hall (*CL* I, 620); and, earlier: 'If, according to you & Hume, impressions & ideas constitute our Being, I shall have a tendency to become a God' (*CL* I, 588).

His God, Wordsworth

The only god in Coleridge's life at this time, however, was Wordsworth. Other friends, like Tom Poole back at Nether Stowey and Charles Lamb in London, stood by appalled at the magnetic force Wordsworth exerted in Coleridge's life. During his time as a journalist in the city, Coleridge had socialized no less energetically than he had worked, getting to know William Godwin and his family and extending his acquaintance to include Mary 'Perdita' Robinson, a poet and once a famous beauty and mistress to the Prince of Wales, to whom Coleridge would dedicate 'A Stranger Minstrel'. Coleridge had stayed with Charles and Mary Lamb in the month before his departure from London, working on his translation of Schiller's *Wallenstein* and reviving the days of drinking, conversation, and general hilarity they had shared at the Salutation and Cat during the winter of 1794–5. It was then, immediately after Coleridge departed for Grasmere, that Lamb complained of Coleridge's having left them 'to go into the North, on a visit to his

God, Wordsworth'.[1] The more forthright Poole had had no reservations about expressing his anxiety directly to Coleridge himself, to which Poole received the following contradictory and revealing reply:

> You charge me with prostration in regard to Wordsworth. Have I affirmed anything miraculous of W.? Is it impossible that a greater poet than any since Milton may appear in our days? ... Future greatness! Is it not an awful thing, my dearest Poole? What if you had known Milton at the age of thirty, and believed all you now know of him?—What if you should meet in the letters of any then living man, expressions concerning the young Milton *totidem verbis* the same as mine of Wordsworth, would it not convey to you a most delicious sensation? Would it not be an assurance to you ... that the greatness was incarnate and personal? (*CL* I, 584)

Coleridge spent three weeks with the Wordsworths at Dove Cottage before moving into Greta Hall, devoting his time to revisions of *The Rime of the Ancient Mariner* to allay Wordsworth's anxieties about the poem's strangeness, and to editorial negotiations with publishers Biggs and Cottle over a reconstructed *Lyrical Ballads*, to be expanded to two volumes and publicly attributed in a way that the first, anonymous edition was not. Because Coleridge's contribution would have shrunk considerably in relation to Wordsworth's by the time they went to press, however, it was decided early on that only Wordsworth's name would appear on the title page. In spite of his marginalization, Coleridge eagerly threw himself into the enterprise over the summer of 1800, still hoping to use the opportunity of a new edition to recover his inspiration. He wrote a handful of original poems but his main aim was to complete the unfinished *Christabel* in time for its inclusion in this second edition of *Lyrical Ballads* along with a host of new poems by the more prolific Wordsworth.

Coleridge did manage a second part, moreover, while projecting (always projecting) a final version of around 1300 lines, roughly twice the 670 odd lines completed (*CL* I, 631). In the end, however, a cryptic note in Dorothy's journal of 6 October records their decision not to go ahead and publish *Christabel* in *Lyrical Ballads*.[2] Different reasons were offered at different times, perhaps the most bizarre being that, given its length, it would so increase Coleridge's contribution to the two volumes that Wordsworth could not then legitimately claim to be the author (*CL* I, 631). The more likely explanation was that Wordsworth (in his own words) 'found that the Style of this Poem was so discordant from my own that it could not be printed along with my poems with any propriety' (*CL* I, 643 and n.2). It is obvious that *The Rime of the Ancient Mariner* was itself only included under sufferance, accompanied as it was by a long and apologetic note of Wordsworth's pointing out to the reader the poem's 'great defects':[3]

first, that the principal person has no distinct character, either in his profession of Mariner, or as a human being who having been long under the controul of supernatural impressions might be supposed himself to partake of something supernatural: secondly, that he does not act, but is continually acted upon: thirdly, that the events having no necessary connection do not produce each other; and lastly, that the imagery is some-what too laboriously accumulated.

Besides having been tidied up, with its archaic spellings and locutions modernized, *The Rime* was to be demoted to the rear of the first volume (it had led the 1798 edition). The unqualified enthusiasm for his 'supernatural' poems offered by discriminating friends like Lamb and distinguished strangers like Byron eventually made it clear to Coleridge just how indifferent Wordsworth had been to their achievement. Writing to Thomas Allsop in 1818, Coleridge was bitter about the way he had been treated:

I have loved with enthusiastic self-oblivion those who have been so well pleased that I should, year after year, flow with a hundred nameless Rills into *their* Main Stream, that they could find nothing but cold praise and effective discouragement of every attempt of mine to roll onward in a distinct current of my own—who *admitted* that the Ancient Mariner, the Christabel, the Remorse, and *some* pages of the Friend were not without merit, but were abundantly anxious to acquit their judgements of any blindness to the very numerous defects. (*CL* IV, 888)

But that was many years later. At the time Coleridge acquiesced willingly enough. It is a tribute to his critical instincts that he was able to recognize Wordsworth's genius and to agitate so effectively for his friend's canonization. It is a tribute to his altruism that he was willing to put aside his own projects – the completion of the translation of *Wallenstein*, for example, for which he had received a £50 advance; a German travel book for Longman (£20); the *Life of Lessing*, still unwritten and still weighing on his conscience – and work in the service of Wordsworth's reputation. Just how much self-persuasion was required for Coleridge to have shelved his prior obligations, however, then or at any time, is a moot point, one that Coleridge often debated with himself. Difficult as it is to exonerate Wordsworth of the charge of self-centredness, in other words, it is worth bearing in mind that the prostration Tom Poole complained of was Coleridge's own choice and that Coleridge did more than anyone to encourage Wordsworth's single-minded fixation on his own poetry and reputation. Coleridge knew well the irrational investments (and the fragility) of a loving friendship like his and Wordsworth's, knew of the human inability to sustain the intensity of love and the way it seeks relief in anger and rejection. After all, he was writing about it – prophetically – at the very time Wordsworth was establishing his ascendancy over him with the new *Lyrical Ballads*, in a passage in *Christabel* that became a universal favourite with the Romantic male reviewers when it was finally published in 1816:

> when he heard the Lady's Tale
> And when she told her Father's Name,
> Why wax'd Sir Leoline so pale,
> Murmuring o'er the Name again,
> Lord Roland de Vaux of Tryermaine?
> Alas! they had been Friends in Youth;
> But whispering Tongues can poison Truth;
> And Constancy lives in Realms above;
> And Life is thorny; and Youth is vain;
> And to be wroth with One, we love,
> Doth work like madness in the Brain:
> And thus it chanc'd, as I divine,
> With Roland and Sir Leoline.
> Each spake words of high Disdain
> And Insult to his Heart's best Brother:
> They parted—ne'er to meet again!
> But never either found Another
> To free the hollow Heart from paining——
>
> They stood aloof, the scars remaining,
> Like Cliffs, which had been rent asunder;
> A dreary Sea now flows between,
> But neither Heat, nor Frost, nor Thunder
> Shall wholly do away, I ween,
> The Marks of that, which once hath been.
> (*Christabel*, Part II, ll. 403–26)

All we can say with certainty is that working so closely with and for Wordsworth not only proved a thankless task, but Coleridge also allowed it to destroy his self-confidence as a poet. As the *Lyrical Ballads* went to press, he was writing of Wordsworth to Francis Wrangham as 'a great, a true Poet – I am only a kind of Metaphysician' (*CL* I, 658). The thought haunted and punished him. 'As to Poetry', he wrote to Thelwall, 'I have altogether abandoned it, being convinced that I never had the essentials of poetic Genius, & that I mistook a strong desire for original power' (*CL* I, 656). Again, writing his own epitaph in the third person to Godwin in early 1801: 'Wordsworth descended on him ... [and] by shewing him what true Poetry was, he made him know, that he himself was no Poet' (*CL* II, 714).

The Preface to *Lyrical Ballads* and the birth of the critic

Another reason given for excluding *Christabel* from the *Lyrical Ballads* was that it made nonsense of the long manifesto Wordsworth had written justi-fying his choice of form and diction in what Coleridge called his 'experi-ment, to see how far those passions, which alone give any value to extraordinary Incidents, were capable of interesting, in & for themselves, in the Incidents of common Life' (*CL* I, 631). It was to this 1800 edition (which, as it happens, did not come out until early 1801) that the famous Preface to *Lyrical Ballads* was added, attacking the élitist affectations of 'poetic diction' – the prevailing language of eighteenth-century poetry – and arguing provoca-tively for the use instead of the language of 'low and rustic life':

> Low and rustic life was generally chosen because in that situation the essential passions of the heart find a better soil in which they can attain their maturity, are under less restraint, and speak a plainer and more emphatic language; because in that situation of life our elementary feel-ings exist in a state of greater simplicity and consequently may be more accurately contemplated and more forcibly communicated; because the manners of rural life germinate from those elementary feelings; and from the necessary character of rural occupations are more easily compre-hended; and are more durable; and lastly, because in that situation the passions of men are incorporated with the beautiful and permanent forms of nature.[4]

As Coleridge suggests in the *Biographia*, it was the Preface to *Lyrical Ballads*, before any individual poem that Wordsworth ever wrote, that brought down the wrath of the reviewers on the enterprise, inspiring in the editor of the *Edinburgh Review*, Francis Jeffrey, a campaign of relentless persecution over twenty years. It was to the Preface, therefore, to the 'long continued contro-versy concerning the true nature of poetic diction' instigated by the Preface (*BL* I, 5), and to Francis Jeffrey and the contemporary reviewers that the *Biographia* addressed itself, evolving its own literary theory by confirming, extending, revising, and denying the claims of the Preface.[5]

When in 1815 Coleridge was dictating the *Biographia*, however, the Preface he analysed so mercilessly at times was Wordsworth's; when the Preface was written he had been happy to own it as 'half a child of my own brain' (*CL* I, 830). Either way, Coleridge had by 1800 already outgrown it. The Preface belonged to the 1790s. When examined in the context of the earlier political writings of the two poets, it can be seen to have assimilated many of their radical ideas, and literature itself can be seen to have assumed most of the responsibility for the social and spiritual revolution to which they still aspired. Christopher Wordsworth made the point in 1851 when he expressed his suspicion that the clue to Wordsworth's '*poetical* theory, in some of its questionable details, may be found in his *political* principles; these had been democratical, and still, though in some degree modified, they were of a republican character. At this period he entertained little reverence for ancient institutions, as such; and he felt little sympathy with the higher classes of society'.[6]

The separation of language and genre by the Augustans into strict hierarchies reflected their general breakdown of the universe and society into rigidly – and, to the young Wordsworth and Coleridge, arbitrarily – distinct classes. Wordsworth and Coleridge saw the language of the bulk of poetry reflecting and perpetuating this social iniquity. The direct connection can be seen in an early note of Coleridge's which records with obvious distaste the precept of Adam Smith that it was the 'Duty of a Poet to write like a Gentleman' (*CN* I, 775). The educated gentlemen to whom the urbane Augustans appealed, and whose language they sought to imitate, were by no means representative of humanity. They may constitute the upper class reading public, the public that pays for 'books of half a guinea price, hot-pressed, and printed upon superfine paper', as Wordsworth defined it, but they were not 'the people'.[7] Coleridge's early conclusions on class distinction were, but for the vehemence and occasional hysteria with which they were expressed, identical to Wordsworth's. 'I *dislike* fine furniture, handsome cloathes, & all the ordinary symbols & appendages of artificial superiority – or what is called, *Gentility*' he wrote to his wife, Sara, probing her social aspirations like a wound (*CL* II, 881). In 'To a Young Ass', one of the *Morning Chronicle* poems that, having helped to establish his reputation for radicalism, would return to haunt him in parodies and satires, Coleridge states his preference for the 'dissonant harsh bray' of the ass over

> Handel's softest airs that soothe to rest
> The tumult of a scoundrel Monarch's Breast
> ('To an Young Ass, Its Mother Being Tethered
> Near It', ll. 35–6)[8]

Besides hierarchy, the unjustified mystery, the lavish waste, and the idolatry that contemporary Dissenting critics like Coleridge found in the Churches of both Rome and England are all seen as characteristic of corrupt poetic diction. The association of idolatry with sensuality linked it metaphorically to a seductive, meretricious, and superficial language reflecting only the vanity of the poet and preventing a direct apprehension of superior reality. Words were substituted for things, 'graven' images claiming attention for their own sake.[9] Coleridge was as fully aware of the religious significance of this inversion of values as he was of the other far-reaching ramifications of what the Preface calls the action and reaction of 'language and the human mind':

> When the material forms or intellectual ideas which should be employed
> to [rep]resent the internal state of feeling, are made to claim attention for

their own sake, then commences Lip-worship, or superstition, or disputatiousness, in religion; a passion for gaudy ornament & violent stimulants in morals; & in our literature bombast and vicious refinements. (*CL* II, 666)

The language of 'low and rustic life' satisfied the criteria developed in the Preface by not being decadent in Wordsworth's and Coleridge's terms – not urban, not effeminate, not élitist: 'from their rank in society and the sameness and narrow circle of their intercourse, being less under the action of social vanity they convey their feelings and notions in simple and unelaborated expressions'.[10] Contemporary upper class readers were not deaf to the challenge in the word 'low' in Wordsworth's tendentious choice of 'low and rustic life'. Nor could they have been insensible to his dubbing this 'the real language of men'.[11] They were being told that their own life and language were elaborate fictions.

As well as being a political and literary challenge, moreover, the rustic language promoted by the Preface was a metaphor for a language of even more pristine integrity. The Preface talks of recovering for poetry a 'far more philosophical language than that which is frequently substituted for it by Poets'.[12] The probable source of the phrase 'philosophical language' is the work once central to Coleridge's Dissenting politics, David Hartley's *Observations on Man*, and it is the influence of Hartley on the theory of language in the Preface that more than anything confirms Coleridge's input:[13]

If we suppose Mankind possessed of such a Language, as that they could at Pleasure denote all their Conceptions adequately, *i.e.* without any Deficiency, Superfluity, or Equivocation; if, moreover, this Language depended upon a few Principles assumed, not arbitrarily, but because they were the shortest and best possible ... this Language might be termed a philosophical one.[14]

Essential to all Hartley's theorizing were his belief in the return of an earthly paradise and, as an Optimist, the related supposition that all association contains a preponderance of pleasure driving mankind towards this millennium. 'Was human Life perfect', Hartley wrote, 'our Happiness in it would be properly represented by that accurate Knowledge of Things which a truly philosophical Language would give us'.[15] Not only did this 'truly philosophical Language' prophesy and reflect perfection, however, it also actively fostered it: 'the Use of Words ... is the principal Means by which we make intellectual and moral Improvements'.[16] Having a language adequate to express what was apprehended would be like having new senses, according to Hartley, encouraging and sharing new perceptions.[17]

It is this idea of poetic language as an agent of millennial progress that lies behind the Preface. Through the ministrations of right-minded poets, a language deriving from 'low and rustic life' would aid in the rectification of man's relationship with nature – Wordsworth's paradise and, when under

the influence of Wordsworth, Coleridge's too. Satirists and antagonistic critics like Francis Jeffrey would have a field day with the Romantic exaltation
of poetry (and of poets) represented by the Preface:

> It is this miserable trick of overrating the importance of all our concep-
> tions, that has made our recent literature so intolerably diffuse and
> voluminous. ... we must have long speculative introductions ... practical
> inferences—historical deductions—and predictions as to the effect of our
> doctrines, or the neglect of them, on the fate of men, and of the universe,
> in all time coming.[18]

By 1800, as I said, Coleridge had already grown out of the Preface he
helped to formulate. Soon he would be expressing his doubts publicly, both
about the theory – 'I rather suspect that some where or other there is a radical Difference in our theoretical opinions respecting Poetry—/ this I shall
endeavour to get to the Bottom of' – and about the poetry that Wordsworth
had written in service to the theory, in which Coleridge discovered 'here &
there a daring Humbleness of Language & Versification, and a strict adher-
ence to matter of fact' (*CL* II, 830). The only figurative language allowed by
the Preface had been that which was produced by passion. Writing to
William Sotheby, Coleridge insisted on less naturalistic and more aesthetic
discriminations: '*metre itself* implies a *passion*, i.e., a state of excitement, both
in the Poet's mind, & is expected in that of the Reader' (*CL* II, 812). Again,
'In point of poetic diction', Coleridge wrote to Tom Wedgwood, 'I am not so
well satisfied that you do not require a certain *Aloofness* from the language of
real Life, which I think deadly to Poetry' (*CL* II, 877).

These intellectual doubts, looking ahead to his wholesale refutation of the
Preface in the *Biographia*, can also be read as Coleridge's way of announcing
his emotional independence from Wordsworth to those of his other friends
concerned about his 'prostration', perhaps even as a belated way of expressing his resentment at Wordsworth's treatment of his own poetry. We know
how little Wordsworth thought of that poetry, and as for Coleridge's other
activity of these years – his journalism – this was rated by the Preface as
worse than useless, in conspiracy with 'sickly and stupid German Tragedies'
and other 'gross and violent stimulants' to 'blunt the discriminating powers
of the mind'.[19]

As the years went by, Coleridge was obliged out of self-defence to become
progressively disillusioned about Wordsworth. Writing to Tom Poole in
1803, for example, he was disturbed to find Wordsworth 'more & more
benetted in hypochondriacal Fancies, living wholly among *Devotees*—having
every the minutest Thing, almost his very Eating & Drinking, done for him
by his Sister, or Wife' – or sister-in-law – '& I trembled, lest a Film should rise,
and thicken on his moral Eye' (*CL* II, 1013). It would be impossible to disen-
tangle envy and resentment from insight in this assessment. A late entry in

Coleridge's notebooks, glossing an earlier note of August 1803 during his, Dorothy's, and Wordsworth's ill-fated tour of Scotland in which he records that he is to separate from the others and 'make [his] own way to Edingburgh' (N227), shows all the wisdom of hindsight: 'O Esteesee! That thou hadst from thy 22nd year made *thy own* way & *alone*'.[20] Coleridge being Coleridge, however, the choice was not really available to him at the time.

Coleridge would go on from the Preface to *Lyrical Ballads* to develop in his Shakespeare lectures a subtler theory of the relation between literature and reality than the one implied in the ideal of linguistic transparency outlined in the Preface, a theory that recovered hierarchies of linguistic utterance ('a certain *Aloofness*') and more clearly privileged the poetic imagination. It would achieve its most compelling expression in the *Biographia*. Coleridge, however, would never renounce his conviction of Wordsworth's greatness. Nor would he attenuate his Romantic claims for the importance of poetry out of deference to the reviewers and satirists. Quite the reverse, for the Preface he later realized had betrayed poetry to nature. Coleridge's literary criticism and literary theory would be his (and our) compensation for the crisis of confidence in his poetry that he experienced in the shadow of the 'giant Wordsworth' he had collaborated to create. His notebooks and letters record one critical insight after another and by January 1804 he is well on the way to writing the *Biographia*:

> Wordsworth is a Poet, a most original Poet—he no more resembles Milton than Milton resembles Shakespere ... he is himself: and I dare affirm that he will hereafter be admitted as the first & greatest philosophical Poet— the only man who has effected the compleat and constant synthesis of Thought & Feeling and combined them with Poetic Forms, with the music of pleasurable passion and with Imagination or the *modifying* Power in that highest sense of the word in which I have ventured to oppose it to Fancy, or the *aggregating* power—in that sense in which it is a dim Analogue of Creation, not all that we can believe but all that we can conceive of the creation. (*CL* II, 1034)

'There Was a Time'

The uncertain provenance and fate of some of the finest lines written during the second half of 1800, as the two poets laboured to revise and extend the '*Lyrical Ballads* by William Wordsworth', are symbolic, reflecting a close dialogue from which Wordsworth would emerge as the supreme poet. Coleridge published a poem entitled 'The Mad Monk' in the *Morning Post* on 13 October 1800, which opened with the following stanzas:

> I heard a voice from Etna's side;
> Where, o'er a cavern's mouth

That fronted to the south,
A chestnut spread its umbrage wide:
A hermit, or a monk, the man might be;
But him I could not see:
And thus the music flow'd along,
In melody most like to old Sicilian song:
'There was a time when earth, and sea, and skies,
        The bright green vale, and forest's dark recess,
With all things, lay before my eyes
        In steady loveliness:
But now I feel, on earth's uneasy scene,
        Such sorrows as will never cease; –
        I only ask for peace;
If I must live to know that such a time has been!'
                    ('The Mad Monk', ll. 1–17)

Published under a pseudonym, the poem appears to have been an imitation or parody of the sentimental Gothic, though of whom exactly – Wordsworth? 'Perdita' Robinson? Joseph Cottle? – no one is certain. Nor are we certain as to who wrote it. Was it Wordsworth's submitted by Coleridge, Coleridge's with help from Wordsworth, or an early Wordsworth poem reworked by Coleridge? 'The final version appears to be a mixture of borrowed material, parody, and a genuinely attempted imitation (by C[oleridge])', writes J. C. C Mays in his edition of the *Poetical Works*, 'a mixture characterised by a distinctive tone of uncertainty'.[21]

The moving lament of the second stanza ('There was a time ... ') would re-emerge two years later as the opening of one of Wordsworth's finest lyrics:

There was a time when meadow, grove, and stream,
The earth, and every common sight
        To me did seem
        Apparelled in celestial light,
The glory and the freshness of a dream.
It is not now as it hath been of yore;—
        Turn whereso'er I may
        By night or day,
The things which I have seen I now can see no more.
(Wordsworth, 'Ode. Intimations of Immortality ... ',
                    ll. 1–9)

'Who that shall point as with a wand, and say', wrote Wordsworth in *The Prelude*, ' "This portion of the river of my mind I Came from yon fountain"?'[22]

Wherever it may have originated, however, the river was by now all Wordsworth.

The final appearance of these lines of loss and regret is in the last major lyric that Coleridge wrote – 'Dejection: An Ode' – appropriately (and ironically) a formal statement of imaginative loss:

> A grief without a pang, void, dark, and drear,
> A stifled, drowsy, unimpassion'd grief
> Which finds no natural outlet, no relief,
>   In word, or sigh, or tear—
> O Lady! in this wan and heartless mood,
> To other thoughts by yonder throstle woo'd,
>   All this long eve, so balmy and serene,
> Have I been gazing on the western sky,
>   And it's peculiar tint of yellow green:
> And still I gaze—and with how blank an eye!
> And those thin clouds above, in flakes and bars,
> That give away their motion to the stars;
> Thos stars, that glide behind them or between,
> Now sparkling, now bedimm'd, but always seen;
> Yon crescent Moon, as fix'd as if it grew
> In its own cloudless, starless lake of blue;
> I see them all so excellently fair,
> I see, not feel how beautiful they are!
>
>   My genial spirits fail,
>   And what can these avail,
> To lift the smoth'ring weight from off my breast?
>   It were a vain endeavour,
>   Though I should gaze for ever
> On that green light that lingers in the west:
> I may not hope from outward forms to win
> The passion and the life, whose fountains are within.

*   *   *

> There was a time when, though my path was rough,
> This joy within me dallied with distress,
> And all my misfortunes were but as the stuff
>   Whence Fancy made me dreams of happiness:
> For hope grew round me, like the twining vine,
> And fruits, and foliage, not mine own, seem'd mine.
> But now afflictions bow me down to earth:
> Nor care I that they rob me of my mirth,
>   But oh! each visitation

> Suspends what nature gave me at my birth,
> My shaping spirit of Imagination.
> ('Dejection: An Ode', ll. 21–46, 76–86)

'Dejection: An Ode' is a severely edited and reorganized version of a much longer, more desultory poem detailing Coleridge's loss of creativity and domestic happiness, the poem we know as 'A Letter to Asra' (more formally, 'A Letter to——[Sara Hutchinson]'). 'A Letter to Asra' evolved in the months after Coleridge visited Gallow Hill near Scarborough in March 1802, where Sara Hutchinson was keeping house for her brother Tom. The trigger, however, was Wordsworth's reading Coleridge the opening stanzas of 'Ode. Intimations of Immortality' on a visit to Greta Hall in April. The unpublished 'Letter' is, as one would expect, much more personal than the formal ode that Coleridge published, more accusatory and self-flagellating, poring over the details of his star-crossed love for Sara Hutchinson and explicitly attributing his failure in part to the misery of cohabitating with an unsympathetic woman. In the kind of symmetry that would seem uncanny or tragically ironic had it not been contrived by Coleridge to confirm his vision of his own life as doomed, 'Dejection: An Ode' was published in the *Morning Post* over the Greek form of his own initials ('Esteesee' = STC) on the very day on which Wordsworth married Sara Hutchinson's sister, Mary – 4 October 1802 – which was also Coleridge's own wedding anniversary.

In many ways 'Dejection: An Ode' is a cunning poem, which is where the irony comes in. Even as the poet deplores his loss of imaginative power he regains it – has *already* regained it: the very lines announcing his indifference to the natural world betray a responsiveness that contradicts that indifference and is at least partly self-redemptive. Moreover, we savour the poem as much for its theoretical statement – as a deliberate expression of Coleridge *on* imagination – as an act or expression *of* imagination, perhaps more:

> O Lady! we receive but what we give,
> And in our life alone does nature live:
> Ours is her wedding garment, ours her shroud!
>   And would we aught behold, of higher worth,
> Than that inanimate cold world allow'd
> To the poor loveless ever-anxious crowd,
>   Ah! from the soul must issue forth,
> A light, a glory, a fair luminous cloud
>   Enveloping the Earth—
> And from the soul itself must there be sent

A sweet and potent voice, of its own birth,
Of all sweet sounds the life and element!
('Dejection: An Ode', ll. 47–58)

Like many Romantic poems it is both – both a poem, that is, and a meditation on poetry. No other Romantic poem, however, has ever been so often
cited and quoted in literary theoretical discussion. At the very moment
Coleridge the poet was undergoing his metamorphosis into Coleridge the
critic, he produced a major confessional poem that is also a major theoretical
statement – one that hovers between the two, refusing to settle exclusively as
either.

The country and the city

In a critical state of mind after the autumn of 1800, having gambled all on
the north and on poetic projects with Wordsworth and then started to
believe for the first time in his life that certain things were out of his imaginative reach – this, remember, is the young man of whom everyone expected
wonderful things – Coleridge retreated into himself, finding solace in fells,
notes, and opium. (And, it should be said, in his children, who appear more
frequently and fondly in his notebooks over these early years of the nineteenth century than at any other time.) Into the first, the fells, he would
erupt in occasional bursts of physical energy that had been and would continue to be characteristic of his life. During these, the lost years, however,
physical exercise was pursued with more than usually manic intensity – like
his extraordinary feat of walking 263 miles in eight days after splitting up
from Wordsworth and Dorothy during their tour of Scotland in 1803 (*CL* II,
982). Still only in his late twenties and early thirties and, though solidly
built, having yet to gain the 'Aldermanic' weight of his later years,[23]
Coleridge could walk for miles and threw himself into often dangerous fell
climbing activities with an abandon that reflected his desperation about his
life and career.
    His second solace, the notebooks, were resorted to more and more fre-
quently and more habitually. Most of the poetry he swore he could not write
appeared here, in casual jottings free from all expectation:

Sept[ember] 29. 1800—after a most tremendous storm of hail / the lower
Half of the lake bright silver / over it & intercepting Borrodale a thick pal-
pable Blue up to the moon / save that at the very top of the blue the
clouds rolled lead-coloured—small detachments of these clouds running
in thick flakes near the moon, & drinking its light in amber and white.—
The Moon in clear azure sky—the Mountains seen indeed, and only seen—
I never saw aught so sublime! (N122)

The thin scattered rain-clouds were scudding along the Sky, above them with a visible interspace the crescent Moon hung, and partook not of the motion—her own hazy Light fill'd up the concave, as if it had been painted & the colours had run.—Dec[ember] 19. 1800. (N137)

'With what eyes these poets see nature!', remarked Hazlitt on joining Coleridge and Wordsworth at Nether Stowey in 'My First Acquaintance with Poets'.[24] Coleridge loved the countryside and his notebooks testify to an acute responsiveness to all its many aesthetic pleasures. On the other hand, he always fared much worse in the country than he did in the city, suffering mentally and physically. He was more exposed to the weather in the country, of course, and winters in the Lake District were cruel. And he was more exposed to Sara, his wife, exacerbating their respective shortcomings and intolerances. But it was more than this. The extraordinarily detailed record offered by his notebooks of perceptions and feelings occasioned by the countryside in its every aspect, mood, and season, for all its apparent objectivity, remains a mental landscape – the phenomenological landscape of an alert, observant, and obsessive mind. Coleridge, as John Rickman unsympathetically but accurately observed, was 'excitable by objects to other men scarce visible or feelable'.[25] Even or especially when Coleridge the observer is at his most responsive – and the rapt attention that he gives to land- or lightscape he is as likely to focus on a passage in a book, or an idea he has come across – his observations are eloquent of the fascination and fixation of narcotic withdrawal. Like the opium-taking that more and more frequently accompanied them, his observations and reflections were, for him, an escape, his notebooks and his opium both symptomatic of the one dis-ease.

In the city, to which he would return periodically, it was different. Living above the editor's office or within call of Daniel Stuart, volunteering for electrocution at Humphry Davy's lectures on chemistry at the Royal Institution (*CN* I, 1099), and invaded by callers whom, even if he wanted to, he could only avoid for so long, Coleridge was accessible and accountable in a way he could too easily avoid in the Lake District. 'By your letter to Southey I understand that you are particularly anxious to see me', Coleridge wrote to Godwin on 19 November 1801, four days after he had arrived in London:

To day I am engaged for 2 hours in the morning with a person in the city—after which I shall be at [Charles] Lambe's—till past 7 at least—I had assuredly planned to walk to Somer's town; but I saw so many people on Monday and walked to & fro so much, that I have been ever since like a fish in air, who, as you know, lies panting & dying from excess of Oxygen/—A great change from the society of W[ordsworth]. & his sister – for tho' we were three persons, it was but one God— —whereas here I have the amazed feelings of a new Polytheist, meeting Lords many, & Gods many – some of them very Egyptian physiognomies, dog-faced Gentry, Crocodiles, Ibises,

&c—tho' more odd fish, than rares aves [i.e., rare birds].—However as to the business of seeing you—it is possible that you may meet me this evening—if not, & if I am well enough, I will call on you—& if you breakfast at 10—breakfast with you tomorrow morning. (*CL* II, 775)

Between his settling in the Lakes and his departure for Malta in 1804, Coleridge returned to London on four occasions, twice taking up temporary lodgings – from mid-November 1801 to the end of February 1802, then again from late January to late March 1804, when he left England in search of health – and maintaining himself by writing for the *Morning Post* and (from February 1804) *The Courier*. And on each occasion throughout what were otherwise for him desperate years he appears to have thrived.

Coleridge thrived because he *survived* in the city in a way that he could not survive in the country, which allowed him too easily to disappear into himself and into his addiction. For all his complaints about the rich food and distraction of company in the city, and all his complaints about the constraints and ephemerality of journalism, the enforced round of dinner parties and the pressure of daily writing (and, later, of regular lecturing) kept him functioning as a social being. Obliged to agonize publicly about the new Cabinet under Prime Minister Addington and about Napoleon and the 'Affairs of France', to remonstrate with his one-time hero Charles James Fox, he had less time to agonize about all the things he had promised but not written, about his failing marriage and frustrated love for Sara Hutchinson. As poor as he was at meeting commitments, the less avoidable daily commitments of society and paid work operated as a control on his tendency to drugs and meditation – always, rightly, associated. Coleridge yearned openly for oneness and wholeness, for balance, reconciliation, integration: for *health* and *sanity* in their root sense. But the country Coleridge yearned for in the sublimely integrated closing vision of 'Frost at Midnight' was just that: a vision. 'I love fields & woods & mounta[ins] with almost a visionary fondness', he had written to his brother when that love had been released by his meeting with the Wordsworths, but the country would never bring him the 'benevolence & quietness' that earlier it had promised (*CL* I, 397).

Coleridge and opium

Clearly by 1800 Coleridge had been taking opium on occasion for many years.[26] Opium, moreover, offered him more than just relief from a variety of real and imagined ailments, it brought the escape and sensual indulgence that he denied so hysterically in confessional notes and letters of later years. 'My sole sensuality was *not* to be in pain!' (N374). It is not possible to believe this when we read the unself-conscious letters of his early years, which are more candid than Coleridge could ever have been once he realized, shamefully, that he was dependent on the physical pleasure and psychological release he was deriving from it. 'I have administered rather a strong Dose of Opium', Coleridge casually reveals to Mary Evans in February 1793, obviously fully aware of the relative strengths of different doses (*CL* I, 52). On 12 March 1796, on the road promoting his *Watchman* and beset by worries, he wrote to John Edwards of resorting to opium under stress:

> Since I last wrote to you, I have been tottering on the edge of madness—my mind overbalanced on the e contra side of Happiness / the repeated blunders of the printer, the forgetfulness & blunders of my associate &c &c abroad, and at home Mrs Coleridge dangerously ill, and expected hourly to miscarry. Such has been my situation for the last fortnight— I have been obliged to take Laudanum almost every night. (*CL* I, 188)

And in a letter to his brother George of March 1798 we find a reference to opium-taking (though the motive for taking it was pain relief) that is so suggestive for our understanding of the recently written 'Kubla Khan': 'Laudanum gave me repose, not sleep: but YOU, I believe, know how divine that repose is—what a spot of inchantment, a green spot of fountains, & flowers & trees, in the very heart of a waste of Sands!' (*CL* I, 394).

It is a measure of Coleridge's innocence of serious addiction that he could so openly have declared the pleasure he was getting from opium, but if the drug itself was not as yet a habit in the 1790s, it was an habitual resort. By 1800 and his taking up residence at Greta Hall, he was well on the way to becoming addicted. Indeed, his decision to 'retire' to the Lakes, driven in the first instance by his yearning for the company of Wordsworth and the circle that included the woman he had fallen in love with, may well have been accelerated or intensified by a desire to avail himself more consistently of the liberating pleasures of opium. Alone in Greta Hall, 13 miles from Dove Cottage and in a marriage 'incompatible with even an endurable Life' (*CL* III, 7), with access to one of the most potent and addictive of all the local concoctions of laudanum, the Kendal Black Drop, Coleridge slipped irretrievably into an addiction that would be a fact of his life from then until his death in 1834.

After 1800, it is not possible to separate Coleridge's personality and thinking from his addiction to opium, though it is equally impossible to identify and measure its effects with absolute precision. His bodily health appreciably deteriorates under its influence (alone testifying to the rapidly increased dosage of these years in the Lake District): 'For the last four months I have not had a fortnight's continuous health', he wrote in January 1801, from which point on his letters become a catalogue of diseases and their symptoms: 'Rheumatic Fever'; 'my left testicle swoln to three times it's natural size'; 'bad eyes, swoln Eyelids, Boils behind my ears, & heaven knows what!'; 'irregular Gout with nephritic symptoms— ... Swoln Knees, & knotty Fingers, a loathy Stomach, & a dizzy Head' (*CL* II, 661, 724). Opium seriously exacerbated any stomach problems he might have inherited from exposure during childhood or the scanty meals at Christ's Hospital: 'The least agitation brings on bowel complaints' (*CL* II, 767). Cramps and constipation bedevil his future existence, leading to an obsession with his bodily functions and some of the most painful narratives of the notebooks (*CN* II, 2091). Dreams, nightmares become more frequent and intense and punitive, and more frequent and intense and punitive again when he tries to moderate his intake of the drug. The most wounded, moving, and naively confessional poem that Coleridge ever wrote unwittingly records the effects of opium withdrawal:

THE PAINS OF SLEEP

Ere on my bed my limbs I lay,
It hath not been my use to pray
With moving lips or bended knees;
But silently, by slow degrees,
My spirit I to Love compose,
In humble trust mine eye-lids close,
With reverential resignation,
No wish conceived, no thought expressed!
Only a *sense* of supplication,
A sense o'er all my soul imprest
That I am weak, yet not unblest,
Since in me, round me, every where
Eternal Strength and Wisdom are.

But yester-night I pray'd aloud
In anguish and in agony,
Up-starting from the fiendish crowd
Of shapes and thoughts that tortured me:
A lurid light, a trampling throng,
Sense of intolerable wrong,
And whom I scorn'd, those only strong!
Thirst of revenge, the powerless will
Still baffled, and yet burning still!
Desire with loathing strangely mixed
On wild or hateful objects fixed.
Fantastic passions! mad'ning brawl!
And shame and terror over all!
Deeds to be hid which were not hid,
Which all confused I could not know,
Whether I suffered, or I did:
For all seemed guilt, remorse or woe,

My own or others still the same
Life-stifling fear, soul-stifling shame!

So two nights passed: the night's dismay
Sadden'd and stunn'd the coming day.
Sleep, the wide blessing, seemed to me
Distemper's worst calamity.
The third night, when my own loud scream
Had waked me from the fiendish dream,
O'ercome with sufferings strange and wild,
I wept as I had been a child;
And having thus by tears subdued
My anguish to a milder mood,
Such punishments, I said, were due
To natures deepliest stain'd with sin:
For aye entempesting anew
Th' unfathomable hell within
The horror of their deeds to view,
To know and loathe, yet wish and do!
Such griefs with such men well agree,
But wherefore, wherefore fall on me?
To be beloved is all I need,
And whom I love, I love indeed.

There had always been a strongly confessional impulse in Coleridge's poetry, as there had been in Coleridge himself. A hundred years before psychoanalysis systematized and theorized the talking cure, Coleridge was its ideal patient. There is little attempt to shape the experience here in 'The Pains of Sleep', or to position his complaint within the kind of quasi-narrative movement traced in the Conversation Poems – beyond a cumulative desperation and the abrupt movement from nightmare to prayer, motivated by the dual expedient of complaint and self-exoneration. Unlike *The Rime of the Ancient Mariner*, the poem does not seriously challenge the faith that it enacts. Like Job and like the *character* of the Ancient Mariner, the intimate Coleridgean speaker remains true to his God in the face of the perverse punishments that are visited upon him, perhaps out of a sense that he is unwilling to disclose of being personally responsible for his own sufferings.

Bodily changes as extreme as those induced by opium so easily become personality changes (Coleridge himself coined the term 'psychosomatic'[27]). Coleridge's statements had never been entirely trustworthy, acutely aware as he was of his audience and desperate as he was to please and impress. But once he becomes addicted we would expect him to lie – to himself, no less than to others – rather than to face the truth. And lie he does on many occasions, habitually: 'the habit of inward Brooding daily makes it harder to confess the Thing, I am, to anyone — least of all to those, whom I most love & who most love me — & thereby introduces and fosters a habit of negative falsehood, & multiplies the Temptations to positive Insincerity' (*CN* II, 3078). The plagiarism that was, for a while at least, a feature of his intellectual claim to attention must have been encouraged by addiction – or perhaps it is more accurate to say that opium encouraged the sense of unreality characteristic of his major transgressions.

To say that opium is inseparable from his thinking, however, also means that we have to concede its influence on some of his most impressive theorizing. Part of that pleasure he derived from opium came from the way of seeing it produced – the 'altered consciousness' that would become such an important part of the attraction of different drugs for a large subculture of Western society in the 1960s and 1970s. Though Coleridge does not openly promote a drug-induced alteration of consciousness, his thinking about creative apperception – 'the power of giving the interests of novelty by the modifying colours of the imagination' (*BL* II, 5) – must have been influenced by his experiences with opium, as the preface to 'Kubla Khan' suggests, no less than by his experience of those other analogues for the imagination – passion and madness (N451; *BL* II, 150).

Malta and Italy

Progressively more ill – so ill that he was convinced he was going to die (*CL* I, 724) – more depressed, more and more deeply addicted to opium and more and more miserable at the thought of home with Sara Coleridge, Coleridge soon began to think of exile as the only cure for his problems this side of the grave. The countries of the Mediterranean had traditionally been treated by the upper class British as anti-inflammatory and decongestant and Southey himself had returned from Portugal in 1801 after a long sojourn designed to restore his failing health. Napoleon had cut off access to large parts of the Mediterranean (Italy would fall to the French while Coleridge was away). At first Coleridge planned to travel with Tom Wedgwood, who really was dying, probably of stomach cancer. Originally it was to be the Azores, before Coleridge finally decided on Malta in the first instance, then on to Sicily and the Italian mainland, encouraged by a London acquaintance, John Stoddart, who had recently assumed the post of Chief Advocate in Malta. By the time Coleridge left London he had a loan of £100 from his friend and correspondent William Sotheby, with Wordsworth standing as security, the best wishes of all his friends – all of them wondering whether he would live to charm them with talk of his experiences – and letters of introduction to the Governor of Malta, Sir Alexander Ball.

Coleridge sailed out of Portsmouth on 9 April 1804 on the merchant ship *Speedwell*, part of a convoy of 35 ships carrying supplies to British and allied ports under guard of the Royal Navy. The passage to Malta might aptly be described as one hell of a journey. After Gibraltar, Coleridge was 'Alone on a wide, wide sea' for the first time, isolated by illness and opium: 'desperately sick, ill, abed, one deep dose after another', his involuntary thoughts plagued by longing for and jealousy over Sara Hutchinson, and his 'Sleep a pandemonium of all the shames and miseries of the past Life from earliest childhood all huddled together' (*CN* II, 2064, 2091). Here again, however, it is extraordinary what compassion and comradeship Coleridge could inspire – in the captain John Findlay, for example, in Mr Hardy, the surgeon who attended him, and even in the ship's mate assisting at the painful enemas he required. (It would be the same on his return journey nearly two and a half years later, when the young artist Thomas Russell and Captain Durkheim of the US merchant ship *Gosport* tended to the ailing, severely constipated Coleridge.)

John Stoddart, too, was delighted by his company when, six weeks after the *Speedwell* had embarked, Coleridge arrived unannounced at his house in Valetta, the capital of Malta. In Stoddart's case there seems to have been some cooling off, but Coleridge had very early on made the acquaintance of Governor Ball and soon won his affection and respect – the last for a set of political papers he helped to produce defining Ball's position with regard to the war in the Mediterranean. It landed Coleridge the job as first under-secretary to the Governor and accommodation in Ball's own household at the Governor's palace – or households, for when the Ball family retreated from the heat to their summer residence at San Antonio, Coleridge went with them. Later, in a recommendation Ball wrote introducing Coleridge to Hugh Elliott, the British Minister at the court of King Ferdinand of Naples, Ball would speak of Coleridge's possessing 'great genius, a fine imagination and good judgement', qualities 'made perfect by an excellent heart and good moral character'. More revealing, however, because less the familiar language of recommendations, was Ball's assuring Elliott that 'You will have much pleasure in his conversation'. Ball obviously enjoyed listening to Coleridge talk. But if we may judge by the notebooks Coleridge, for his part, seems unusually to have listened to Ball as well.

Like his journalism, Coleridge's activities as Ball's secretary offered him protection from himself, though his determination to shake himself free of opium and 'spite all horrors to go through one month unstimulated Nature' came to nothing on an island where drugs were all too readily available (*CN* II, 2091). He was walking a tightrope – no day without its extrovert activity to occupy his mind, 'No night without its guilt of opium and spirits' (*CN* II, 2387) – but he managed to stay focussed and effective for the 15 months he was employed. Eventually he rose to the position of acting Public Secretary, 'the next civil dignity to the Governor' and worth £600 a year, a position suddenly made available by the death of the incumbent. He handled the job well enough to be encouraged to apply for a permanent position in the Maltese civil service and at different stages and in certain moods seriously considered remaining in exile (*CL* II, 1171).[28] However, letters, memories, and the shocking news of Dorothy and William's brother John Wordsworth's death by drowning during a storm that overturned the ship he captained, reminded Coleridge of where his allegiances lay, and of the fact that he was here only for repair and recreation. From early 1805 Coleridge fully intended to go home.

Knowing what he *should* do, on the other hand, only made the decisive action of either returning or staying impossible. He lingered. Eventually he would return to England, but nowhere near as soon as he had given his family and friends to expect. With the arrival of the new Public Secretary in September 1805 he had been relieved of his duties and able to travel to Sicily and from there to mainland Italy. Once there, however, in spite of the French invasion of Italy and proscriptions against British travellers, he chose to remain, until finally departing nine months later in late June 1806 having charmed the captain of the *Gosport*. Without having accomplished any of the tasks he had set himself, least of all the task of recovering his health, and having lost to fortune and the plague what little he had managed to write outside his notebooks in abortive attempts to relay his manuscripts back to England, Coleridge arrived back in England on 17 August 1806.

Coleridge returns to the Anglican establishment

That Coleridge should have chosen Malta in the first place is symbolic, war with France having been precipitated in March 1803 by Britain's asserting her sovereignty over the island in the face of French demands to evacuate. The history of Malta immediately prior to Coleridge's arrival had been as impossibly complicated as its racial and cultural mix. A political and diplomatic football because of its strategic position in the Mediterranean and the fact of its having an impregnable fortress, it had been wrested from the Catholic Order of St John by Napoleon before his Egyptian campaign in 1798. A French garrison under General Vaubois was later in that year besieged in the fortress, and from then until 1803 the French, the Russians, the British, the Neapolitans, and the now dispersed and impoverished Order of St John (under Russian protection) argued the toss, with a *consiglio popolare* or popular council of the native Maltese themselves occasionally getting a look in. From 1800, however, once Vaubois surrendered to Britain's General Pigot as a 'representative' of Malta's legal suzerain, King Ferdinand of Naples, the British retained effective control over Malta and a dominant interest in the island's traffic.

According to the terms of the Peace of Amiens drawn up in March 1802, however, Malta was to be returned to the Order of St John and to become a neutral power, with the British withdrawing their troops within three months. This they had been reluctant to do. At the end of 1802, Bonaparte had informed the British ambassador in Paris that 'on Malta depended the question of peace or war' and that 'on no terms would England be permitted to retain Malta'.[29] Suddenly the retention or relinquishment of Malta became critical to the future of Britain and her empire. Under Coleridge's urging, the attitude of Stuart's *Morning Post* had swung around to that of the conservative newspapers to support the government against the arguments of pacifists like Charles James Fox – once a hero of Coleridge's and worthy of a complimentary copy of *Lyrical Ballads*[30] – who denied that Malta was worth the war with France. Napoleon still insisted on its evacuation by the British, as London insisted on the evacuation of Switzerland and Holland by France, and the war with France that had begun in 1793 was resumed on 16 May 1803 after an uneasy peace. Admiral Nelson had no great conviction as to the strategic importance of Malta and argued at length with Alexander Ball over the issue, but Nelson nevertheless defended its retention in a letter to the Prime Minister, Henry Addington: 'I consider Malta as a most important outwork of India, that it will ever give us great influence in the Levant, and indeed all the southern parts of Italy. In this view, I hope that we shall never give it up'.[31]

Coleridge's choice of Malta, then, reflected the extent to which he had become more conservative and belligerent in his attitude to global politics. All his life Coleridge had sought one surrogate after another for the father he had lost so suddenly, and with such disturbing consequences, as an eight-year-old. Over the early years of the nineteenth century, with the crisis of confidence he suffered on failing to match up to expectation and with his loss of autonomy to opium, Coleridge more and more sought repose in the paternalistic institutions from which he had fled as a radical youth – in short, in the Anglican establishment. In letters before he left England to his new friends, Sir George and Lady Beaumont, Coleridge had melodramatically confessed to the many sins of his Jacobinical youth, throwing himself on their mercy (and their patronage) (*CL* II, 998–1005). A baronet and representative of the inherited aristocracy, the conservative Beaumont, who had initially found Coleridge's critical views of government disturbing, had suddenly become the unwitting object of Coleridge's prodigal need to offload his youthful delinquencies, to ingratiate himself and regain the acceptance of the establishment.

Beaumont, in other words, was shaping up as next in the long line of Coleridge's surrogate fathers. On Malta itself, there was Alexander Ball: 'Sir A.B. behaves to me with really personal fondness, and with almost fatherly attention', he confided in Daniel Stuart (*CL* II, 1168). There was a difference, however, in that Ball, as the governor of a small but strategic part of the British Empire, was the closest Coleridge had yet come to executive power, to the authority of the State. For Coleridge, Ball was a dramatic example of how the dispensing power of privilege was and (more to the point) *should* be exercised – with 'purity and strict propriety', he recalled in his periodical

The Friend, an 'evenness' of temper, and 'attentive and affectionate manners'.[32] Ball soon became for Coleridge, in the language of Renaissance treatises on ideal statecraft, 'the abstract Idea of a wise & good Governor' (*CL* II, 1141), and Coleridge's eulogy in *The Friend* imagines him as just such an exemplary statesman: 'the virtues of Sir Alexander Ball, as a master, a husband, and a parent, will form a no less remarkable epoch in the moral history of the Maltese than his wisdom, as a governor, has made in that of their outward circumstances'.[33] Coleridge had long ago discovered the deep emotional attraction of patriotism and with *The Courier* become more politically conservative, but Coleridge's real conversion to the Anglican establishment took place on Malta when Alexander Ball offered a human and (in Coleridge's Burkean terms) *admirable* incarnation of State power. It was an affirmation of the patriarchy – 'master', 'husband', 'parent', 'governor' – towards which he had once displayed such ambivalence, fawning and mocking by uncertain turns. Coleridge's attitude to Church and State would never be uncritical, but from here on an unshakeable commitment to their priority and survival is manifest in all his thinking.

Coleridge and religion

As corollary or condition of this return to the Anglican establishment, Coleridge also sought finally and emphatically to embrace an orthodox Anglican religion. He had long ago expressed his distrust of the Unitarianism adopted at Cambridge under the inspiration of Priestley and Frend: 'How is it that Dr Priestley is not an atheist?', he had asked Rev. John Edwards in March 1796, long before he gave up preaching in Unitarian chapels:

> He asserts in three different Places, that God not only *does*, but *is*, every thing.—But if God *be* every Thing, every Thing is God—: which is all, the Atheists assert—. An eating, drinking, lustful *God*—with no *unity* of *Consciousness*— —these appear to me the unavoidable Inferences from his philosophy—Has not Dr Priestley forgotten that *Incomprehensibility* is as necessary an attribute of the First Cause, as Love, or Power, or Intelligence? (*CL* I, 192)

More and more, the *rational* religion offered by Priestley's Unitarianism, denying the mysterious and the miraculous, appeared to Coleridge a contradiction in terms, as reductive and indifferent as Godwinian atheism. What had once seemed so simple and sublime a solution – a single deity, co-extensive (and co-existent) with His universe, 'something *one* & *indivisible*' (*CL* I, 349) – began to strike him as cold and question-begging. The idea of the unity (and thus interchangeablity) of God with his creation – 'God all in all! | We and our Father ONE!'[34] – robbed Coleridge of a personal relationship with his God. 'Socianism [i.e., Unitarianism] Moonlight', he wrote in his notebooks in late 1799, 'Methodism &c A Stove! O for some Sun that shall unite Light & Warmth' (*CN* I, 467). From then on, the 'moonshine heartless Head-work' of Unitarianism becomes a leitmotif – or, more accurately, a recurring gripe – in Coleridge's formal and informal writings (*CN* II, 2892). His heart would not own it: 'The strongest argument for [Chri]istianity the weak Argument that do yet persuade so many to believe – i.e., it fits the human heart' (N174).

It was the same with the otherwise attractive philosophy of Spinoza, whose version of pantheism held sway over Coleridge's imagination around the turn of the century (and, some would say, on and off all his life). All of them, all pantheisms, insofar as they conceived of human beings as at one and consubstantial with the material universe (*CL* I, 177), necessarily dehumanized humanity in Coleridge's terms, robbing it not just of its personal relationship with God but also of free will and meaningful responsibility. Throughout his life, the 'important subjects' identified by Coleridge in a letter of January 1796 to Josiah Wade never changed:

> whether we be outcasts of a blind idiot called Nature, or the children of an all-wise and infinitely good God; whether we spend a few miserable years on the is earth, and then sink into a clod of the valley, or only endure the anxieties of mortal life in order to fit us for the enjoyment of immortal happiness. (*CL* I, 177)

A large part of the reason why the philosophy of Kant 'took possession of [him] as with a giant's hand' (*BL* I, 153) was its affirmation of God, freedom, and immortality, not as the logical conclusions of our reasoning (or 'understanding' as he would call it, after Kant's *Verstand*), but as 'regulative', *a priori* ideas necessary to make sense of human conscience. 'Conscience unconditionally *commands* us to attribute *reality* and actual *existence*, to those ideas and those only, without which the conscience itself would be baseless and contradictory, to the ideas of Soul, of Free-will, of Immortality, and of God!'[35]

Indeed, the part that 'proof' and the intellect had to play in all this was itself questionable. Not only was Coleridge concerned to find a religious solution that would satisfy his emotional needs in a way that a cerebral Unitarianism would not, he also became convinced that 'faith in the existence of a God, not only as the *ground* of the universe by his essence, but as its maker and judge by his wisdom and holy will' could or rather *should* never be 'wholly independent of the will':

> Our feelings almost necessitate it; and the law of conscience peremptorily commands it. The arguments, that at all apply to it, are in its favor; and there is nothing against it, but its own sublimity. It could not be intellectually more evident without becoming morally less effective; without counteracting its own end by sacrificing the *life* of faith to the cold mechanism of a worthless because compulsory assent. (*BL* I, 203)

The more Coleridge struggled ineffectually with opium and with life, the more important it was for him to credit himself and all individuals with responsibility for their own fate. It was Coleridge's sense of sin and of his own sinfulness – 'For the good that I would I do not: but the evil which I would not, that I do' (Romans 7:19) – that impelled his return to an orthodox Anglican belief in the trinity (Tri-unity) of God and in the divinity of Christ, who 'by a mysterious action' intervenes on our behalf to secure our redemption (*CL* II, 1189). If we may believe a letter written to his brother George a year prior to his departure for Malta – and Coleridge was always inclined to mould and modify his beliefs according to his correspondent – he was already well under way to conversion before exile and isolation precipitated its completion:

My Faith is simply this—that there is an original corruption in our nature, from which & from the consequences of which, we may be redeemed in Christ—not as the Socinians say, by his pure morals or excellent example merely—but in a mysterious manner as an effect of his Crucifixion—and this I believe—not because I *understand* it; but because I *feel*, that it is not only suitable to, but needful for, my nature and because I find it clearly revealed.—Whatever the New Testament says, I believe—according to my best judgment of the meaning of the sacred writers.—Thus I have stated to you this whole of the Change which has taken place in me. (*CL* II, 807)

Exactly how orthodox Coleridge was theologically either then or in later life is a matter of debate. Certainly his initial approach to Trinitarianism was, to quote Basil Willey, 'along the high metaphysical road', unrecognizable to the ordinary believer in the historical humanity of Christ.[36] Christ as the Logos is God's 'Idea' of himself, a projected image or alter ego 'co-existing with, & yet filiated', in which God 'beholds well-pleased his whole Being' (*CL* II, 1195). At the same time as he embodied a kind of divine narcissism, Christ is also the head of a composite (and very abstract) body of humanity (*CL* II, 1197). Later, the whole mass of his dense and discontinuous argumentation in the *Opus Maximum* – 'the principal Labour of my Life since Manhood' – would be directed towards an intellectual justification of the Trinity.[37] 'But the belief', as Willey goes on to say, 'was far more to him than a matter of metaphysical speculation'.[38] During the many, many hours of suffering and self-loathing that were to follow – as in 1810 when a rupture with Wordsworth reminded him of his utter aloneness – he coped by rehearsing his religious beliefs in a 'Confessio Fidei' (a declaration of his faith) and calling on Christ as his redeemer:

1. I believe, that I am a Free Agent, inasmuch as, and so far as, I have a will which renders me justly responsible for my actions, omissive as well as commissive. Likewise that I possess Reason, or a Law of Right and Wrong, which uniting with my sense of moral responsibility constitutes the voice of Conscience.

2. Hence it becomes my absolute Duty to believe, and I do believe, that there is a God, that is, a Being in whom Supreme Reason and a most holy Will is coincident with an infinite Power. ...

3. My Conscience forbids me to propose to myself the Pains and Pleasures of this Life, as the primary motive or ultimate end of my actions. ...

4. I believe, and hold it as a fundamental article of Christianity, that I am a fallen creature; that I am of myself capable of moral evil, but not of myself capable of moral good, and that Guilt is justly imputable to me prior to any act, or assignable moment of time, in my Consciousness. I am born a child of Wrath. This fearful Mystery I pretend not to understand—I cannot even conceive the possibility of it—but I know, that it is so! My Conscience, the sole fountain of certainty, commands me to believe it. ...

5. I receive with full and grateful Faith the assurance of Revelation, that the Word which is from all eternity with God and is God, assumed our human nature in order to redeem me and all mankind from this our connate Corruption.

6. I believe that this assumption of Humanity by the Son of God was revealed & realized to us by the Word made Flesh, and manifested to us in Christ Jesus; and that his miraculous Birth, his agony, his Crucifixion, Death, Resurrection, and Ascension, were all both Symbols of our Redemption ... and necessary parts of the aweful process.

7. I believe in the descent and sending of the Holy Spirit, by whose free grace alone obtained for me by the merits of my Redeemer I can alone be sanctified and restored from my natural inheritance of Sin & Condemnation be a Child of God, and an Inheritor of the Kingdom of God. (*CN* III, 4005)

There are traces elsewhere in this entry of Coleridge's reading of the seventeenth-century Church of England clergyman and theologian Robert South's *Sermons Preached Upon Several Occasions* (*CN* III, 4005n.). More and more the orthodox Anglican divines would become part of his vast and voracious reading, as religion came to dominate his thoughts and writing.

Orthodoxy itself, like patriarchy in the State, became a kind of self-affirming commitment, an act of faith never 'wholly independent of the will'. And the transfer of his theological allegiances to Anglican Trinitarianism was facilitated by his transferring his *emotional* allegiances in his hour of need to the Anglican establishment of his childhood and his father, the Rev. John Coleridge: 'that venerable Countenance and Name which form my earliest recollections and make them *religious*' (*CL* V, 462). Beginning with essays in his periodical *The Friend*, through vital passages of the *Biographia Literaria* and the two Lay Sermons of 1816 and 1817) to *Aids to Reflection* (1825) and *On the Constitution of the Church and the State* (1830), Coleridge's published works from here on would be dedicated to the rationalization and humanization of the Church establishment into which he had been born. Ultimately, he would become its greatest and most influential apologist, after his heroes Robert South, Jeremy Taylor, and Richard Hooker in the seventeenth century.

7
'The One Proteus of the Fire and the Flood': Critic for Hire

Coleridge may have returned to England in mid-August of 1806, but it was not until late October that he worked up the courage to confront his friends and family – at least, those friends and family living in the north of England. It took him a month even to write to his wife, who in 1803 had been joined at Greta Hall by her sister and Robert Southey and their family. The Wordsworths, with whom Coleridge communicated more promptly, received only complaints about his health and a succession of excuses. The main reason he gave the Wordsworths for his lingering in the South was a paralysing antipathy to domesticating with his wife,[1] and judging by the intensifying repulsion recorded in letters and notebooks there was a great deal of truth in this (*CL* II, 1178, 1200, 1203; *CN* II, 2398). Though Coleridge had been talking about it on and off for many years, his priority now was a separation. But Dorothy Wordsworth's reaction to Coleridge after three years apart in late October suggests that a consciousness of his own visible decline may have been another reason for Coleridge's reluctance to return to the Lake District, however sympathetic his friends might have been:

> We all went thither to meet him and never never did I feel such a shock as at first sight of him. We all felt exactly in the same way— ...
> He is utterly changed; and yet sometimes, when he was animated in conversation concerning things removed from him, I saw something of his former self. But never when we were alone with him. He then scarcely ever spoke of anything that concerned him, or us, or our common friends nearly, except we forced him to; and immediately he changed the conversation to Malta, Sir Alexander Ball, the corruptions of government, anything but what we were yearning after. All we could gather from him was that he must part from her or die and leave his children destitute, and that to part he was resolved.
> ... that he is ill I am well assured, and must sink if he does not grow happy. His fatness has quite changed him—it is more like the flesh of a person in a dropsy than one in health; his eyes are lost in it.[2]

On the other hand, London seemed blessedly free of emotional complications. Coleridge had no hesitation about catching up and staying with Charles and Mary Lamb in London and visiting Daniel Stuart at Margate. From them we hear of no disappointment or regret. Perhaps the main difference was that, while Stuart would always welcome copy for *The Courier*, still they greeted Coleridge with no demands or expectations, either for themselves or of him. Sara Coleridge, on the other hand, was anxious to regain a husband and the respectability that, for her, attended upon it. Southey no doubt sought help with looking after Coleridge's family and the Wordsworths were anxious to get Coleridge's thoughts on William's *magnum opus*, *The Recluse*. Amid the emotional riot of Coleridge's raw need for Wordsworth's affection and respect it would be wrong to lose sight of Wordsworth's need for Coleridge's critical input and approval. Wordsworth's *Recluse* to a large extent had been Coleridge's own brainchild – a sublime, summary work by the great philosophical poet of the age which he had been urging Wordsworth to write for some eight years now, promising him direction and ideas. Coleridge's only contribution to date, however, had been incinerated (or so he claimed) with the body of Major Adye, the friend and courier who had died of the plague returning with Coleridge's letters and papers to England in 1805 (*CL* II, 1165, 1169).

Until he could face his northern conscience, then, Coleridge installed himself in the offices of *The Courier* and wrote long letters of excuses to his wife and thoughts on religion to others. More and more, his actions (and inactions) would be determined by the incidents, ideas, and people that he sought to avoid, instead of being determined by things that he sought. Avoidance of the pathological kind that Coleridge practised invariably compounds itself, frequently leading to a kind of paralysis. In the effort to avoid his wife Sara he found himself unable to do anything, except lie about all the things he was doing. It was the same with his correspondence, where a desire to avoid the obligations brought by letters from his friends and family – the obligation to answer the letter itself in the first instance, and then the further obligation to act on any pain or information it may contain – led to his delaying opening them: 'I have sunk under such a strange cowardice of Pain', he confessed to Josiah Wedgwood, 'that I have not unfrequently kept letters from persons dear to me for weeks together unopened' (*CL* III, 19). After Malta this became a settled habit, and it was not long before he was only able to open those letters immediately that he knew to be innocent of obligation.

Finally, however, on 23 October 1806, he left for the north to negotiate a separation with his wife, just as the Wordsworths (and Sara Hutchinson) were setting out for the south to Coleorton, a house in Leicestershire belonging to the Beaumonts. Having secured Sara Coleridge's unwilling agreement to a permanent separation, Coleridge and Hartley joined them there for Christmas. The literary significance of this reunion was, inevitably, all Wordsworth's way. Coleridge was treated to a reading of Wordsworth's

'Poem addressed to Coleridge': the full, thirteen-book autobiographical epic we call *The Prelude*, intended as introductory to *The Recluse* and, because *The Recluse* remained incomplete, never published in Wordsworth's own lifetime.[3] When Coleridge celebrated Wordsworth's achievement in an ambitious meditative poem of his own, one that imitates and paraphrases the original, he captured the conflicting pain and pleasure that the whole experience of Wordsworth in sublime stride must have been for him:

> Ah! as I listened with a heart forlorn
> The pulses of my Being beat anew:
> And even as Life returns upon the Drowned,
> Life's joy rekindling roused a throng of Pains—
> Keen Pangs of Love, awakening as a babe
> Turbulent, with an outcry in the heart;
> And Fears self-willed, that shunned the eye of Hope;
> And Hope that scarce would know itself from Fear;
> Sense of past Youth, and Manhood come in vain,
> And Genius given, and knowledge won in vain;
> And all which I had culled in Wood-walks wild,
> And all which patient toil had reared, and all,
> Commune with *thee* had opened out—but Flowers
> Strewed on my corse, and bourne upon my Bier,
> In the same Coffin, for the self-same Grave!
> ('To William Wordsworth, Composed after the
> Night of His Recitation of a Poem on the
> Growth of an Individual Mind', ll. 61–75)

The poem, otherwise more generous than this painfully self-reflective passage suggests and certainly more acute in its interpretative paraphrase, ends as so many of Coleridge's late works will end, not in an act of communion as in the Conversation Poems, but 'absorbed' in lonely prayer.

Along with the joy of recovering moments of their old intimacy and intellectual excitement over this Christmas period shared with the Wordsworths at Coleorton went some painful misunderstanding and mutual disenchantment. The intense emotional and imaginative investment Coleridge had made in a relationship with Sara Hutchinson while alone in Malta and Italy – a relationship he remained incapable of realizing – now expressed itself as pathological jealousy, focussed on a fantasy of Wordsworth's and Sara's involvement. All their plans for Coleridge in the future, including Coleridge's own, revolved around his sharing a house with the Wordsworths, but it was slowly becoming apparent to everyone that this was likely to create more problems than it would solve.

Coleridge then moved around for the year 1807, mainly in the south. After April in London with the Wordsworths he renewed old friendships in Bristol, where his wife was staying with her family, before they all went on to visit Tom Poole in Nether Stowey for the summer, hoping – vainly as it turned out – to visit Coleridge's own family in Ottery St Mary. It was while in the West, at Bridgwater, that Thomas De Quincey introduced himself, having pursued Coleridge from London through Bristol and Stowey. De Quincey, having just abandoned his degree at Oxford – later he would write *Confessions of an English Opium-Eater* and become one of the distinguished essayists of the period – would be another in the long line of young writers and intellectuals whose infatuation with Coleridge by reputation was only confirmed at their first meeting:

> Coleridge, like some great river, the Oreallana or the St Lawrence, that, having been checked and fretted by rocks and thwarting islands, suddenly recovers its volume of waters, and its mighty music, — swept at once, as if returning to its natural business, into a continuous strain of eloquent dissertation, certainly the most novel, the most finely illustrated, and traversing the most spacious fields of thought, by transitions the most just and logical, that it was possible to conceive.[4]

I am quoting here from the extensive memoirs De Quincey would write of the friendships he developed over the next ten years with Coleridge and Wordsworth – if either his prostration before Wordsworth or his ambivalent discipleship with the damaged Coleridge could be called a friendship. In biographical studies published after Coleridge's death in 1834, De Quincey would comment with the acuteness and cunning of a fellow addict on Coleridge's opium habit and as a scholar and plagiarist familiar with German literature and ideas on Coleridge's plagiarism of German literature and ideas. In July 1807, however, De Quincey had only flattery and assistance of the most material kind to offer: an anonymous loan of £500 on generous terms, mediated by Coleridge's friend and ex-publisher Joseph Cottle (who successfully urged that it be commuted to £300), and his company for Sara Coleridge and the children on their journey to Bristol, and again in October on their return to the Lake District where for the time being De Quincey would settle.

The literary lecturer

After De Quincey escorted Sara Coleridge to Bristol, Coleridge spent the remainder of a lazy summer in Nether Stowey with Poole, who in late August received a letter from Humphry Davy urging him to urge Coleridge to commit to a series of lectures in London:

> The managers of the Royal Institution are very anxious to engage him; and I think he might be of material service to the public, and of benefit to

his own mind, to say nothing of the benefit his purse might receive. In the present condition of society, his opinions in matters of taste, literature, and metaphysics must have a healthy influence; and unless he soon becomes an actual member of the living world, he must expect to be brought to judgment for 'hiding his light'.[5]

Public lectures on cultural and scientific topics flourished in England during the Napoleonic wars, when a number of institutions sprang up to house and foster them. Davy himself had had huge success at the Royal Institution, where in 1802 Coleridge had attended his lectures on chemistry, which were so popular they created traffic jams in the street outside.[6] Davy had first suggested to Coleridge that he should offer a set of lectures not long after he returned from the Mediterranean (CL II, 1187). Fresh from the Italian galleries and churches and from his intimacy with painters like the American Washington Allston, Coleridge had planned (in his head at least) a set of 'Lectures on the Principles common to all the Fine Arts' (CL II, 1181). Southey and Wordsworth, however, both with Coleridge's return to the Lake District on their respective agendas, appear to have talked him out of it.

Now it was time. The wonder is that he should have delayed so long, given the success of his political lecturing in 1795, given his developing interest in literary criticism and theory, stimulated by his reading of Kant and the post-Kantian German aestheticians, and given the fact that what was being asked of him was only a more formal version of the talking he had in fact been doing all his life. Responding promptly to Davy's letter to Poole, Coleridge proposed a series of lectures, not on the 'fine arts' generally this time, but on 'the Principles of Poetry', drawing on canonical and characteristic writers since (and including) Chaucer: 'the whole result of many years' continued reflection on the subjects of Taste, Imagination, Fancy, Passion, the source of our pleasure in the fine Arts in the *antithetical* balance-loving nature of man, & the connection with moral excellence' (CL III, 30). And so it was settled.

It was also in 1807, in late October, just as he was about to quit Bristol for London and his lectures, that Coleridge fell violently ill dining out with Charles Lamb's friend and another ex-student of Christ's Hospital, John Morgan, whose Unitarian father had been one of Coleridge's supporters during his Bristol days in the mid-1790s. (Morgan the son, on the other hand, was, like Coleridge, in retreat from Unitarianism and would express his gratitude to Coleridge for 'making me able to defend at least in my own mind the Orthodox religion against the Unitarian philosophy'.[7]) Coleridge spent the next three weeks on the Morgans' sofa in receipt of their solicitous 'attentions and indulgences' (CL III, 47). It was a rehearsal for the moment when, after the rupture with Wordsworth in 1810, the three of them – John and his wife Mary, and her sister Charlotte Brent – would become Coleridge's surrogate family. Or surrogate for the Wordsworths, who had already become his surrogate family. From the beginning, Coleridge remarked on the similarities between the triangular William, Mary, and Sara Hutchinson on the one hand, and John, Mary, and Charlotte on the other, and when Coleridge left he presented Mary and Charlotte with lines that were an open invitation to repeat the arrangement some time in the future:

> Alas for some abiding place of love,
> O'er which my spirit like the mother dove,
> Might brood with warming wings!
> ('To Two Sisters: A Wanderer's Farewell',
> ll. 3–5)

For the moment, however, his new literary life beckoned. Coleridge left for London on 22 November 1807, settling into rooms that Daniel Stuart had arranged for him above the offices of *The Courier* in the Strand. His London friends, Davy especially, eagerly anticipated his mesmerizing the nation's most distinguished audience in the lavish 500-seat lecture theatre of the Royal Institution. Delays, however, occasioned in part by Davy's contracting prison fever, meant that the lecture series could not begin until 15 January 1808. When it did begin, moreover, it began inauspiciously, with Coleridge collapsing immediately after the first lecture. 'Acrid scalding evacuations, and if possible worse Vomitings' caused the postponement of one lecture after another – the opium-induced malfunctioning of his stomach and bowels again, exacerbated by 'Hensbane', 'Rhubarb and magnesia' and compounded, surely, by anxiety at the thought of so demanding an audience (*CL* III, 51). 'He ain't well that's certain', as Lamb laconically put it.[8] By the end of March only three of the promised course of twenty five winter lectures had been delivered, and by early June, when he gave his last, only twenty at the most.[9] On 13 June he wrote apologizing to the Secretary of the Royal Institution that illness obliged him to abandon them altogether (*CL* III, 117).

Incomplete and uneven this first series of lectures may have been, but having dispensed with the kind of formality that the Royal Institution expected and overcome the worst of his anxiety Coleridge was soon giving some intimation both of his powers of eloquence and of his responsive critical intelligence.[10] He never again repeated the mistake of reading out a passage of over twelve hundred words, as he did from the aesthetician Richard Payne Knight in his first lecture![11] Abandoning a written script for notes which even then he might set aside to indulge his digressive impulses, Coleridge began to take risks – risks that, admittedly, only sometimes came off: 'He spoke without any Assistance from a manuscript', wrote Edward Jerningham after the course was over, obviously referring to the later 1808 lectures, 'and Therefore said several Things suddenly, struck off from the Anvil, some of which were entitled to high Applause and others incurred mental Disapprobation'.[12] But the closer he was able to bring the lecture form to his extempore talk, the more likely he was to engage the audience, many of them already disposed to indulge his idiosyncrasies.[13] Henry Crabb Robinson, who had attended some of this first series, made the point four years later while attending Coleridge's lectures on Shakespeare and Milton at the Surrey Institution:

The difference was not great between his conversation which is a sort of lecturing & soliloquizing and his lectures which were colloquial – And in which he was himself aware it was impossible for him to be methodical. And those hearers who enjoyed him most, probably enjoyed most his digressions. The same subjects haunted his mind for many years.[14]

Even the disapproving Wordsworth had to concede that Coleridge 'seemed to give great satisfaction' when he came down to London in late February 1808 with the express purpose of removing the stricken Coleridge to the Lakes, and then stayed to hear Coleridge's third and fourth lecture.[15] More to the point, Coleridge himself rediscovered his own elocutionary and theatrical powers and recovered his confidence in himself during these early lectures. In a note dated 16 May, Joseph Farington relayed Prince Hoare's experience of Coleridge on Milton:

When Coleridge came into the Box there were several Books laying. He opened two or three of them silently and shut them again after a short inspection. He then paused, & leaned His head on His hand, and at last said, He had been thinking for a word to express the distinct character of Milton as a Poet, but not finding one that wd. express it, He should make one 'Ideality'. He spoke extempore.—[16]

So much confidence did Coleridge regain that lecturing arguably became a temporary vocation – not immediately, for he had hatched a scheme for another journal, but later, from 1811 to 1814, when his lectures gave commitment and continuity to the darkest years of his life, then again in 1818–19. In all, he would deliver well over a hundred lectures on literature and aesthetics. Along with journalism it would become a ready source of income, but more than that it gave Coleridge an appreciative audience of the kind he rarely got in reviews and magazines.

Given the number of lectures he delivered, Coleridge's range of exemplary reference is surprisingly narrow, certainly when compared with his own omnivorous reading habits and the informal if undeveloped comments we find on a myriad of writers in his notebooks, letters, and marginalia. In the lectures, on the other hand, there was Shakespeare, Shakespeare, and Shakespeare. Aside from the occasional (very occasional) lecture on Dante, Cervantes, and Spenser, the only other poet to receive more than cursory treatment was Milton. Even when declaring his intention to comment on a wide historical range of writers, as in 1808, once Coleridge ascended the podium a canon that was already small enough in itself shrank considerably. After one lecture on taste, in 1808, and eleven on Shakespearean drama, Coleridge finally got around to two on Milton: 'But the word poetry was not used till the lecture was two-thirds over', Henry Crabb Robinson reported to Mrs Clarkson, 'nor Milton's name till ten minutes before the close'. And the topic of the next (the fifteenth) lecture? 'Shakespeare's superiority over other poets'.[17]

The obsession with Shakespeare (bardolatry) was as much if not more characteristic of the period – the audience – than it was of Coleridge, and their appreciation no doubt encouraged this exclusiveness. However we account for it, the result in Coleridge's case is a wealth of suggestive ideas and readings that, when worked up into a body of commentary, has made him one of the great critics of Shakespeare. Like Coleridge's other writings, however, especially the *Biographia*, his Shakespeare criticism has been contaminated by evidence of plagiarism, sometimes extensive and sometimes crucial. The wholesale borrowings all appear later – such as his definitions of 'wit' and 'humour' from Jean Paul Richter's *Vorschule der Aesthetik* and whole passages on aesthetics from Schelling's 'Über das Verhaltniss der bildenden Kunste zu der Natur', both in his 1818 lectures on European literature.[18] The critical moment came with Coleridge's acquisition of a copy of A. W. Schlegel's *Vorlesungen über dramatische Kunst und Litteratur*, published in Heidelberg in 1809 and 1811, before his ninth lecture in the 1811–12 series (mid December 1811). All of Coleridge's speculative literary history in the lectures from 1812 onwards is derivative and he resorted to Schlegel to help him formulate some of the central theoretical distinctions often associated with Coleridge's own name (like that between mechanical and organic form[19]). To quote R. A. Foakes: 'Coleridge certainly used Schlegel's lectures freely towards the end of the 1811–12 course and relied upon them heavily in the courses he gave in 1812 and 1813'.[20]

The issue has been bedevilled by the debate begun in Coleridge's own time, and to which Coleridge himself publicly contributed, as to whether or not the Germans were the first to affirm and critically substantiate Shakespeare's 'judgement' – countering the common eighteenth-century view that Shakespeare was a child of nature who wrote instinctively and artlessly. It is a minor point, as it happens, and both Coleridge and the Germans had been anticipated by occasional English critics (like John Dennis) much earlier in the previous century. Coleridge's extreme sensitivity on this point was in part personal, in part nationalistic – even Wordsworth, after all, in his 'Essay, Supplementary to the Preface' to his *Poems* (1815), had given the German critics priority[21] – but mostly it was a displaced anxiety about the status of his whole critical oeuvre. At some level, Coleridge must have known that by plagiarizing he was making everything he had to say susceptible to doubt. Now that a chronological order has been established for the relevant documents comprising Coleridge's

Shakespeare criticism it seems fair to say that most of Coleridge's ideas about the plays themselves and about what they represented aesthetically were developed by the time of the first, 1808 series.[22] But the years 1810–14 were the worst years of Coleridge's addiction, when he learnt better than anyone that he was not to be trusted.

Again like Coleridge's other writings – like his informal 'writings', this time, including his table talk – Coleridge's Shakespeare criticism has required extensive editorial assembly and reconstruction, the most recent and authoritative text being that for the Collected Works by R. A. Foakes. None of Coleridge's literary lectures was published in his own lifetime (though the idea of doing so was mooted occasionally). Only for some of the lectures do we have a complete set of Coleridge's lecture notes, and even in these cases they can hardly be said to account for all that transpired. These lecture notes, other notebook jottings, occasional newspaper reports of the lectures (some of which were remarkably generous in their coverage, depending on what else was making news at the time), Coleridge's own marginalia to various editions of Shakespeare (used at times as lecture notes), accounts given in the letters of friends, like those of Henry Crabb Robinson to Catherine Clarkson – these are our more or less sketchy, more or less reliable sources for Coleridge on Shakespeare. We do, however, have a relatively complete shorthand account of the lectures of 1811–12 from the pens of J. Tomalin and John Payne Collier, engaged for that purpose, and at other times different shorthand recorders were employed. Though 'even the most enthusiastic of Coleridge's admirers could in all probability make only partial record of his lectures', as Foakes concludes, the same will always be true of his conversation.[23] Some things are simply not recoverable. What we have, however, allows us confidently to trace a large and developing (if sometimes suspect) body of criticism.

Coleridge on Shakespeare

'Metaphysics and psychology', as Coleridge says in the Biographia, 'have long been my hobby-horse' (BL I, 85). Two paradoxical tendencies stand out in Coleridge's Shakespeare criticism because they stand out in Shakespearean drama: the tendency towards detailed psychological realism and the tendency towards poetic sublimation. This combination of truth and transcendence made Shakespeare the ideal subject for Coleridge's determination to bring 'the whole soul of man into activity' (BL II, 15–16). The psychological realism of Shakespearean drama challenged his interpretative ingenuity (it was Coleridge who coined the term 'practical criticism'), while its poetry encouraged his irrepressible impulse to theoretical extrapolation. The two of them together, such apparently 'opposite and discordant qualities', helped him beyond the naiveties and suspicion of art in the Preface to Lyrical Ballads to his affirmation of imagination.

Coleridge enjoyed starting with what he took to be the largely unquestioned assumption of Shakespeare's 'fidelity to Nature':

> Whatever Play of Shakespeare's we had selected, there is one preliminary point to be first settled, as the indispensable Condition not only of just and genial Criticism, but of all consistency in our opinions.—This point is contained in the words, probable, natural. We are all in the habit of praising Shakespear, or of hearing him extolled for his fidelity to Nature. Now what are we to understand by these words, in their application to the Drama?[24]

At one extreme, Shakespeare's 'fidelity to Nature' suggests a total transparency of the artistic medium of the kind aspired to in the Preface: 'the power of so carrying the Eye of the Reader as to make him almost lose the consciousness of words—to make him *see* every thing', as Coleridge phrases it in a discussion of *Venus and Adonis*.[25] Coleridge rarely attributes this power to Shakespeare and rarely places any value on the power itself (the qualifying 'almost' expresses his reservations). In drama, however, this fidelity to the phenomenal world can take the form of psychological realism, and Coleridge was fond of adducing proofs of what on one occasion he called 'the re-creating psychologic (if not omni-, yet) hominiscience of *"the Myriad-minded"* Bard' (*CL* III, 428).

It is easy to see why Coleridge has gained the reputation of being the first great character critic and, of all his readings, it is that of Hamlet – Hamlet the character, that is, rather than *Hamlet* the play – which has proved most influential, critically and theatrically. Here are Collier's notes for the lecture Coleridge delivered on 2 January 1812:

> He meant to pourtray a person in whose view the <external> world and all its incidents <and objects> were comparatively dim, and of no interest of themselves, and which began to interest only when they were reflected in the mirror of his mind. Hamlet beheld external objects in the same way that a man <of vivid imagination> who shuts his eyes, sees what has previously made an impression upon his organs.
>
> Shakespeare places him in the most stimulating circumstances that a human being can be placed in: he is the heir apparent of the throne: his father dies suspiciously: his mother excludes him from the throne by marrying his uncle. This was not enough but the Ghost of the murdered father is introduced to assure the son that he was put to death by his own brother. What is the result? Endless reasoning and urging—perpetual solicitation of the mind to act, but as constant an escape from action— ceaseless reproaches of himself <for his sloth>, while the whole energy of his resolution passes away in those reproaches. This, too, not from cowardice, for he is made one of the bravest of his time—not from want of

forethought or quickness of apprehension, for he sees through the very souls of all who surround him, but merely <from> that aversion to action which prevails among such as have a world within themselves.[26]

Hamlet is a victim of his own restless intellect and self-reflective introspection, paralysed not in spite of, but precisely because of his being 'deeply acquainted with his own feelings, painting them with such wonderful power & accuracy'. With every new provocation to action Hamlet 'still yields to the same retiring from all reality' and 'seizes hold of a pretext for not acting':

he is all meditation, all resolution <as far as words are concerned>, but all hesitation & irresolution when called upon to act; so that resolving to do everything he <in fact> does nothing.

Hamlet is also a victim of his own noble imagination, overcome by 'a sense of imperfectness' in a world incommensurate with his high ideals. It is this, more than anything, that makes Coleridge's Hamlet so characteristically Romantic, treading as he does the fine line between vision and narcissism. And it is this that makes Hamlet, for Coleridge, Shakespeare's greatest creation. Coleridge may revert to a moral reading of the play as an affirmation of action as 'the great end of existence', but all the emotional weight of Coleridge's extended analysis is on Hamlet's side. The Prince of Denmark remains more heroic for having retired from reality than he could ever have been indulging in the vulgar activism of a Fortinbras.

The reason for this critical sleight of hand is not hard to find. Coleridge's friends all recognized the extent to which his Hamlet was modelled on himself, indeed Henry Crabb Robinson doubted 'whether he did not design an application to himself': 'Somebody said to me, this is a Satire on himself; No, said I, it is an elegy'.[27] Later in life, Coleridge, too, is reported to have conceded that he had 'a smack of Hamlet'.[28] Hamlet is said to have retired into his mind, just as Coleridge had retired into his, transmuting a political into an ideal world in protest against inhibitions placed on his imagination. (Coleridge might also have remarked that, like him, Hamlet was given to erupting into extraverted, indeed manic activity at times.) Whether it was self-satire, self-elegy, or self-justification – and there seems an element of all three involved – it required a careful editing of the play *Hamlet* in the interests of a Coleridgean apologetics. If Hamlet's imagination heroically isolates him from the action, Coleridge exaggerates that isolation, no less than he ignores much of the selfishness and *schadenfreude* ('malicious joy') that offended August Wilhelm Schlegel.[29]

Coleridge's practical criticism largely comprises subtle analyses of character motivation designed as 'proof of Shakespeare's minute knowledge of human nature'.[30] It was hardly surprising, given the interest in the human psyche manifest in his notebooks, that he should seek in Shakespeare subjects for analysis. The unique vividness of Shakespearean characterization, a theme of Shakespeare commentary from the very beginning, has never been successfully subordinated to formalist or materialist analysis, even in our own day. What was implicit from the beginning had become explicit in the work of such eighteenth-century critics as Maurice Morgann, who was convinced that certain passages in Shakespeare could not 'be sufficiently explained in words, without unfolding the whole character' – which is precisely what he attempted with Falstaff – and that it was 'fit to consider [Shakespeare's characters] rather as Historic than Dramatic beings'.[31]

Coleridge's sense of his own critical distinction in the area of character psychology led him to focus on this aspect of the plays. The very rare reservations that he expresses about Shakespeare's judgement always concern some apparently 'unnatural' passage, either psychologically improbable or out of character. The speech of Aufidius in *Coriolanus* I, x, 12–24 is an example; Oliver's confessed hatred of his brother in *As You Like It*. Faced with such a challenge, however, Coleridge self-consciously retains his 'deep Faith in Shakespeare's Heart-lore', taking it for granted that both instances are to be found 'in nature' and that these natural counterparts must have escaped his notice.[32] So with Prospero's elaborate periphrasis in *The Tempest* I, ii, 412–13:

> The fringed curtain of thy eye advance
> And say, what thou seest yond?

'As a paraphraze of "Look what is coming", it certainly did appear ridiculous', but Coleridge rallies: 'different modes of expression it should be remembered frequently arose from dif[ference] of situation & education', and 'this solemnity of phrazeology was in Coleridge's opinion completely in character with Prospero'.[33] Suddenly its very artificiality becomes a guarantee of its authenticity. It is, after all, 'too venturous to charge a speech in Shakespear with want of truth to Nature'.[34]

The dangers of so undiscriminating a faith in Shakespeare's 'Heart-lore' are obvious and Coleridge's attempts to read Shakespearean drama as transcending its own poetic and dramatic conventions rarely convincing. His pressing for psychological and linguistic realism, however, represents only one aspect of his Shakespearean criticism. There are other discussions in which the Aristotelian demand for probability informing his defence of character consistency, far from being interpreted as a kind of literal verisimilitude, is a demand for the 'semblance of truth' only (to quote the *Biographia*), 'sufficient to procure for these shadows of imagination that willing suspension of disbelief for the moment, that constitutes poetic faith' (*BL* II, 7). This famous idea of a 'Poetic Faith before which our common notions of philosophy give way' – a feeling 'much stronger than historic faith' – began its life in a discussion of *The Tempest* in 1811–12.[35] Just as Aristotle had stated his preference for 'likely impossibilities' over 'unconvincing possibilities',

Coleridge warned only against too flagrant a violation of probability: 'tho' the imagination may supersede perception, yet it must be granted an imperfection (tho' even here how easily do we tolerate it?) to place the two in broad contradiction to each other'.[36]

The German playwright Kotzebue and Shakespeare's contemporaries Beaumont and Fletcher might violate this rule of probability, argues Coleridge, but Shakespeare is always careful to exclude the arbitrary from the central characters and central events of his plays.[37] The *locus classicus* of this argument is to be found in Coleridge's commentary on *King Lear*, in which two fantastic hypotheses threaten the audience's participation in the dramatic illusion. The first is the story itself: 'a gross improbability'. In Shakespeare's defence, Coleridge counters that the fable was 'so rooted in the popular faith' that it had assumed the validity of an unquestioned myth – a likely impossibility – and 'a few facts were only necessary ... to put an end to all doubt as to their incredibility'. The other potentially disturbing element is the two sisters, Goneril and Regan, a species of 'wickedness in an outrageous form'. Again, however, the matter was out of Shakespeare's hands: the fable had 'compelled' the otherwise faithful dramatist to introduce them. All the more important is it, then, to prevent a central character like Edmund from 'passing into utter *monstrosity*', and this time Coleridge's defence of Shakespeare is a cogent, detailed analysis of the 'preformation of Edmund's character' in the first scene, which is made to compensate for the motiveless malice of the elder sisters. It is a fine set piece in which Coleridge combines his talent for psychological analysis with an understanding of the play as performance, while betraying his own theatrical sense of narrative. 'From the first drawing up of the curtain', says Coleridge, Edmund has stood before the audience 'in the united strength and beauty of earliest Manhood':

Our eyes have been questioning him. Gifted thus with high advantages of person, and further endowed by Nature with a powerful intellect and a strong energetic Will, even without any concurrence of circumstances and accident, Pride will be the Sin that most easily besets him/. But he is the known and acknowledged Son of the princely Gloster—Edmund therefore has both the germ <of Pride> and the conditions best fitted to evolve and ripen it into a predominant feeling. Yet hitherto no reason appears why it should be other than the usual pride of Person, Talent and Birth, a pride auxiliary if not akin to many Virtues, and the natural ally of honorable [impulses]. But alas! In his own presence his own father takes shame to himself for the frank avowal—that he is his Father—has blushed so often to acknowledge him that he is now braz'd to it. He hears his Mother and the circumstances of his Birth spoken of with a most degrading and licentious Levity—described as a Wanton by her own Paramour, and the remembrance of the animal sting, the low criminal gratifications connected with her Wantonness and prostituted Beauty assigned as the

reason, why 'the Whoreson must be acknowledged.'—This and the consciousness of its notoriety—the gnawing conviction that every shew of
respect is an effort of courtesy which recalls while it represses a contrary
feeling—this is the ever-trickling Flow of Wormwood and Gall into the
wounds of Pride—the corrosive Virus which inoculates Pride with a
venom of its own, with Envy, Hatred, a lust of that Power which in its
blaze of Radiance would hide the dark spots on his disk—pangs of shame,
personally undeserved, and therefore felt as wrongs—and a blind ferment
of addictive workings towards the occasions and causes, especially
towards a Brother whose stainless Birth and lawful Honors were the constant remembrancers of *his* debasement, and were ever in the way to prevent all chance of its being unknown or overlooked—&—forgotten.[38]

All this, and so much more – on primogeniture, on Edmund's banishment
for his father's shame – as Coleridge suddenly erupts into an imaginative
explication of Gloucester's introduction of Edmund in the first scene of *King
Lear*. With such compellingly plausible characterization as this and such suggestive concentration, argues Coleridge, Shakespeare succeeds in preserving
the dramatic illusion, and the 'sort of temporary Half-Faith, which the
Spectator encourages in himself & supports by a voluntary contribution on
his own part' – the 'poetic faith' of the *Biographia* – remains unshaken.[39]

Coleridge sees himself as adjudicating between, on the one hand, what he
calls the 'delusion' sought by confining the action to one time and place in
the interests of verisimilitude (the neoClassical 'unities') and, on the other, a
disillusioned alertness to the play's fictionality:

Here I find two extremes in critical decision—The French, which evidently
presupposes that a perfect delusion is to be aimed at. ... The opposite, supported by Dr Johnson, supposes the auditors throughout as in the full and
positive reflective knowledge of the contrary. In evincing the impossibility
of Delusion he makes no sufficient allowance for an intermediate State,
which we distinguish by the term, Illusion.[40]

When Coleridge admits as the only necessary requirement of a play, not
consistency, but *apparent* consistency – 'without any of the *effects* of
improbability'[41] – he is also seeking a compromise between slavish forms
of realism and what he considers the annoying arbitrariness of the utterly
improbable 'pantomimic tragedies and weeping comedies of Kotzebue and
his imitators' (*BL* II, 185). The drama is, after all, neither a copy nor a trav-
esty of the familiar world, it is an imitation:

But a moment's reflection suffices to make every man conscious of what
every man must have before felt, that the Drama is an *imitation* of reality
not a *Copy*—and that Imitation is contra-distinguished from Copy by this,

that a certain quantum of Difference is essential to the former, and an indispensable condition and cause of the pleasure, we derive from it; while in a Copy it is a defect, contravening its name and purpose.[42]

The 'certain quantum of Difference' distinguishing an imitation from a copy can be understood in terms of Coleridge's further distinction between 'meditation' and 'observation', two opposed ways of experiencing before experience itself is transmuted into art. Mere observation leads to an uncreative copying, reproducing 'images of sight and sound, and other sensible impressions'. 'Without a delicate tact for these', Coleridge concedes, 'no man ever was, or could be either a musician, or a poet', but we require more of genius.[43] Shakespeare, pre-eminently, drew his characters 'from meditation rather than observation, or rather by observation which was the child of meditation'.[44] The result was a set of characters that were 'all Shakespere, & nothing Shakespere' (*CN* II, 2086, 40). Coleridge is still trying to reconcile the two paradoxical responses to Shakespearean drama with which we began, the sense we have that it is 'so true to nature – that you never can conceive his characters could speak otherwise than they do in the situation in which they are placed', and the certainty that it is 'so peculiar that if you read but a few detached lines you immediately say this must be Shakespear'.[45] For the truth is, 'No character he has drawn could so properly express himself as in the language put into his mouth'.[46]

The residual, Protean divinity of Shakespeare in his drama is in the poetry – *is* the poetry. It is the trademark left by the work of the meditative imagination, through and by means of which nature is recreated as drama: 'Here Shakespeare adapts himself to the situation so admirably <and as it were put himself into the situation> that through poetry, his language <is the language> of nature'.[47] 'Shakespeare was pursuing two Methods at once', wrote Coleridge in his treatise on method; 'besides the psychological Method, he had also to attend to the poetical'.[48]

Coleridge's definition of this 'subtle spirit' of imagination is not always clear – it is not always clear in his Shakespeare criticism, for example, how imagination differs from passion or feeling.[49] It is rare, moreover, that Coleridge invokes the imagination in his 'practical criticism' and when he does he tends to draw his illustrations from the poems, *Venus and Adonis* and the sonnets (*CN* III, 3290; *BL* II, 19–28). Still, its effects – modifying, unifying, animating, idealizing, reconciling – are as familiar as the dignity Coleridge accords it. For Coleridge, the activity of the imagination not only differentiated an imitation from a copy, it was also largely responsible for the artistic coherence that sustained the 'willing suspension of disbelief' exercised by the play's audience:

Yet still the consciousness of the Poet's Mind must be diffused over that of the Reader or Spectator—but he himself, according to his Genius, elevates

us, & by being *always in keeping* prevents us from perceiving any strangeness, tho' we feel great exaltation.[50]

The critical currency of the phrase 'willing suspension of disbelief' confirms that the idea of aesthetic attention as a self-willed, sustained illusion
that Coleridge developed in his Shakespeare criticism has largely been
accepted as accurate.[51] In exploring the creative complicity between this aesthetic receptivity of the reader or audience and the imagination of the poet,
Coleridge extended his investigation well beyond Shakespeare's 'deep and
accurate science in mental philosophy'.[52] Though Shakespeare's command
of that 'science' would remain the motivating assumption behind his practical criticism, Coleridge has used the lazy identification of Shakespeare with
nature, current since Shakespeare's own lifetime, to develop a literary theory
that can accommodate not just all of Shakespeare's plays – the comedies
along with the histories and tragedies; *The Tempest* as well as *Hamlet* – but all
poetry and all art.

The Friend

Coleridge may have discovered a vocation during his 1808 lectures on the
principles of poetry but by June, when he wrote to the board of the Royal
Institution crying off the series, he was physically ill (again) and mentally
very disturbed, writing letters of pent-up, paranoid accusation to Wordsworth
and of slightly less paranoid resentment to his brother George (*CL* III, 101–5).[53]
He offered to refund £40 of the £60 already advanced by the Royal Institution
towards the agreed fee of £140 (who would not hear of it and voted to pay
him a further £60 as an appropriate portion [*CL* III, 117–18, 118n.]) and
went off to convalesce, first at Stuart's house in Margate, then at Bury St
Edmond with Thomas and Catherine Clarkson. Coleridge had negotiated a
review of Clarkson's *History of the Abolition of the Slave Trade* in the *Edinburgh
Review* with its editor, Francis Jeffrey, otherwise so antagonistic towards
Coleridge and those he identified as the Lake poets.[54] Jeffrey had guardedly
accepted the proposal then proceeded to suppress some of Coleridge's more
enthusiastic support for Clarkson and to insert praise for William
Wilberforce and a passage seriously doubting the contribution of Pitt, which
Coleridge had argued elsewhere in the article. In his darker or more partisan
moments, Coleridge would see these alterations as characteristic of Scottish
or Whig chicanery (or of both): sceptical, disrespectful, and manipulative
(*CL* III, 272).[55]

Writing to Jeffrey himself, however, Coleridge was prepared to accept it as
Jeffrey's editorial right: 'your character and interest, as the known Editor of
the Review are pledged for a general consistency of principle in the different
Articles with each other' (*CL* III, 148). As it happens, it was a right that Jeffrey

exercised with all but a handful of contributors, but for our purposes it was a right that Coleridge at the time was coveting for himself. Already, even while winding up his lectures, he had been planning his next venture: an edifying periodical for an unedifying age, one that – unlike Jeffrey's Whig *Edinburgh Review* and Leigh Hunt's liberal *Examiner*, and (this above all) unlike Cobbett's populist *Political Register* – would counteract the tendencies of modernity, rather than pander to them, rising above the clamours of contemporary politics and contemporary personalities to investigate true principles:

> I do not write in this Work for the *Multitude*; but for those, who by Rank, or Fortune, or official Station, or Talents and Habits of Reflection, are to *influence* the Multitude. I write to found true PRINCIPLES, to oppose false PRINCIPLES in Criticism, Legislation, Philosophy, Morals, and International Law. ... Cobbett sells his weekly Sheet for ten pence—Now this differs from mine in two points mainly. First: he applies himself to the Passions that are gratified by Curiosity, and sharp—often calumnious—personality; by the Events and political Topics of the Day, and the names of notorious Contemporaries.—Now from all these I abstain altogether—nay, to strangle this vicious Temper of mind by directing the Interest to the noble germs in human nature is my express and paramount Object. (*CL* III, 143)

As always, Coleridge's intentions are eloquent. In an age of periodicals, his periodical would neutralize all the others, reforming the political reformers by opposing everything they did and symbolized. Instead of countering the resistance of a new reading public to what was distinguished and difficult and demanded intellectual and imaginative exertion, newspapers, magazines, and Reviews were identifying and conspiring with the reading public, encouraging its complacency and philistinism (*BL* I, 59). Coleridge's periodical, to be entitled *The Friend*, announced itself in its Prospectus as a 'Weekly Essay'. Later its title page would describe it more popularly as a 'Weekly Paper', but a 'Weekly Paper' paradoxically 'Excluding Personal and Party Politics, and the Events of the Day'. In short, it had none of his earlier *Watchman*'s aspirations 'To supply at once the places of Review, Newspaper, and Annual Register!!!'.[56] 'The subjects were generally chosen, obstinately in defiance of popular taste', De Quincey later wrote; 'they were treated in a style which avowed contempt for the popular models'.[57]

Having found temporary control of his opium habit and a measure of 'Tranqullity—by Ease from the Sting of Self-disapprobation' amongst Quaker friends of the Clarksons on his way north, Coleridge threw himself into the enterprise with that manic energy he seemed always to discover when the future seemed hopeless and his body and soul exhausted (*CL* III, 135). Various prospectuses were written and dispatched to his wide acquaintance and Wordsworth, Lamb, and Southey (amongst others) were all conscripted to write letters on *The Friend*'s behalf – and this in spite of the fact that none of them had any faith in Coleridge's ever managing to get it into print. 'Of the Friend and Coleridge', wrote Wordsworth to Daniel Stuart, 'I hear nothing':

> and am sorry to say I hope nothing. I think it is too clear that Coleridge is not sufficiently master of is own efforts to execute anything which requires a regular course of application to one object. I fear so—indeed I am assured that it is so—to my great sorrow.[58]

But still all of them exerted themselves on Coleridge's behalf. In this sense alone, *The Friend* was aptly named: all his friends were involved in the promotion and many of them got caught up in the production. Southey and Wordsworth contributed material, for example, but more than anyone it was Sara Hutchinson who made it happen.[59]

Coleridge was living in the Wordsworth household again, now at Allan Bank in Grasmere. The atmosphere of lively chaos created by the presence of the Wordsworth children and visits from his own, De Quincey's lingering presence, and the coming and going of visitors offered its own kind of support. The geography, however, made producing a periodical a near impossible challenge. Coleridge had to organize the subscription, printing, and distribution at an awkward distance from all developed modes of communication and production. Because there was no direct postal link between Grasmere and Penrith where *The Friend* was being printed, Coleridge on several occasions had to walk miles over Helvellyn via Grisedale Tarn – 'our most perilous & difficult Alpine Pass' (*CL* III, 211) – to ensure that copy got through to the printer. With impractical but irrepressible determination, Coleridge spent six months lurching from one disappointment to another – 'vexations, hindrances, scoundrelisms, disappointments' (*CL* III, 173) – before finally setting it all up. (Originally planned for January, the first issue came out on 1 June 1809.) Then, after four numbers, Sara Hutchinson took over as prompt and amanuensis, for like the *Biographia* six years later much of *The Friend* was dictated. Without this vital assistance it would never have survived as long as it did and it folded when Sara eventually retreated, exhausted in herself and unable to rally Coleridge, just before the last number came out ten months and twenty eight issues after the first.[60]

The Friend not only relied on friends, however, it also sought to make friends, though Coleridge had a strange way of endearing himself. In a characteristic piece of Coleridgean indirection, the Prospectus is cast as a letter to a friend, sharing confidences that amount to an explanation and justification of the enterprise:

> It is not unknown to you, that I have employed almost the whole of my Life in acquiring, or endeavouring to acquire, useful Knowledge by Study, Reflection, Observation, and by cultivating the Society of my Superiors in Intellect, both at Home and in foreign Countries. You know too, that at

different Periods of my Life I have not only planned, but collected the Materials for, many Works on various and important Subjects: so many indeed, that the Number of my unrealized Schemes, and the Mass of miscellaneous Fragments, have often furnished my Friends with a Subject of Raillery, sometimes of Regret and Reproof. Waiving the Mention of all private and accidental Hindrances, I am inclined to believe, that this Want of Perseverance has been produced in the Main by an Over-activity of Thought, modified by a constitutional Indolence, which made it more pleasant to me to continue acquiring, than to reduce what I had acquired to a regular Form.

Coleridge then goes on (at length) about his own writing practices before finally getting around to 'the Weekly Essay, of which you will consider this Letter as the Prospectus'. The sheer length of the Prospectus (about 1500 words) and its leisured convolution are alone a trial of the reader's (and potential customer's) patience, but Coleridge also openly declares his determination 'to run Counter to many Prejudices of many of my Readers' by 'upholding the Principles both of Taste and Philosophy, adopted by the great Men of Europe from the Middle of the fifteenth till toward the Close of the seventeenth Century'.[61] Coleridge is throwing down his ideological antiquarianism as a gauntlet. In all, winding its curvilinear path between ingratiation and alienation – tempting his readers into his study by threatening to disqualify them as readers – the Prospectus gives some indication of the far greater trial of their patience that the essays themselves will often make.

Southey found in the familiarity of the Prospectus 'a sort of unmanly *humblification*'.[62] Jeffrey, on the other hand, counselled him not to seem 'so awfully impressed with the importance of [his] task'.[63] Together they capture that uncertain mixture of humility and self-importance that will characterize the Coleridgean persona in all his later prose works. There is a similar explosion of impatience with his readers in the *Biographia* – disqualifying them from ever understanding the ideas he appears to be at pains to explain – and both can be compared with the notorious outburst of his letter to his wife Sara in 1802 protesting his superiority over her (*CL* II, 888).[64] This mixture of unctuous ingratiation and self-defensive arrogance reflects (as it had always reflected) Coleridge's anxiety about his own genius, as well as about the fate of genius generally in a society becoming progressively more democratic. His reply to a correspondent in number 11 conveys a sense of insult in the face of the expectations and limitations of his contemporaries that will become an obsession:

I dare not flatter myself, that any endeavours of mine, compatible with the duty I owe to Truth and the hope of permanent utility, will render THE FRIEND agreeable to the majority of what is called the reading Public. I never expected it. How indeed could I, when I was to borrow so little from passing Events, and absolutely excluded from my plan all appeals to personal curiosity and personal interests. Yet even this is not my greatest impediment. No real information can be conveyed, no important errors rectified, no widely injurious prejudices rooted up, without requiring some effort of Thought on the part of the Reader. But the obstinate (and toward a contemporary Writer, the contemptuous) aversion to all intellectual effort is the mother evil of all, which I had proposed to war against, the Queen Bee in the Hive of our errors and misfortunes, both private and national. The proof of the fact, positively and comparatively, and the enumeration of its' various causes will, as I have already hinted (P. 75) form the preliminary Essay of the disquisition on the elements of our moral and intellectual faculties. To solicit the attention of those on whom these debilitating causes have acted to their full extent, would be no less absurd than to recommend exercise with the dumb bells, as the only mode of cure, to the patient paralytic in both arms.[65]

What this passage also reveals is the extent to which the qualifications of his readership, far from being merely preliminary or promotional, *is* Coleridge's subject matter. The opening number not only expands on the theme but also includes the Prospectus itself, as a way of underlining its importance. The gambit opening his second number – 'Conscious that I am about to deliver my sentiments on a subject of the utmost delicacy' – might stand for any or all of his essays, insofar as a consciousness of his readers and of the politics of cultural transmission pervades and sometimes preoccupies them. (Vying with this for its representative quality might be a sentence in Coleridge's discussion of Martin Luther and ghosts: 'I will endeavour to make my meaning more clear to those of my Readers, who are fortunate enough to find it obscure in consequence of their own good health and unshattered nerves', the multiple ironies of which reflect on every level of Coleridge's literary life.[66]) The very shift in direction witnessed in *The Friend* from number 11 onwards – 'I shall do my best, and even make all allowable sacrifices, to render my manner more attractive and my matter more generally interesting' – is, we are told, in grudging response to pressure from his readers.[67]

The cultural and intellectual qualifications of his readership and of the reading public is not by any means the only issue in *The Friend*. Not only does it contain stand-alone material like Wordsworth's 'Essay on Epitaphs' and passages from *The Prelude* published for the first time, as well as a selection of discrete poems, mostly by Wordsworth and Coleridge,[68] but from its turgid foray into the liberty of the press in numbers 3 to 6 to its closing, unfinished essay 'Sketches and Fragments of the Life and Character of the Late Sir Alexander Ball' (21–22, then 26–7), *The Friend* touches on a multitude of topics in its often obscure, meandering course and illuminates a good many of them. Coleridge described the actor Edmund Kean's performances as like reading Shakespeare 'by flashes of lightning' and so his *Friend* throws out flashes of lightning on topics as diverse as censorship, language, taxation, 'rights and duties', travel-writing, ghosts, education, childhood, and (defensively, for here Coleridge is actively rewriting his past) Jacobinism and the French Revolution.[69] Implicitly or explicitly, the conservative political theorist Edmund Burke is busy throughout – as are Immanuel Kant and the seventeenth-century divine Richard Hooker[70] – especially in the more politically focussed early numbers. There are also many reflections on poetry and the imagination and the best of these will find their way into the *Biographia*.[71]

Some topics, moreover, are illuminated by more than flashes, like his discussion of 'the heroic LUTHER' when comparing the triumvirate Voltaire, Rousseau, and Robespierre with its Coleridgean counterpart Erasmus, Luther, and Munster (though Coleridge was indebted for his biographical notice of Luther to the German travel writer Jonas Ludwig von Hess[72]). Here again it is interesting to watch the way Coleridge works from parallels with his own life:

It is evident from his Letters that he suffered from great irritability of the nervous System, the common effect of deranged digestion in men of sedentary habits, who are at the same time intense thinkers: and this irritability added to, and revivifying the impressions made upon him in early life, and fostered by the theological Systems of his Manhood, is abundantly sufficient to explain all his Apparitions and all his nightly combats with evil Spirits.[73]

But still we are reminded of Poole's early reflections on Coleridge's lack of perseverance, the ease with which he is distracted from the topic in hand and his disinclination to move beyond or past what he saw as the 'evil Spirits' in contemporary culture. Henry Crabb Robinson would complain of one of the 1811–12 lectures that Coleridge 'wasted his time on the introduction to the introduction' and *The Friend* (reissued in 1812 and again, reorganized and rewritten, in 1818) would establish Coleridge's reputation for obscurity and elaborate inconsequentiality, both of which were justified.[74] William Hazlitt, Coleridge's greatest, if at times also his most cruel and wilfully unsympathetic critic, put it brilliantly:

What is his Friend itself but an enormous Title-page; the longest and most tiresome Prospectus that ever was written; an endless preface to an imaginary work; a Table of Contents that fills the whole volume; a huge bill of fare of all possible subjects, with not an idea to be had for love or money? One number consists of a grave-faced promise to perform something impossible in the next; and the next is taken up with a long-faced apology for not having done it. Through the whole of his work, Mr Coleridge appears in the character of the Unborn Doctor; the very Barmecide [i.e., 'phantasm'] of knowledge; the prince of preparatory authors!

> He never is—but always to be *wise*.
>
> He is the Dog in the Manger of Literature, an intellectual Mar-Plot who will neither let anyone else come to a conclusion, nor come to one himself.[75]

Of course there are ideas to be had in *The Friend*, for both love and money. The sense of disappointed expectation, however – one that reflects Hazlitt's own bitter disappointment in Coleridge's not living up to the impossible things he seemed to promise to the young 19-year-old when the two had first met – the accusation that Coleridge never progresses beyond preliminary caveats and definitions that are designed to establish his knowledge and authority (and are thus more ideologically than philosophically revealing), these are not unreasonable.

The break with Wordsworth

The Friend failed, gradually alienating too many of its 500-odd subscribers with its irregular issue, dense argumentation, and occasionally perverse editorial strategies, like leaving sentences unfinished until the next number. Coleridge's determination to persist with it, while arguably heroic in itself, ended by taking a great toll on his friendships with those constrained to assist in its production – with Thomas Clarkson, who had rallied all his Quaker friends to subscribe (Coleridge's pro-war stance had offended the pacifist Quakers amongst his subscribers);[76] with Stuart who at considerable trouble and some cost to himself had supplied the stamped paper for the first 20 issues; but most of all with the Wordsworths and the Hutchinsons. It was the first, and only, concerted effort made by all members of the Wordsworth household to support the homeless Coleridge in his deepening addiction, his often infantile craving for affection and reinforcement, and his extreme changes of mood. An exhausted Sara Hutchinson had been obliged to withdraw from Grasmere on 5 March 1810 to a farm her brothers had bought in Wales and within the month Coleridge, too (as Dorothy observed), had effectively withdrawn:

> We have no hope of him—none that he will do any more than he has already done. If he were not under our Roof, he would be just as much the slave of stimulants as ever; and his whole time and thoughts, (except when he is reading and he reads a great deal), are employed in deceiving himself, and seeking to deceive others. He will tell me that he has been writing, that he has written half a friend; when I know that he has not written a single line. The Habit pervades all his words and actions, and you feel perpetually new hollowness and emptiness. I am loth to say this, and burn this letter, I entreat you. I am loth to say it, but it is the truth. He lies in bed, always till after 12 o'clock, sometimes much later; and

never walks out—Even the finest spring day does not tempt him to seek the fresh air; and this beautiful valley seems a blank to him. He never leaves his parlour except at dinner and tea, and sometimes supper, and then he always seems impatient to get back to his solitude—he goes the moment his food is swallowed. Sometimes he does not speak a word, and when he does talk it is always very much and on subjects as far aloof from himself and his friends as possible.[77]

The misunderstanding that actually precipitated the break between Coleridge and Wordsworth occurred later and has gone down on record as a misunderstanding about the precise wording of a warning that Wordsworth issued to a wealthy lawyer friend of theirs, Basil Montagu, who had offered to accommodate Coleridge in London over the winter of 1810–11. When Sara Hutchinson had left Grasmere, Coleridge suspected William and Dorothy of conspiring in her withdrawal. It was true. Dorothy was convinced that work on *The Friend* had 'harassed and agitated her mind continually, and we saw that he was doing her health perpetual injury'.[78] Then, when they arrived in London in late October, Montagu appears to have told Coleridge that (in the words of Coleridge's notebooks) Wordsworth had 'authorized M[ontagu]. to tell me, he had no Hope of me!—O God! what good reason for saying this?' (N504). Coleridge explained it to other friends a little over a year later as a commission to tell Coleridge, not only that he had 'no Hope' of him, but that he had 'for years passed ... been an absolute nuisance in the family' (*CL* III, 376, 382).

Coleridge immediately left the Montagus for Hudson's Hotel in Covent Garden to dwell on the insult he had received and to rehearse his own constant support for an ungrateful Wordsworth. Correspondence with the Wordsworths stopped and two years would be spent engaging one friend after another in the sorry business of trying to establish the exact commission Wordsworth had in fact given Montagu on 18 October 1810. The truth is that a friendship already very unequal in its needs and demands, and already under great strain, had been exhausted by Coleridge's residence at Allan Bank during the production of *The Friend* and, though diplomatically patched up in the summer of 1812, would never recover. As Coleridge predicted at the time of their reconciliation, there would always remain 'an immedicable *But*' (*CL* III, 437).

8
'To Preserve the Soul Steady': The Sage of Highgate

Setting a pattern for the next six years of his and Coleridge's life, John Morgan came to the Hudson Hotel to reclaim Coleridge the moment he heard about his breakdown, packing up Coleridge's belongings and moving him into the household Morgan shared with his wife Mary and her sister Charlotte Brent at Hammersmith on the outskirts of London. There Coleridge would continue until a sudden access of scrupulosity or a painful scene of one kind or another, usually involving his drinking or drug taking, drove him out on his own for a period or (less often) into the house of another friend. And when that happened, Coleridge would write letters blending acute self-analysis with maudlin apologies and after a while Morgan would come to reclaim him again, a situation that would be reversed momentarily in 1813 when, by exerting himself in borrowing and lecturing, Coleridge would recall Morgan from his bankrupt retreat in Ireland.[1]

So began the period generally agreed to have been the worst in Coleridge's life, culminating in the crisis of December 1813 and followed by a decisive, if gradual and unspectacular turn-around that saw him finally established in the household of Dr James Gillman of Highgate until his death in 1834.[2] Just how bad Coleridge was during this period following the break with Wordsworth depends on the nature of our evidence. Coleridge's notebooks and letters suggest moments of insanity and thoughts of suicide, as he stared 'down into the grave (on the brink of which I am now probably tottering)' (*CN* III, 4006). Wordsworth, however, in the first instance at least, failed to appreciate the extremity of Coleridge's suffering and the significance of his silence for the simple reason that reports from Lamb suggested Coleridge's condition was far from critical:

> Coleridge has powdered his hair, and looks like Bacchus, Bacchus ever sleek and young. He is going to turn sober, but his Clock has not struck yet, meantime he pours down goblet after goblet, the 2d to see where the 1st is gone, the 3d to see no harm happens to the second, a fourth to say there's another coming, and a 5th to say he's not sure he's the last.

Neither Lamb nor his sister Mary mentioned anything of Coleridge's being distraught when they wrote to the Wordsworths, indeed Mary made a point of saying 'he has been very cheerful'.[3] There is no need to doubt the depth of Coleridge's despair, but like every suffering addict and depressive Coleridge maintained his sanity and resolve by exaggerating that suffering and over-dramatizing his struggles. Where there is room for complaint, after all, there is always hope. 'The worst is not', Edgar reminds us in Shakespeare's *King Lear*, 'so long as we can say "This is the worst" '.[4] Coleridge said it a lot over these years, and for his own sake, no less than for the sake of his audience of random acquaintances and sympathetic friends, turned his survival into an heroic narrative of extreme difficulties overcome. This was his way of coping.

Two other things are also suggested by the discrepancy between Coleridge's account of his own condition and the account given by his London friends. The first is that his buoyancy had less to do with what Richard Holmes calls 'the performance he was putting on' and more to do with Coleridge's extreme mood swings – or, more positively, with Coleridge's almost miraculous powers of recovery.[5] 'Yet how Coleridge does rise up, as it were, almost from the dead!', Dorothy Wordsworth had written to Lady Beaumont in January 1808.[6] And so he did, sometimes within the hour. But this did not guarantee that by midnight he would not be in despair again: 'Whirled about without a center—as in a nightmair—no gravity—a vortex without a center' (*CN* III, 3999).

The second thing that the discrepancy suggests is that London society and its daily exigencies were working their magic again. To his familiar conversationalists Godwin, Stuart, and Charles and Mary Lamb, he had added Henry Crabb Robinson, a friend since his first lecture series, and Washington Allston, who had arrived in London from Italy where together he and Coleridge had toured the galleries and talked the sun down. Crabb Robinson recalled having been kept 'on the stretch of attention and admiration from half past three till twelve o'clock. On politics, metaphysics and poetry, more especially on the regency, Kant and Shakespeare, he was astonishingly eloquent'.[7] There were no guarantees. Coleridge was always prone to drug overuse, physical collapse, and despair, and he fell heavily when he did fall. But each time he managed to rise up 'as it were, from the dead', over the years working his way through one crisis after another and, later, one medical practitioner after another in search of a solution to the drug addiction he became increasingly willing to confess.

No doubt, when it came, this increasing willingness to confess – by 1814 arguably a proneness to confess – also contributed to his ultimate survival. We should never discount the therapeutic function of the many confessional acts performed by Coleridge over the dark years from 1810 to 1816, when able at last to acknowledge the extent and strength of his opium abuse. The open parade of his habit and his guilt before objective medical professionals, in the first instance, had a profoundly liberating effect on him. Here, in his doctors, were strong men of the kind Coleridge envied and idolized, scientific men with whom he could share his fascination with things mental and physical, all the while objectifying and distancing his illness and extending his private mythology of larger-than-life characters and improbable incidents for his friends. Then, from 1814, one after another of these friends would become his more or less willing audience, as Coleridge warmed to the task of explaining what manner of man he was: 'The Mariner hath his will'.

Not only was Coleridge able to function socially for much of the time, he was also remarkably productive for a man on the brink. He began a second spate of journalistic and 'auxiliary' editorial work for editor T. G. Street on *The Courier* from May to September 1811, writing over ninety articles before being laid low by a crisis at Hammersmith and an opium-induced collapse. Street sacked him in October when he failed to produce a long-promised series of character studies of leading statesmen. But still, only one month later, Coleridge was back on his feet and delivering his second series of literary lectures, this time for the London Philosophical Society at Scot's Corporation Room in Fleet Street. These are the best chronicled and documented of all his literary lectures, Coleridge by now claiming a number of accomplished shorthand newspaper men among his acquaintance. Henry Crabb Robinson and John Payne Collier both wrote for *The Times*, as had the latter's father, John Dyer Collier, before switching to *The Morning Chronicle*. (Morgan engaged John Payne Collier, Crabb Robinson engaged a J. Tomalin, to take notes for publication or posterity.) Because of the running coverage Coleridge received in the press, because of the reputation he had acquired from his Royal Institution lectures in 1808, and because he took the trouble to promote the series, these lectures were well attended, better attended than Coleridge himself seems to have realized (*CL* III, 343). Between then and 1814, moreover, he repeated the performance on six occasions: at Willis's Rooms and the Surrey Institution in London, then, later, in Bristol and Clifton. On every occasion there were problems and compromises – whole lectures lost to inexplicable and unjustified digression or cancelled through illness; a culpable reliance on the criticism of A. W. Schlegel that had come his way – but still, in the next lecture, the next week, the next series, Coleridge would rise again.[8] 'The man is absolutely incorrigible', Crabb Robinson decided after a lecture on *Romeo and Juliet* dissolved into a defence of corporal punishment, 'without pretending to find the least connection between that topic and poetry'. 'But', he was forced to conclude, 'his *vitia* [vices] are, indeed, *splendida*'.[9]

In 1812, he made a last trip to the Lake District (driving steadfastly through Grasmere and past the Wordsworths' without stopping) in order to recover unbound copies of *The Friend* for a London reissue. With Southey, he published anonymously a collection of notes and observations the two had had in hand since 1806, entitled *Omniana* – an important and not often enough remarked concession to the fact that his genius lay in brief and illuminating commentary, not in systematic research and the patient unfolding of an ambitious dissertation. The vast majority and vastly more tedious entries are Southey's, and Southey had been hounding him for some time to expedite the volume. *The Friend* of 1812 and most of the *Omniana* may have been old material but Coleridge did not stop disseminating his ideas and seeking some financial return on his intellectual efforts.

This he would gain in abundance with his revised version of the play he had read to William and Dorothy Wordsworth at Racedown at the beginning of their intimacy in 1797. *Osorio* had since become, more abstractly, *Remorse*, and the same Theatre Royal (known as Drury Lane) that had rejected the play in 1797 was suddenly 'confident of its success'.[10] It was not the same theatre, as it happens, because Drury Lane had burnt down in 1809. The same company, but with a different committee and in a new building, Drury Lane was opening for its first season since the conflagration.

As the undergraduate Coleridge's phantom flights to London to catch Mrs Siddons suggest, and as the wealth of theatrical commentary and criticism and of journalistic reference confirms, London had a thriving theatrical culture throughout the period. Theatre, however, is often omitted from accounts of the literary life of the Romantic period, for a variety of reasons. Outside straightforward reviewing, dramatic criticism has always been uncertain as to how best to deal with production and performance, but there were other factors bearing on its neglect by literary historians. For a start, there was the multimedia nature of most contemporary productions – plays were one part of a programme of entertainments[11] – and the huge size of the theatres and the correspondingly large scale of their productions (in which ships might be floated across the stage) tended, like Hollywood today, to emphasize spectacle at the expense of language. In his *Memoirs* of 1806, the dramatist Richard Cumberland was indignant:

> Since the stage of Drury Lane and Covent Garden have been so enlarged in their dimensions as to be henceforward theatres for spectators rather than playhouses for hearers, it is hardly to be wondered at if their managers and directors encourage those representations, to which their structure is best adapted. The splendour of the scenes, the ingenuity of the machinist and the rich display of dresses, aided by the captivating charms of music, now in a great degree supersede the labours of the poet.[12]

Add to this the discouraging effects of Shakespeare idolatry, the vogue of 'closet dramas' (like those of Joanna Baillie) written to be read rather than performed, and the paucity and limited theatricality of dramatic writings by major authors – and it is perhaps hardly surprising that Romantic literary history has neglected the stage.

Only the two 'patent' or major theatres mentioned by Cumberland existed, both claiming from the monarch an inherited right to perform spoken drama in order to fend off the challenge of the London minor theatres. The government, moreover, kept a close eye on their offerings, requiring scripts to be cleared by the Lord Chamberlain before they were allowed performance. In recognition of the power of the theatre to enact and communicate anxieties or even openly encourage subversion, plays considered to pander to topical controversy or resentments were simply refused.

Verse drama other than Shakespeare and a handful of well-tried favourites (Rowe, Otway, Dryden, Congreve, Addison) were a huge gamble, and those comparatively few contemporary plays that *were* staged rarely remained in performance more than ten consecutive nights. In Coleridge's pseudo-Shakespearean blank verse Gothic tragedy –

> ALVAR   The Past lives o'er again
> In its effects, and to the guilty spirit
> The ever-frowning Present is its image.
> (*Remorse*, I, 274–6)

– two brothers Don Ordonio and Don Alvar vie for the love of one woman, Donna Teresa. The evil Ordonio – 'His proud forbidding eye, and his dark brow' (I, 81) – attempts to have Alvar murdered and to seduce Teresa until Alvar, very much alive, returns in disguise to manipulate a satisfactory resolution. (In the original, Ordonio/Osorio is remorsefully imprisoned; in *Remorse*, Coleridge reluctantly agreed to his being stabbed on stage by a Moorish heroine of her people, Alhadra.) As Coleridge's revised title suggests, his real interest originally lay in the psychological ramifications of transgression and guilt, part of his and Wordsworth's – indeed, if we may judge by its centrality to the Gothic mode, part of the period's – obsession at the time, as *The Rime of the Ancient Mariner* attests:

> ORDONIO   remorse! remorse!
> Where got'st thou that fool's word? Curse on remorse!
> Can it give up the dead, or recompact
> A mangled body? mangled – dashed to atoms!
> Not all the blessings of a host of angels
> Can blow away a desolate widow's curse!
> And though thou spill thy heart's blood for atonement,
> It will not weigh against an orphan's tear!
> (*Remorse*, V, 170–7)

Crabb Robinson thought that Coleridge indulged 'in those metaphysical and philosophical speculations becoming only in solitude and with select minds', as if Coleridge had transposed his notebooks onto the stage.[13] And certainly the play has its moments of elaborate indirection:

> ALVAR   Yon insect on the wall,
> Which moves this way and that its hundred limbs,

Were it a toy of mere mechanic craft,
It were an infinitely curious thing!
But it has life, Ordonio! life, enjoyment!
And by the power of its miraculous will
Wields all the complex movements of its frame
Unerringly to pleasurable ends!
Saw I this insect on this goblet's brim
I would remove it with an anxious pity!

ORDONIO What meanst thou?

ALVAR   There's poison in the wine.

In spite of the necessary verbosity of verse drama, however, and in spite of the inwardness and agonizing of the two brothers – and here, of course, especially for Coleridge, Hamlet was a seductive, if dangerous model – there were ample opportunities for theatricality on a large scale that were exploited by the managers. The conjuring scene in the middle of the play, for example, became a set piece in which the theatre's 'machinist' indulged in some spectacular special effects.

Like many writers, Coleridge became fascinated with the theatrical transformation of his own words, relying on Drury Lane's superior stage sense and making all the modifications required of him. (The success in the theatre of the death scene he had abominated surprised and gratified him [CL III, 428].) He threw his energies into the production even while delivering his lectures at the Surrey Institution. When it opened, on 23 January 1813, it opened to boisterous acclaim that spilled over into his lectures (where he was applauded on entrance) – acclaim that none of his other works had ever received. 'In terms of profit and public recognition', writes J. R. de J. Jackson, 'it was Coleridge's most successful literary enterprise'.[14] The reviewers, on the other hand, were harder to please, but still Coleridge had the privilege of watching the play run for 20 nights and earn him an astonishing £300, after which the published script went into what for him was an unprecedented third edition:

the Remorse has succeeded in spite of bad Scenes, execrable Acting, & Newspaper Calumny. ... I shall get more than all my literary Labors put together, nay, thrice as much, subtracting my heavy Losses in the Watchman & the Friend—400£: including the Copy-right. (CL III, 436, 437)

All this helped to allay Coleridge's renewed fears for his and his family's future since Josiah Wedgwood had written on 9 November 1812 withdrawing his half of the £150 Wedgwood annuity that Coleridge had been paying to his wife. Just as the more sanguine amongst his friends started to imagine that Coleridge had turned a corner in his career, however, Morgan's fortunes collapsed and the exertion involved in touring Bristol lecturing and borrowing on the Morgans' behalf, coupled with the inevitable return of heavy opium consumption, crushed Coleridge as quickly and effectively as the success of his play had seemed to revive him. That was in December 1813. It was more than a year before he was able to begin the process of recomposition that became the *Biographia Literaria*.

Coleridge's apostasy and obscurity

The reissue of *The Friend*, the confidence Coleridge felt in organizing one series of lectures after another, the spread of his success with *Remorse* into the lecture theatre – all suggest that Coleridge's reputation was growing. And so it was, but not always in ways that Coleridge welcomed. Largely against the will of one determined to stay out of – or, as Coleridge would have it, stay above – the petty cavillings of personality and politics, he found himself heavily implicated in the culture wars of the period, cited and ridiculed by the radicals and liberals of the next generation for his political apostasy and conservative apologetics. On 25 November 1810, Leigh Hunt's *Examiner* had announced Coleridge's intention to write again for *The Courier* on behalf of the government in a notice that had neatly drawn up the battle lines:

> Mr. Coleridge, once a republican and a follower of Tom Paine, is now a courtier and a follower of Spencer Parcival [*sic*]. Not succeeding in persuading the public to read the crampt and courtly metaphysics of his lately deceased paper the *Friend*, he now takes his revenge by writing against the popular judgment in the hireling daily prints. — But even here he is as harmless as ever; for what with the general distaste to such writings, and what with the difficulty getting at Mr. Coleridge's meaning, he obtains but very few readers.[15]

Coleridge had been, as we know, both more and less radical than the term 'republican' suggested, and was only occasionally a follower of Paine's deist, 'unalienable Rights' radicalism.[16] The *Examiner*'s cartoon sketch of the 'crampt and courtly metaphysics' of *The Friend* is apposite, however, identifying as it does an ideological dimension to Coleridge's obscurity, which would fast become proverbial: 'I wish he would explain his Explanation' (Byron).[17] From *The Friend* on, and especially after the defeat of Napoleon in 1815 with Britain more and more divided on vital issues of reform, Coleridge would feature as 'a political reactionary who knows he has a vested interest in not being understood', to quote Marilyn Butler.[18]

Apposite, too, therefore, was *The Examiner*'s remarking the dramatic change that Coleridge's allegiances had undergone since the 1790s, in spite of his disingenuous attempts to mask it. The assassination of Prime Minister Spencer Perceval in May 1812 seemed to operate as an accelerant to his growing conservatism. Coleridge indulged in righteous horror at what he saw as 'the atrocious sentiments universal among the Populace' in response to Perceval's murder – at their appearing cruelly to welcome it as an opportunity for introducing reforms postponed by the war – and he used the occasion as proof of suspicions he had harboured from the beginning of the darkly corrupt and ill-educated sensibilities of the mass of the population. Suddenly, writing to Southey, he is reminded of

> that theme which no one I meet seems to feel as they ought to do—and of which I find scarcely any, but ourselves, that estimate according to it's true gigantic magnitude—I mean the sinking down of Jacobinism below the middle & tolerably educated Classes into the Readers & all-swallowing Auditors in Tap-rooms &c, of the Statesman, Examiner, Cobbet, &c. (CL III, 410)

Coleridge had always, even in the Bristol days, deferred with Burke to the *necessarily* irrational element in all our social and political arrangements, but now he could be blatantly unreasonable, allowing the acrimony and paranoia that affected his personal relations to infect his political thinking. 'Great changes of opinion upon such subjects, are apt to be *violent* also', wrote his old friend John Thelwall, reviewing Coleridge's career in December 1818, 'and violence is, in our estimation, but an indifferent proof of their deep-felt and conscientious sincerity'.[19]

Biographia Literaria

Far from damping or deflecting the growing critical opposition Coleridge faced in the liberal and radical press, the *Biographia Literaria* served only to confirm and encourage it. His major confrontation with the educated reading public of his day, Coleridge used it to set the record straight, as he saw it: to express his frustration at his own and Wordsworth's treatment at the hands of their contemporaries, to dispel what we would call the 'urban myth' of a school to which he and Southey and Wordsworth belonged, and in the process to project into a public sphere that had been giving him so much grief the romanticized image of himself nurtured in his notebooks and letters. Since *The Friend*, Coleridge had been facing an attack on not one, but two fronts. Criticized, on the one hand, for his growing political and cultural conservatism, he was also still being ridiculed for his association with the radical experimentation of Wordsworth's *Lyrical Ballads* and their Preface. 'Abuse me they must', he complained to Southey after *The Times* reviewed his *Remorse* unfavourably:

> the old infamous Crambe bis millies cocta [heated up leftovers] of the 'sentimentalities, puerilities, whinings, meannesses (both of style & thought)'

in my former Writings—but without (which is worth notice both in these Gentlemen, & in all our former Zoili [critics]), without one single Quotation or Reference in proof or exemplification ... they might (as at the first appearance of my Poems they did) find indeed all the opposite vices; but if it had not been for *the Preface* to W's Lyrical Ballads would themselves have never dreamt of affected Simplicity & Meanness of Thought & Diction—. This Slang has gone on for 14 or 15 years, against us—& really deserves to be exposed. (*CL* III, 433)

Accordingly, Coleridge's stated concern at the opening of the *Biographia* is to vindicate or 'exculpate' himself in the face of an unjust campaign of persecution in the periodical press. He is quick to qualify, however, and to insist on what he calls 'additional purposes': 'the statement of my principles in Politics, Religion, and Philosophy, and the application of rules, deduced from philosophical principles, to poetry and criticism' (*BL* I, 5). But if Coleridge had 'additional purposes' he also had an ulterior motive, one that, for all the difficulty of his occasional prose, was clearly apparent to many of his contemporaries.

The *Biographia* is, as I suggested in my Prologue, a complex, uneven, often contradictory document. After the first four chapters a fragmentation of interests occurs, with the biography, the philosophy, and the literary criticism going their separate ways. It is even arguable that it is only in the first chapter that we find that perfect blending or reconciliation of interests that makes Coleridge's decision to write his 'metaphysical works, as *my Life*, & *in* my Life' a brilliant and innovatory one (N237). Here the various and casual details are engaging in their own right and at the same time subservient to Coleridge's main arguments about poetic language and poetic genius; here the technique of the *Biographia* most resembles that of the Conversation Poems.

It is, however, ill-sustained. In the second chapter, Coleridge's personal grievances threaten the delicate balance of biography and criticism and in the third, the chapter on Southey, Coleridge is repaying old debts and the tone of his defence is correspondingly flat and perfunctory. Southey patently did not interest Coleridge enough, either as a man or as a poet, for his case to have become culturally or critically significant. It is only in the fourth chapter, and then only momentarily, that Coleridge regains a profound interpenetration of the personal and the impersonal. After that follow the controversial chapters on (and of) metaphysics, disrupted by extensive biographical digressions – variously interpreted as a ruse to minimize the extent of his plagiarisms and, more simply, as 'cold feet'[20] – before being quixotically terminated in chapter 13. Even the comparatively homogeneous final chapters on the theory and practice of Wordsworth have to survive footnotes and digressions, outbursts of indignation and warning and apology, and the sudden interpolation of a cherished theory or opinion. Finally, the whole book has to survive makeweight chapters on Coleridge's visit to Germany and on Charles Maturin's *Bertram* that Coleridge imported to meet the requirement of length.

The understandable abbreviations made by the *Biographia*'s various editors after the 1847 edition of his daughter, Sara, and son-in-law, Henry Nelson Coleridge, were made on the Coleridgean assumption that there exists an Idea – 'living, seminal, formative, and exempt from time' (*BL* I, 97n.) – by which the *Biographia* is organized from within; that we have only to prune certain 'inorganic' or unworthy parts and this organization and its 'indwelling' Idea or principle will be revealed. And over time various critical commentators have followed them in this search for 'unity' or 'integrity' within the miscellaneous.[21] There is no organic or occult unity in the *Biographia*, as it happens – other than as what Jerome Christensen calls 'a floating object of desire'[22] – but Coleridge's biographical sketches of his literary life and opinions can be shown to have an argumentative coherence when read as a discontinuous, annotated allegory on the literary marketplace and culture of early nineteenth-century Britain. For it is with literary culture *as* a marketplace that the *Biographia* is preoccupied – with the new, more democratic literary or print culture enabled and encouraged by new technologies and evolving under the stimulus of market forces.

On genius

The surest sign of the inadequacy of this new culture had been its failure to recognize and celebrate the 'FIRST GENUINE PHILOSOPHIC' poet, William Wordsworth, and the first genuine philosopher-critic, Samuel Taylor Coleridge (*BL* II, 156). Against the conspiracy he apprehended between the new reading public created by an unconstrained free enterprise and the periodical reviews that serviced this new public, Coleridge defends the claims of 'genius':

THE VISION AND THE FACULTY DIVINE (*BL* II, 260; I, 241)[23]

The *Biographia*, before anything else, is a sustained attempt to establish the priority and authority of Wordsworth's and of his own genius, and in doing so to secure from the reader a humility or deference which presumes itself ignorant of the author's understanding unless or until the author's ignorance is understood (*BL* I, 232–3). Which is why Coleridge is content to retain the metaphysical chapters he appears so whimsically to abandon. Their primary function is to convince the reader of the author's philosophical genius; in a gesture known to the High Renaissance as *sprezzatura*, to intimate rather than to elaborate the artist's powers. That way, Coleridge could have his metaphysical cake and eat it too, impressing readers with his intellectual credentials without being obliged to argue his case. (Responsibility for expounding the onto-theological principles necessary to guarantee and regulate his critical practice is shifted onto his unfinished *Logosophia* [*BL* I, 304, 136, 161, 263].)

As its title suggests, however, Coleridge's *Biographia Literaria* is a defence of literary life generally, not just of the author's own literary life – which explains the change from 'Autobiographia literaria' used prior to publication in a letter to his friend and medical advisor, Dr Robert Brabant (*CL* IV, 578). The note of desperation that we hear so frequently throughout the discussion of contemporary culture in the *Biographia* results from the fact that, according to Coleridge, literary life in his sense – the disinterested pursuit of perfection – urgently *needed* defending. He believed it was being undermined by the very institutions which should have been encouraging and ennobling it (the reviewers, that is, and their reading public).

This preoccupation, not to say obsession, of Coleridge's with the threat posed to high-minded literary endeavour by a developing print culture is manifest in many of what seem to be random, even anomalous details or digressions in the text. Coleridge's apparently random confrontation with 'a rigid Calvinist, a tallow chandler by trade' in the tenth chapter (*BL* I, 180–2) is a case in point. Coleridge is recounting his experience as a young ideologue touting his periodical *The Watchman* on a pilgrim's progress around the Midlands and trying for all he is worth to convince the sceptical (as his epigram from John's Gospel declares) 'That All may know the TRUTH; And the TRUTH may make us FREE'. The processing of tallow or animal fat for candle and soap making was a foul smelling trade and Coleridge recalls suffering down wind throughout what must have seemed an interminable sales pitch, only to be told that the 32 pages of each eight-day issue were 'more than I ever reads, Sir! all the year round' (*BL* I, 182). The episode is allegorical, at once a parody and a paradigm in a whole series of significant confrontations that take place in the *Biographia* between genius on the one hand – 'the noble living and the noble dead'[24] – and an uncomprehending (mis)reading public on the other. 'Fit audience find, though few', as Milton expressed it in *Paradise Lost* (VII, 31) in a phrase that would become a leitmotif in the work of both Coleridge and Wordsworth (*BL* II, 147).

The tallow chandler's failure to understand the prophet Coleridge recalls the vision of Milton in his blindness and old age in the second chapter – unacknowledged; misunderstood; unrewarded (*BL* I, 36–7). It prefigures the hypothetical confrontation between Coleridge the metaphysician and his puzzled and resistant readers in the letter from the fictional 'friend' used to arrest the philosophical dissertation (*BL* I, 300–4). It also prefigures the ideological impasse between Coleridge and the philistine French officers over Michaelangelo's statue of Moses – for Coleridge a composite symbol of high Renaissance culture, for the French officers a smutty diversion – the analogy elaborated in the twenty first chapter to stigmatize the imaginative poverty of *Edinburgh Review* editor Francis Jeffrey's influential criticism of Wordsworth's poetry (*BL* II, 116–18).

Coleridge's last word on Wordsworth

That Coleridge should centre his argument about the inadequacy of prevailing cultural arrangements on the misunderstood poetic genius of Wordsworth makes the *Biographia* his last and his major tribute to his lapsed friend. From the beginning of his literary lecturing, Coleridge had been promising to use the poetry of Wordsworth as exemplary in a public forum, and in 1808 Dorothy Wordsworth was expressing hope that this would be the vital promotion that her brother's work needed.[25] The promised lectures on the modern poets – then and later – never eventuated, let alone the lecture devoted exclusively to Wordsworth that Coleridge seemed to intimate. Now was his chance to clear his conscience and establish once and for all what he had been protesting in the privacy of his letters and notebooks: that his contribution to their friendship had always been self-effacing. Looking first at Wordsworth's imaginative powers, then at his poetry, Coleridge's tribute to Wordsworth in the first instance is the tribute of sustained critical attention, of a kind that he had never lavished on any writer before, other than Shakespeare – and even then, arguably, never as systematically.

'The least of what I have written concerns myself personally', Coleridge assures the reader in the opening paragraph, and insofar as Wordsworth's poetry and ideas occupy the bulk of the second volume this is confirmed by our reading. It was not all flattery, however, and if the sheer *extent* of the attention helped to secure Wordsworth's reputation it was also true that the reputation it helped to secure was for the poetry that Coleridge privileged. The fact that Wordsworth himself could not see past Coleridge's criticism of his Preface to *Lyrical Ballads* and of the 'matter-of-factness' of his poetry has always seemed ungrateful, but Coleridge in the *Biographia* showed no more sympathy for Wordsworth's 'experiments' than Wordsworth had shown for his 17 years earlier.[26]

It has to do with the way Coleridge positions his own argument in relation to that of Francis Jeffrey and the reviewers, against whose attacks he defends Wordsworth. The Preface had become the basis of contemporary opposition to Wordsworth and was dictating the reviewers' choices of 'typical' Wordsworth passages, directing their attention to the worst, most prosaic poetry: 'drivelling', 'childish', 'namby-pamby'.[27] In order to separate himself from the myth of a Lake school of poets – a school characterized by 'sentimentalities, puerilities, whinings, meannesses (both of style & thought)', as Coleridge reminded Southey – Coleridge's strategy was not to defend the boldness of Wordsworth's challenge to contemporary taste, but to concur with the reviewers' rejection of his 'affected Simplicity & Meanness of Thought & Diction' (*CL* III, 433). What this necessitated was a systematic refutation of the controversial claims of the Preface and a systematic renunciation of the 'daring Humbleness' that horrified many of Wordsworth's other contemporaries (*CL* II, 830). Coleridge also shared Jeffrey's conditioned distaste for the 'unworthy objects' and characters of Wordsworth's poetry, and chose willfully to ignore the revolution in subject matter effected by Wordsworth – a revolution comparable, and directly related, to the revolution in poetic language. In doing so, Coleridge refused the basic challenge to feel, without 'gross and violent stimulants',[28] that the Wordsworthian sensibility offered – and continues to offer – to the reader; the lesson 'that *everything* can be poetic, if it is *perceived* poetically, *felt* poetically'.[29]

Jeffrey and Coleridge on Wordsworth

At his most conservative, the *Edinburgh* reviewer Jeffrey had treated Wordsworth and the Lake poets as vulgar revolutionaries, 'furnishing themselves from vulgar ballads and plebeian nurseries' – which was exactly what Wordsworth had had in mind.[30] The observation, though acrimonious, was not unjustified. Their appeal to the 'middling and lower orders' had struck Jeffrey not only as subversive, but also as absurd, especially in an author 'who has had occasion to indite odes to his college bell, and inscribe hymns to the Penates'. The arts 'do not take their models from what is ordinary', he protested, 'but from what is excellent'.[31] To overlook a refined and liberal education and seek excellence in 'a different and a scantier *gradus ad Parnassum*' is to turn one's back upon the achievements of civilization.[32]

It was not so much to the art that Wordsworth did use that Jeffrey objected, however, as to the art he did not use. '*Their* simplicity', Jeffrey complained of the Lake poets,

> does not consist, by any means, in the rejection of glaring or superfluous ornament, — in the substitution of elegance to splendour, or in that refinement of art which seeks concealment in its own perfection. It consists, on the contrary, in a very great degree, in the positive and *bona fide* rejection of art altogether.[33]

Again it was acrimonious, but Jeffrey was one of the few contemporary critics to appreciate the seriousness of Wordsworth's revolt against language and literature. (Later, in the *Spirit of the Age* [1825], Hazlitt would confirm this revolt in a spectacular fashion.[34]) The problem with the Preface for Jeffrey was its failure to recognize that all human languages were artificial, relying on convention for their meaning; that the choice was not between meretricious art and noble nature, but between different kinds (classes) of art. The reviewer of *Poems in Two Volumes* in *The Satirist* summarized most cogently and comprehensively the case against Wordsworth on behalf of the majority of reviewers:

> Of this grand system of poetry, which was thus first discovered by Mr. William Wordsworth, about the year of our Lord 1800, and was of course altogether unknown to Homer, Virgil, Shakespeare, Milton, and Dryden, the grand principle was, that nature could only be represented with fidelity by a close imitation of the language, and a constant adoption of the phrases, made use of by persons in the lowest stages of life: as if language were not entirely factitious and arbitrary; as if men in all ranks

and situations were not the creatures of habit; as if the expressions of the meanest individuals were not the result of the education which they receive, while those of the higher orders are rendered natural by long usage to the well-informed and accomplished part of mankind.[35]

Not 'natural', note, but 'rendered natural to' (second nature).

But Jeffrey and the early critics of the Preface were not the only ones ultimately provoked to 'direct hostility' by the calculated affront of the Preface to what passed as poetry and good sense – and, by implication, to what passed as reality.[36] The point at which the theory of language in the Preface became revolutionary was, as we saw, the point at which Coleridge, too, by 1802 at the latest, had separated himself from the Preface.[37] When in the *Biographia* Coleridge advocates a 'natural language, neither bookish, nor vulgar', he echoes a typical Augustan compromise (*BL* I, 22).[38] Good sense, it seems, dictated the language of Chaucer, Gower, Herbert, and, surprisingly, 'elegant and unaffected women'. Herbert he calls an '*exquisite* master of this species of style, where the scholar and the poet supplies the material, but the perfect well-bred gentleman the expressions and the arrangement' (*BL* II, 92, 93). The contempt for Adam Smith's dictum that it is a poet's duty to write like a gentleman is a long way in the past.[39] With this entirely different ideal of linguistic purity in mind, Coleridge criticizes Wordsworth for having confused a *lingua communis*, plain and unpretentious, with the language of the rustic:

> the poet, who uses an illogical diction, or a style fitted to excite only the low and changeable pleasure of wonder by means of groundless novelty, substitutes a language of *folly* and *vanity*, not for that of the *rustic*, but for that of *good sense* and *natural feeling*. (*BL* II, 55)

By 1815 and the composition of the *Biographia*, Coleridge was emphasizing the classical virtues of perspicuity and propriety in the idea of a simple language,[40] where the Preface had emphasized transparency and transcendence.

Coleridge had always been sceptical about what Wordsworth in *The Excursion* called 'the poetry of common speech'.[41] A whimsical note in an early letter captures his attitude to the democratization of poetic ability: 'all men are poets in their way, tho' for the most part their ways are *damned bad ones*' (*CL* II, 768). In the *Biographia* itself, determined to establish that most poets are damned bad poets and most readers damned bad readers, Coleridge pursues a perversely literal-minded examination of rustic language to the point where, in exposing its absurdity as a poetic language, he becomes himself slightly absurd, and very patronizing:

> Let the management of the POOR LAWS in Liverpool, Manchester, or Bristol be compared with the ordinary dispensation of the poor rates in

agricultural villages, where the *farmers* are the overseers and guardians of the poor. If my own experience have not been particularly unfortunate, as well as that of the many respectable country clergymen with whom I have conversed on the subject, the result would engender more than scepticism concerning the desireable influences of low and rustic life in and for itself. (*BL* II, 45)

In all the depreciating analyses of 'low and rustic life' in the *Biographia*, it becomes apparent that Coleridge's scepticism is directed, not just towards rustic sensibility and understanding, but towards nature's formative powers as well. Five years after his leaving the Lake District and breaking up with Wordsworth, Coleridge is expressing his resentment over their rupture by systematically denying values that Wordsworth had held dear – continued to hold dear. Instead of seeing nature as being conducive to rectitude, it is now a rectitude developed in the classroom that is seen as conducive to the influence of nature. Nature preaches only to the converted. In the late 1790s, when he was addressing Hartley in 'Frost at Midnight', Coleridge had been content to 'Let Nature be your Teacher', according to the axiom of Wordsworth's 'The Tables Turned' (l. 16). By the time of the *Biographia*, he was insisting on a more traditional pedagogy, deferring throughout to various clergymen and teachers. It is part of Coleridge's message to a post-Waterloo Britain and all his arguments point to the need for the guiding and educating class he would later call a 'clerisy'.[42]

Coleridge in the *Biographia* continually sides with the *status quo* – 'that state of association, which actually exists as *general*', as he calls it (*BL* II, 130) – against the radical tenets of the Preface. While he denies a monopoly on 'the best part of language' to rustics and other inferior social classes, however, Coleridge is not, like Jeffrey and the Augustans, interested in transferring it to another social class. As he wrote in an early letter to Tom Poole, 'There are favoured *Individuals*, but not *Classes*' (*CL* I, 480). This characteristically Romantic notion informs Coleridge's revised theory of poetic language in the *Biographia*, distinguishing it both from the theory of the Preface and from the assumptions of Jeffrey and the reviewers. 'Education, or original sensibility, or both, must pre-exist' to render an individual susceptible to the influence of nature (*BL* I, 45). Education may account for the 'refinement' necessary to raise the mind above vulgarity and degradation, but it could not account for the language of genius.

Accordingly, the best part of language for Coleridge is not the language of low and rustic life – or 'of conversation in the middle and lower classes of society',[43] or of real life, or of prose – chosen because each was the closest thing to nature that Wordsworth could think of. On the contrary, the best part of language is formed by the 'voluntary appropriation of fixed symbols to internal acts, to processes and results of imagination' (*BL* II, 54). For the Preface, the poet is 'a man speaking to men', for Coleridge he is emphatically a *poet* speaking to men, distinguished not merely by a greater sensitivity to nature, but also by the characteristic operation of his mind on that nature. After all, 'What is poetry? is so nearly the same question with, what is a poet? that the answer to one is involved in the solution of the other' (*BL* II, 15). When Wordsworth made the mistake of wanting the question of what poetry is to be nearly the same as the question of what nature is, he failed to account for this operation, and for what was to become for both him and Coleridge the most noble of all the mind's faculties, the imagination:

> The poet, described in *ideal* perfection, brings the whole soul of man into activity, with the subordination of the faculties to each other, according to their relative worth and dignity. He diffuses a tone, and spirit of unity, that blends, and (as it were) fuses, each into each, by that synthetic and magical power, to which we have exclusively appropriated the name of imagination. This power, first put into motion by the will and understanding, and retained under their irremissive, though gentle and unnoticed, controul (*laxis effertur habenis* ['carried on with slackened reins']) reveals itself in the balance and reconciliation of opposite and discordant qualities: of sameness, with difference; of the general, with the concrete; the idea, with the image; the individual, with the representative; the sense of novelty and freshness, with old and familiar objects; an more than usual state of emotion, with more than usual order; judgement ever awake and steady self-possession, with enthusiasm and feeling profound or vehement; and while it blends and harmonizes the natural with the artificial, still subordinates art to nature; the manner to the matter; and our admiration of the poet to our sympathy with the poetry. (*BL* II, 15–17)

This *wonderful* passage, in the Coleridgean sense, represents the culmination of years of intensive thinking about the nature of poetry in the wake of the mental crisis that seemed to depress, if not entirely destroy his own poetic talent around the turn of the century. Into it, Coleridge typically channelled all the poetry of which he was still capable.

With this exalted faculty in mind, Coleridge directs the attention of the reviewers away from the poetry of Wordsworth's that, after Jeffrey, he sees as *merely* simple, and towards the 'impassioned, lofty, and sustained diction, which is characteristic of his genius' (*BL* II, 8) – towards, that is, the great blank verse of the years 1798 to 1805 (most of which, incidentally, had yet to be published). Of the five criticisms levelled at Wordsworth in chapter 22 of the *Biographia*, all but one are variations of bathos expanded from misgivings Coleridge expressed to Southey in his letter of 1802 in which he remarked 'here & there a daring Humbleness of Language & Versification' in Wordsworth's poetry (*CL* II, 830).[44] Occasional notes in the *Diaries* of Henry Crabb Robinson suggest that this disenchantment of Coleridge's became a regular element of his discussions of Wordsworth.[45]

Jeffrey had rightly seen the Preface as 'a kind of manifesto', and felt that Wordsworth's poetry was 'written avowedly for the purpose of exalting a system'.[46] The vast majority of Wordsworth's reviewers shared Jeffrey's belief.[47] When Wordsworth, on the other hand, 'is led to abandon his system', Jeffrey argued, 'he does always write good verses'.[48] So Coleridge in the *Biographia* contrasts the prosaic or trivial lines written 'because the poet *would* so write' with the more figurative or dignified verse written 'because he could not so entirely repress the force and grandeur of his mind' (*BL* I, 120). The motivation for Coleridge's refutation of the Preface thus lies as much in his conviction that its theory corrupted Wordsworth's poetry as it lies in Coleridge's middle-aged social and political beliefs. Wordsworth was being distracted by his own theory and by carping reviewers – both – from his true task of composing 'the FIRST GENUINE PHILOSOPHIC POEM' (*BL* I, 156). The carping reviewers, in their turn, were as blind to Wordsworth's genius as Napoleon's army officers to the genius of Michaelangelo (*BL* II, 118).

Defending literary life

Like so many major documents of literary theory – Aristotle's anti-Platonic *Poetics*, for example, Sir Phillip Sidney's anti-Puritan *Apology for Poetry*, and Percy Bysshe Shelley's anti-materialist *Defence of Poetry* – the *Biographia* was responding to what it saw as a direct attack upon poetry. Like these and other testaments, it can be read as a local and immediate 'apology' that at the same time aspires to a transhistorical or transcendental affirmation. While thus endeavouring to define poetry for all times and all places, however, it never fully extricates itself from the historical conditions which nurtured and motivated it, nor ever loses sight of the specific cultural corruptions against which it defines itself. 'All our notions', as Coleridge himself observed, are 'husked in the phantasms of Place & Time, that still escape the finest sieve & most searching Winnow of our Reason & Abstraction' (*CN* I, 334).

In terms familiar from dark satire like Alexander Pope's *The Dunciad*, the *Biographia* envisages the works of Shakespeare and Milton and Wordsworth overwhelmed by an incalculable number of sentimental and sensational poems and novels and magazines in the indiscriminate expansion of the book trade. Coleridge takes up the burden of the *Critical Review* and the rest of the conservative press of the late eighteenth century in striking out against the '*manufactory*' of the novel, for example, instigated by a consumer culture in which 'the booksellers, those pimps of literature' pander to the voracious, undiscriminating appetites of a reading public 'not overly delicate in their choice of food' and storming the circulating libraries for 'everything that is new'.[49] This anxiety informs the simile Coleridge chooses to 'illustrate the present state of our language' – and, by extension, of our literature – in the second chapter of the *Biographia*:

a press-room of larger and smaller stereotype pieces, which, in the present anglo-gallican fashion of unconnected, epigrammatic periods, it requires but an ordinary portion of ingenuity to vary indefinitely, and yet still produce something, which, if *not* sense, will be so like it, as to do as well. Perhaps better: for it spares the reader the trouble of thinking; prevents vacancy, while it indulges indolence; and secures the memory from all dangers of intellectual plethora. Hence of all trades, literature at present demands the least talent or information. (*BL* I, 39)

On the market forces 'that tended to make the writer only a paid worker in the print factory' – to quote Alvin Kernan – 'and his work only a commodity',[50] Coleridge demonstrates a combination of characteristic insight and willful naivety, obliged as he is to play the double game of being experienced in and informed about this new economic world on the one hand, and yet at the same time indifferent, indeed openly hostile towards it. Coleridge shares his insight with most of his contemporaries. As we have seen, changes in the economic structure of authorship – the shift from literary patronage to the publishing marketplace – had been a common topic of cultural speculation from at least the middle of the eighteenth century.[51] The *Biographia* offers 'opinions' on authorial privacy and integrity, and on publicity, profit, and literary prostitution, that were fast becoming clichés.

Coleridge's naivety, on the other hand, is at once more congenial and more calculating. He projects himself in the *Biographia* as a literary Don Quixote, an idealist in both the colloquial and the philosophical sense and a relic from another, nobler world of chivalry, patronage, and the purest of motives – a golden world variously invoked in anecdote and quotation as a Burkean paradise before the advent of lawyers and 'sophisters, œconomists, and calculators'.[52] If the extent of his preoccupation with the culture of print in the *Biographia* is not always apparent, Coleridge's affected indifference to the business of writing is itself partly responsible. And there is certainly some truth in the Coleridgean persona of the quixotic idealist not made for this world. Coleridge's financial dealings could hardly be said to have been a resounding success, propped up as they invariably were by his friends. (It is interesting to read in William St Clair's recent study of Romantic publishing how badly Coleridge was shortchanged in negotiating terms for the *Biographia* itself, for example.[53]) Still, the naive, quixotic Coleridge remains no less tendentious a figure than the portrait of a benign James Boyer. It is the same with Coleridge's special pleading in the *Biographia* on behalf of creative genius – on behalf of the poet Wordsworth and of himself as a philosopher-critic. Coleridge, as I said, had a message for a conflicted nation.

All this special pleading, with its resistance to materialism and commercialism and utilitarianism, would prove enormously influential on subsequent cultural thinking in Britain and on Anglo-American literary scholarship, informing its defence of humane letters. It would also inform its individual and generic priorities, making Wordsworth and poetry central to Romantic humanist endeavour. Indeed, it is only comparatively recently that the mature Coleridge's Tory interpretation of Romanticism has been seriously challenged and we have been obliged to look more sceptically upon Coleridge's attempts to rescue creative literature from the marketplace and from the culture wars of his own period.[54] While its assumptions and conclusions have been challenged, however, no one has challenged its creative influence on the study of literature in the English language.

The years of infamy

The *Biographia* opened with Coleridge's puzzling over the source of his notoriety in the periodical press:

> It has been my lot to have had my name introduced both in conversation, and in print, more frequently than I find it easy to explain, whether I consider the fewness, unimportance, and limited circulation of my writings, or the retirement and distance, in which I have lived, both from the literary and political world. (*BL* I, 5)

When Coleridge had written this in 1815 he was being disingenuous and playing down the many claims he had made on the public's attention – keeping faith only with the private and retiring half of his split existence. We know that in the 1790s, for example, he had published poetry consistently in the high profile periodical press, as well as publishing numerous separate volumes: (with Southey) *The Fall of Robespierre* (1794); his *A Moral and Political Lecture* (1795), *The Plot Discovered* (1795), and *Conciones ad Populum* (1795), and his journal *The Watchman* (1796); *Poems on Various Subjects* (1796), *Sonnets from Various Authors* (1796), *Poems by S. T. Coleridge* (1797), and *Fears in Solitude* (1798). The *Lyrical Ballads* was admittedly published anonymously, but it was precisely because Coleridge was anxious about his reputation for radicalism that they chose to publish it that way (*CL* I, 412). Later, in 1800, came his translations of Schiller, then in 1803 another edition of his poetry. In 1809–10 he brought out *The Friend* (which, as we saw, brought him again to the attention of the public intellectuals), in 1811–12 he had a number of his public lectures further publicized by reprints in the major London newspapers, and in 1813 his *Remorse* was extensively reviewed, first as a performance, then as a publication. Nor, while protesting 'the retirement and distance, in which I have lived, both from the literary and political world', does Coleridge allude to the open secret of his contributions as a journalist to the leading dailies *The Morning Post* and *The Courier*.

It was true, on the other hand, that the circulation of his individual publications had been limited in comparison with writers like Walter Scott and,
more recently, Lord Byron, both of whom had been outselling all previous
poets. It was true that little had come out of the lost years between 1804 and
1808, when Coleridge started lecturing and conceived *The Friend*. It was also
true that after 1802 Coleridge's name had been most frequently introduced in
the press, not for anything he had actually written, but indiscriminately, as
one of a collective of 'Lake poets' (occasionally and ignominiously, merely as
a disciple of the now estranged Wordsworth). Still, whichever way we choose
to look at it, Coleridge was not quite the wallflower he tries to make out.

If his protest about how little he had brought to the attention of the public was disingenuous in 1815, however, by the time of the actual publication
of the *Biographia* in July of 1817 it must have seemed a bizarre claim to many
of his readers, friends and enemies alike. By that time, not only had his two
'lay sermons' to a troubled country been added to the list of his publications
but all the poems that would establish his reputation as a unique poet were
at last in print. In April 1815, Coleridge had written an embarrassingly florid
and self-abasing letter soliciting Byron's 'good Will, not unlike that with
which a Swan instinctively takes up the weakling Cygnet into the Hollow
between its wings' – soliciting his patronage, in effect. 'Anxiety', as Coleridge
went on to say, 'makes us all ceremonious' (*CL* IV, 560). In response, Byron
had encouraged Coleridge to publish *Christabel* (*CL* IV, 602–3n.) and written
to Tom Moore urging him to review Coleridge's collected poems favourably
in the *Edinburgh Review* whenever they should appear (which Moore, incidentally, did not do).[55] Then with characteristic largesse, Byron also sent
Coleridge £100 in February 1816. It was after that, just two weeks before
Byron left England for good in April 1816, that the two of them finally met
and Byron was treated to Coleridge's reciting 'Kubla Khan'. The result of all
the mutual flattery that passed between them and of Byron's exertions on
Coleridge's behalf was that *Christabel*, 'Kubla Khan', and 'The Pains of Sleep'
were published together in a single, 64-page volume by John Murray, one of
London's leading publishers (if only by virtue of his being Byron's publisher). The two 'lay sermons' – the first entitled *The Statesman's Manual; or,
The Bible the Best Guide to Political Skill and Foresight* (1816) and 'Addressed to
the Higher Classes of Society', the second entitled *A Lay Sermon Addressed to
the Higher and Middle Classes on the Existing Distresses and Discontents* (1817) –
came out in December 1816 and April 1817 respectively.

More to the point, however, by the time of the *Biographia*'s publication in
July 1817, all these works had received extended, high profile reviews in
places like Jeffrey's *Edinburgh Review* and Hunt's *Examiner* – and all had been
almost uniformly savaged. Ironically, then, at the time the *Biographia* was
being composed, its attack on periodicals was more accurate as a creative
prophecy with regard to his own imminent career than it was as a history
of his reputation before 1815, especially if one takes into account the

respectful reception of his poetry in the 1790s before the *Lyrical Ballads* provoked such a strong reaction. Indeed, the *Biographia* would itself provoke vicious reprisals – from Hazlitt in the *Edinburgh*, for example, and John Wilson ('Christopher North') in *Blackwood's Edinburgh Magazine* – and though Coleridge's two-volume 'collected poems', *Sibylline Leaves*,[56] published by Rest Fenner at the same time as the *Biographia*, fared better with the reviewers, the usual complaints about Coleridge's sentimentalities and obscurities and apostasy were paraded. 'It was Coleridge's misfortune', writes J. R. de J. Jackson in his Critical Heritage volume on Coleridge's reception, 'to present the bulk of his writing to the public at the very time that the cut and thrust of reviewing was at its height'.[57] It was his double misfortune to have made precisely that change in literary culture so central to his critique in *The Friend* and the *Biographia*. It would not be until around 1820 that Coleridge's reputation, as a poet at least, would finally take a turn for the better,[58] a turn confirmed by the reception of the 1828, 1829, and 1834 editions of his *Poetical Works*.

The last years

In one sense, the composition of the *Biographia* spelled the end of Coleridge's literary life, in another sense it marked its beginning. It depends entirely on what we mean by 'literary' and 'literature'. It was the beginning in the sense that the years from 1815 saw the run of publications we have been discussing, and the run would continue. 1818 would add an extensively revised and reorganized version of *The Friend*, another dramatic piece (rejected by Covent Garden and Drury Lane) *Zapyola: A Christmas Tale in Two Parts*, and his 'preliminary' *Treatise on Method*, introductory to the *Encyclopaedia Metropolitana* (which it was proposed he should edit and for which he attempted to evolve an elaborate taxonomy). Then, in 1825, came Coleridge's extended moral and meditative annotations to the sermons of Robert Leighton, full title: *Aids to Reflection in the Formation of a Manly Character, on the Several Grounds of Prudence, Morality, and Religion, illustrated by Select Passages from Our Elder Divines, Especially from Archbishop Leighton*. His other original publication before his death in 1834, aside from the publication of some political pamphlets and in 1825 of a lecture *On the Prometheus of Aeschylus* delivered to the Royal Society of Literature in fulfillment of the conditions of his receipt of a pension of 100 guineas p.a., was his 1829 vision of the Anglican establishment, *On the Constitution of the Church and State*.

In terms of 'creative' or 'imaginative' literature, however, though Coleridge continued to write poetry until his death, there is nothing to stand beside the lyrics he wrote in his twenties. The significant poetry published in the last 17 years of his life had all been written and published long before. Coleridge might add the marginal gloss to *The Rime of the Ancient Mariner* in

1817 and rework it for subsequent editions, but this was brilliant tinkering. So with his literary criticism after the *Biographia*. Aside from occasional insights that have entered the Coleridge canon – like the distinction between symbol and allegory in *The Statesman's Manual*[59] – Coleridge had said his piece. The truth is that he became far more interested in religious symbolism than in literary symbolism. Central though religion and spirituality had always been to his thinking, he began to focus his mind more and more exclusively on religious issues. The major work that he promised himself and his public – the consummation of all his intellectual efforts, he tells us, his *Logosophia* or *Opus Maximum* – was also known for a while (and perhaps most appropriately) as the 'Assertion of Religion':

> the whole Scheme of the Christian Faith, including *all* the Articles of Belief common to the Greek and Latin, the Roman and the Protestant Church, with the threefold proof, that it is *ideally*, *morally*, and *historically* true, will be found exhibited and vindicated in a proportionally larger Work, the principal Labour of my Life since Manhood, and which I am now preparing for the Press under the title, Assertion of Religion, as necessarily *involving* Revelation; and of Christianity, as the only Revelation of permanent and universal validity.[60]

This is not to suggest that Coleridge renounced literature or literary issues, for he remained actively engaged with them in conversations and notes and marginalia that mushroomed during these final years. The one meeting between Coleridge and the poet John Keats that Keats recorded in a letter of April 1819 to his brother and sister-in-law in America captures the variety and extent – as well as the associative but progressive movement – of Coleridge's thinking out loud on topics directly related to the imagination and the status of 'the imaginary':

> Last Sunday I took a Walk towards highgate and in the lane that winds by the side of Lord Mansfield's park I met Mr Green our Demonstrator at Guy's in conversation with Coleridge—I joined them, after enquiring by a look whether it would be agreeable—I walked with him at his alderman-after dinner pace for near two miles I suppose In those two Miles he broached a thousand things—let me see if I can give you a list—Nightingales, Poetry—on Poetical sensation—Metaphysics—different genera and species of Dreams—Nightmare—a dream accompanied by a sense of touch—single and double touch—A dream related—First and second consciousness—the difference explained between will and Volition—so m[an]y metaphysicians from a want of smoking the second consciousness—Monsters—the Kraken—Mermaids—southey believes in them—southeys belief too much diluted—A Ghost story—Good morning—I heard his voice as he came towards me—I heard it as he moved away—I had heard it

all the interval – if it may be called so. He was civil enough to ask me to call on him at Highgate Good Night![61]

Even in his talk, however, and in the informal writings that literary scholarship would spend the second half of the twentieth century recovering in full, we note a marked shift after 1815 towards metaphysical and specifically theological enquiry, one confirmed by Coleridge's choice of reading.

Coleridge's main or immediate influence on the nineteenth century – and it was powerful – came through his discussions of society, religion, and theology with the many new disciples that gathered around him in the asylum he eventually found at Dr James Gillman's. After another breakdown precipitated by the overconsumption of opium, Coleridge presented himself on 12 April 1816 to Gillman at Moreton House on Highgate Hill, then a village outside and overlooking London. Dr Joseph Adams, who had been attending Coleridge, had written to Gillman a few days before of Coleridge's desire 'to fix himself in the house of some medical gentleman, who will have courage to refuse him laudanum':

> As he is desirous of retirement, and a garden, I could think of no one so readily as yourself. Be so good as to inform me, whether such a proposal is absolutely inconsistent with your family arrangements. I should not have proposed it, but on account of the great importance of the character, as a literary man. His communicative temper will make his society very interesting, as well as useful.[62]

Gillman 'had no intention of receiving an inmate' into his house, but after one evening of 'captivating' conversation, 'looked with impatience for the morrow': 'I felt indeed almost spell-bound, without the desire of release'.[63] Again, 'the Mariner hath his will'. Two days later Coleridge arrived with the proof sheets of *Christabel* in his hand intending to stay for a month until he had overcome his addiction. When the Gillmans moved to another house in Highgate seven years later in November 1823 – Number 3, The Grove – Coleridge, still with them, stayed with them. Another surrogate for the families he could not abide.

As Coleridge's reputation grew the world, by and large, came to him in his retirement, 'a kind of Magus', wrote Thomas Carlyle, 'girt in mystery and enigma'.[64] There were the sceptical, like Carlyle himself, and there were the curious, like John Stuart Mill. There were old friends, sceptical enough after a lifetime of Coleridgean caprice but still devoted, like Charles Lamb and Henry Crabb Robinson. Mostly, however, Coleridge preached to the infatuated: to his new disciples Joseph Henry Green, H. F. (Henry) Cary (translator of Dante), C. A. Tulk, Thomas Allsop, John Hookham Frere, along with nephews John Taylor Coleridge and Henry Nelson Coleridge, and daughter Sara (who married Henry Nelson, her first cousin). All of these last came to listen and record, acting as notetakers, amanuenses, and later editors. Julius Hare, F. D. Maurice, Arthur Hallam, and Richard Monckton Milnes came as emissaries of the intellectual discussion group, the Cambridge Apostles. From America came Ralph Waldo Emerson, James Fenimore Cooper, and Emma Willard.

Coleridge died on 25 July 1834 in the attic 'Bed and Bookroom' at The Grove he had chosen for himself eleven years earlier, the room where he had conducted so many 'Attic nights' of endless '*One*versazioni' on everything that had come within his purview – which at one time or another had been just about everything in the intellectual universe of the Romantic period (*CL* V, 368; VI, 790).

Epilogue

'No one on earth has ever LOVED me', a distraught Coleridge confided in his notebooks, in voluntary exile in Hudson's Hotel after Basil Montagu had passed on a version of Wordsworth's message about how insufferable Coleridge had been to live with (*CN* III, 4006). He was wrong. No one had ever loved him enough to satisfy his insatiable needs, perhaps – 'The whole craving of his moral being was for love', wrote his disciple Thomas Allsop[1] – but Coleridge was almost universally admired and loved. Not at all times, by any means. Most of his friends found him – as Lamb found him – alternately enchanting and infuriating: 'The rogue gives you Love Powders, and then a strong horse drench to bring 'em off your stomach that they mayn't hurt you'.[2] Thomas Middleton, Robert Southey, Tom Poole, Joseph Cottle, Josiah Wade, John Thelwall, Tom Wedgwood, Humphry Davy, William Godwin, Daniel Stuart, John Morgan, Henry Crabb Robinson – none of them would have expressed it in Lamb's inimitable way, but every one of them knew the affection and frustration of being Coleridge's friend. And for all of them, Wordsworth included, the affection survived the frustration. For Lamb especially, the poetry, too, came with love powders:

He is at present under the medical care of a Mr Gilman (Killman?) a Highgate Apothecary, where he plays at leaving off Laud[anu]m.—I think his essentials not touched, he is very bad, but then he wonderfully picks up another day, and his face when he repeats his verses hath its ancient glory, an Arch angel a little damaged. … [he recited 'Kubla Khan'] so enchantingly that it irradiates & brings heaven & Elysian bowers into my parlour while he sings or says it.[3]

In this sense at least, Coleridge led a charmed life. His suffering – his addiction and loneliness and desperation – is apparent and should never be underestimated, but the wonder is surely that he should have survived at all, given the extremes of physical and mental derangement he was to reach on occasion. Other addicts have known much sadder endings. George Burnett – one of the original pantisocrats, who having been caught up in the excitement of the enterprise was severely disappointed and depressed by its failure – ended up in the Marylebone Workhouse and was dead at 35.[4] Though laudanum was available over the counter and therefore free of the financial legacy of illegality, in the quantities most addicts required it would still have been cripplingly expensive. The opium-eater De Quincey, who could afford to offer Coleridge £500 pounds in 1807, was imprisoned for debt in the Canongate Toll-booth in Edinburgh in 1831. Though he was released the same day on grounds of ill health, thereafter the threat of imprisonment for debt hung over him constantly and his existence became a complex and fugitive one.

Debt and self-destruction were by no means inevitable. The lives of prominent contemporaries like James Mackintosh and William Wilberforce demonstrate that it was possible to contain an addiction and to remain productive, as Coleridge did for the last eighteen years of his life. But that required money and emotional support. Coleridge started with nothing and, as we have seen, accumulated debts throughout his life. On every occasion, however, there were family or friends to help him out. If the alacrity with which Coleridge sought and accepted money suggests that he thought the world owed him a living, it is also true to say that the world thought so, too. From his debts at Cambridge to his board at the Gillmans, he was covered. And this timely financial support was nothing compared to the emotional support he always found.

The affection and allegiance that Coleridge inspired across a huge range of utterly disparate people was the greatest tribute paid to him by his contemporaries. His thinking and his talking, abstracted and self-generative as it was, was in the end inseparable from his personality, from his humanity. De Quincey made the point in one of the series of articles he wrote on Coleridge's death:

> If, generally speaking, poor Coleridge had but a small share of earthly prosperity, in one respect at least, he was eminently favoured by Providence; beyond all men who ever perhaps have lived, he found means to engage a constant succession of most faithful friends; and he levied the services of sisters, brothers, daughters, sons from the hands of strangers — attracted to him by no possible impulses but those of reverence for his intellect, and love for his gracious nature. How, says Wordsworth —
>
> > — How can *he* expect that others should
> > Sow for him, reap for *him*, and, at his call,
> > Love him, who for himself will take no thought at all?

How can he, indeed? It is most unreasonable to do so: yet this expectation, if Coleridge ought not to have entertained, at all events he realized. Fast as one friend dropped off, another, and another, succeeded: perpetual relays were laid along his path in life, of judicious and zealous supporters; who comforted his days, and smoothed the pillow for his declining age, even when it was beyond all human power to take away the thorns which stuffed it.[5]

And just as his friends forgave him everything, so subsequent scholarship has forgiven him everything – largely for the same reasons, I suspect, of 'reverence for his intellect, and love of his gracious nature'. Scholarship has forgiven him his plagiarism, for example, often arguably when it should not have, and scholarship has heeded his plea in the *Biographia* and forgiven him his failure to fulfil the promise of his early career: 'By what I *have* effected, am I to be judged by my fellow men; what I *could* have done, is a question for my own conscience' (*BL* I, 221).

Indeed, since his death, academic scholarship has gone much, much further. Beyond forgiving Coleridge for what he did not publish it has set about rescuing him from the ephemerality of his own massive informal output: publishing all his lectures, letters, notebooks, table talk, and marginalia, and converting a modest published works into the voluminous collected works of which even the publisher of *Omniana* never would have dreamed. Not content merely to publish, moreover, scholars and commentators since Sara and Henry Nelson Coleridge have also set about editing, revising, cross referencing, and collating to establish what Coleridge thought and felt in ways that, ironically, Coleridge himself found impossible. As each glossarist imposes a satisfying coherence on the tale, another comes along to disrupt and complicate, but the commitment to the tale and its teller remains constant. No writer in English has been as well served as Coleridge by the culture he collaborated to create. That has been our tribute.

Notes

Prologue: Literary Life, 1815

1. Howard Mumford Jones, *Revolution & Romanticism* (Cambridge, MA: Harvard University Press, 1974), p. 286n.
2. Samuel Taylor Coleridge, *Biographia Literaria*, with an introduction 'On Criticism and the "Biographia Literaria"' by Arthur Symons (London and Toronto: J. M. Dent & Sons, 1906), p. x.
3. See *Shorter Works and Fragments* (CC), I, 625–85 (p. 625).
4. Holmes, *Darker Reflections*, p. 349.
5. 'My First Acquaintance with Poets', in *William Hazlitt: Selected Writings*, ed. Jon Cook (Oxford and New York: 1991), pp. 211–30 (pp. 212–13).
6. See, for example, amongst Coleridge's Collected Works, the two-volume *Shorter Works and Fragments* (CC).
7. J. H. Haeger, 'Anti-Materialism, Autobiography, and the Abyss of Unmeaning in the *Biographia Literaria*', in *Coleridge's Biographia Literaria: Text and Meaning*, ed. Frederick Burwick (Columbus: Ohio State University Press, 1989), pp. 75–87 (p. 77).
8. 'Seem to have made up my mind to write my metaphysical works, as *my Life*, & *in my Life* — intermixed with all the other events/ or history of the mind & fortunes of S. T. Coleridge' (September–October 1803), N237.
9. Jerome Christensen, ' "Like a Guilty Thing Surprised": Coleridge, Deconstruction, and the Apostasy of Criticism', in *Coleridge's Biographia: Text and Meaning*, ed. Burwick, pp. 171–90 (p. 185).
10. Wordsworth to Thomas Noon Talfourd, 11 April 1839, *Wordsworth Letters: The Late Years 2*, p. 969.
11. Wordsworth to Thomas De Quincey, 6 March 1804, *Wordsworth Letters: The Early Years*, p. 454.
12. See the opening line of 'The Two-Part *Prelude* of 1799', *The Prelude*, p. 1.
13. 'My nature requires another Nature for its support, & reposes only in another from the necessary Indigence of its Being', note of November 1803 (*CN* I, 1679).
14. M. G. Cooke, 'Quisque Sui Faber: Coleridge in the *Biographia Literaria*', *Philological Quarterly* 50 (April 1971), pp. 208–29 (p. 223).
15. *Coleridge 'Biographia Literaria' Chapters I–IV, XIV–XXII, Wordsworth Prefaces and Essays on Poetry 1800–1815*, ed. George Sampson (Cambridge: Cambridge University Press, 1920), p. v.
16. Compare Hazlitt: 'I observed that he continually crossed me on the way by shifting from one side of the foot-path to the other. This struck me at the time as an odd movement; but I did not at that time connect it with any instability of purpose or involuntary change of principle, as I have done since', 'My First Acquaintance with Poets', in *Selected Writings*, ed. Cook, p. 218.

Chapter 1 'The Discipline of His Taste at School': Christ's Hospital and Cambridge

1. Gillman, pp. 4–5.
2. Holmes, *Early Visions*, p. 4.
3. For discussion of these and other forms of publishing in the eighteenth and early nineteenth century, see William St Clair, *The Reading Nation in the Romantic Period* (Cambridge: Cambridge University Press, 2004), pp. 161–8.
4. Ashton, p. 16.
5. Gillman, pp. 17, 20.
6. Gillman, p. 20.
7. In a MS note amongst the Abinger papers, as quoted in Ashton, p. 14.
8. Wordsworth describes Newton 'Voyaging through strange seas of Thought, alone' in *The Prelude* (1850), III, 63.
9. In his 'On the Living Poets', in *Lectures on the English Poets*, published with *The Spirit of the Age* (London and Toronto: J. M. Dent & Sons, 1910), pp. 143–68 (p. 167).
10. Coleridge in an article in *The Courier*, 15 July 1811, *Essays on His Times* (CC), II, 225–8 (p. 226).
11. See Richard Holmes, *Shelley: The Pursuit* (London: Penguin, 1987), p. 18.
12. Holmes, *Early Visions*, p. 26.
13. Leigh Hunt, *Autobiography*, revised edition [1859], ed. J. E. Morpurgo (London: The Cresset Press, 1949), p. 56.
14. As quoted in Ashton, p. 19.
15. See, for example, *Church and State* (CC), pp. 46–7.
16. Lamb, 'Recollections of Christ's Hospital' (1813), in *The Works of Charles and Mary Lamb*, ed. E. V. Lucas, in 6 vols (London: Methuen & Co., 1912), I, 162–74 (pp. 171, 172).
17. Charles Lamb, 'Christ's Hospital Five and Thirty Years Ago' (1820), in *The Works of Charles and Mary Lamb*, II, 14–26 (p. 15).
18. These figures, from the investigation of the parliamentary committee set up by Brougham in 1816, were released in 1819. See Alan Richardson, *Literature, Education, and Romanticism: Reading as Social Practice, 1780–1832* (Cambridge: Cambridge University Press, 1994), p. 45. For a contemporary account, listing 500 such schools, see Nicholas Carlisle, *A Concise Description of the Endowed Grammar Schools in England and Wales* (London, 1818).
19. Johnson's own 'Scheme for the Classes of a Grammar School', with its exclusively classical language teaching, is included by Boswell in his *Life of Johnson*, ed. R. W. Chapman, rev. J. D. Fleeman, World's Classics (Oxford: Oxford University Press, 1980), pp. 71–2.
20. From his syllabus for a school for boys in the Lake District, as quoted in Jennifer Wallace, *Shelley and Greece: Rethinking Romantic Hellenism* (London: Macmillan, 1997), p. 66.
21. See my entry under 'Dissenting Academies' in the *Oxford Companion to the Romantic Age* or, for more information, H[erbert] McLachlan, *English Education under the Test Acts: Being the History of Non-conformist Academies 1662–1820* (Manchester: Manchester University Press, 1931).
22. As quoted in Roy Porter, *English Society in the Eighteenth Century*, revised edition (Harmondsworth: Penguin, 1990), p. 164.

23. Kenneth Johnston, *The Hidden Wordsworth: Poet, Lover, Rebel, Spy* (New York: Norton, 1998), p. 176.
24. See Britain on 'Education', in *An Oxford Companion to the Romantic Age*, pp. 166, 168. For an astute contemporary account of the 'Public schools', see the article by the reviewer and wit Sydney Smith (himself an old boy of Winchester) in the *Edinburgh Review* XVI, no. 32 (August 1810), pp. 326–34.
25. Quoted in 'Christ's Hospital Five and Thirty Years Ago', *The Works of Charles and Mary Lamb*, II, 23–4.
26. Hunt, *Autobiography*, p. 74.
27. Coleridge's own account of the Christ's Hospital regime can be found in a letter to Thomas Poole, 19 February 1798, in the *Collected Letters* (*CL* I, 387–9).
28. Kenneth Curry, *Southey* (London and Boston: Routledge & Kegan Paul, 1975), p. 10.
29. Holmes, *Shelley: The Pursuit*, pp. 19–20.
30. Lamb, 'Christ's Hospital Five and Thirty Years Ago', *The Works of Charles and Mary Lamb*, II, 24–5.
31. Plotinus, *The Enneads*, trans. Stephen MacKenna, rev. B. S. Page (London: Faber and Faber, 1969), pp. 409–10 (V. 5, § 8).
32. John Milton, *Of Education* (1644), in *Milton's Prose Writings*, intro. K. M. Burton, Everyman's Library (London: J. M. Dent & Sons, 1958), p. 323.
33. 'You think it worth your while to hazard your son's innocence and virtue for a little Greek and Latin?' In his *Some Thoughts Concerning Education* (1692), as quoted in S. J. Curtis, *History of Education in Great Britain*, fifth edition (London: University Tutorial Press, 1963), p. 114.
34. For the battle over working men's education, see E. P. Thompson, *The Making of the English Working Class* (Harmondsworth: Penguin, 1980), pp. 817–19.
35. *Oxford Companion to the Romantic Age*, p. 166.
36. E. P. Thompson, *Witness Against the Beast: William Blake and the Moral Law* (Cambridge: Cambridge University Press, 1993), p. xiv.
37. R. D. Anderson, *Education and the Scottish People 1750–1918* (Oxford: Clarendon, 1995), p. 2.
38. Stephen Gill, *William Wordsworth: A Life* (Oxford: Clarendon, 1989), p. 39.
39. Johnston, *The Hidden Wordsworth*, p. 129.
40. Holmes, *Early Visions*, p. 49.
41. Mr Collins is a foolish, fawning character in Jane Austen's novel *Pride and Prejudice*.

Chapter 2 'The Progress of His Opinions in Religion and Politics': The Radical Years

1. On 'primogeniture, which disinherits every other member of the family, to heap unwholesome abundance upon one', see William Godwin, *Enquiry Concerning Political Justice*, ed. Isaac Kramnick (Harmondsworth: Penguin, 1976), p. 473.
2. As quoted in Gillman, p. 53.
3. *Sors misera servorum in Insulis Indiæ; Occidentalis* ('The Unhappy Fate of the Slaves in the West Indian Islands'), ll. 45–56, as reprinted in *Poetical Works* (CC) I (Part 1), pp. 72–84 (p. 77).
4. See Coleridge's essay 'Enthusiasm for an Ideal World' in *The Friend* (CC), I, 223.

5. 'The Unanimous Declaration of the Thirteen United States of America, 4 July 1776', as reprinted in *Revolutions 1775–1830*, ed. Merryn Williams (Harmondsworth: Penguin, 1971), pp. 45–51 (p. 45).
6. Richard Price, *A Discourse on the Love of Our Country*, reprinted in *Burke, Paine, Godwin, and the Revolution Controversy*, ed. Marilyn Butler (Cambridge: Cambridge University Press, 1984), pp. 23–32 (p. 29).
7. Tom Paine, *The Rights of Man*, as reprinted in *Burke, Paine, Godwin, and the Revolution Controversy*, pp. 107–21 (pp. 110, 114–15).
8. See Ben Ross Schneider, *Wordsworth's Cambridge Education* (Cambridge: Cambridge University Press, 1957), p. 143.
9. Edmund Burke, *Reflections on the Revolution in France: A Critical Edition*, ed. J. C. D. Clark (Stanford, CA: Stanford University Press, 2001), p. 238.
10. *Appeal from the New to the Old Whigs*, in *Edmund Burke on Politics and Society*, ed. B. W. Hill (London: Fontana, 1975), pp. 360–74 (pp. 373–4).
11. There are, needless to say, many more books devoted to this period of British and European history than it would be possible to list. See, amongst my suggestions for Further Reading at the end of this volume, works by Jennifer Mori, Ian R. Christie, R. K. Webb, J. Steven Watson, the volume of scholarly essays edited by H. T. Dickinson, and (for the European context) E. J. Hobsbawm. *Revolutions 1775–1830*, ed. Merryn Williams (Harmondsworth: Penguin, 1971) offers a comprehensive anthology of excerpts from contemporary documents and treatises and two convenient anthologies of polemical and other responses to the French Revolution are available in *Burke, Paine, Godwin, and the Revolution Controversy*, ed. Marilyn Butler (from which I have been quoting) and Stephen Prickett's *England and the French Revolution* (Basingstoke and London: Macmillan, 1989).
12. See Nicholas Roe, *Wordsworth and Coleridge: The Radical Years* (Oxford: Clarendon, 1988), p. 164.
13. *A Letter from the Right Honourable Charles James Fox to the Worthy and Independent Electors of the City and Westminster* (London, 1793), as quoted in Roe, *Wordsworth and Coleridge: The Radical Years*, p. 100.
14. Kenneth Johnston, *The Hidden Wordsworth: Poet, Lover, Rebel, Spy* (New York: Norton, 1998), pp. 178–9.
15. The Whiggism, that is, of liberal reformer Charles James Fox, referring to his support for appeasement with France. Foxite Whiggism was more sympathetic to the populist cause in France. At home, the Whigs sought to reform and increase the powers of the House of Commons, supported the toleration and emancipation of Catholics and Dissenters, and distrusted monarchical privilege and power.
16. Henry Gunning, *Reminiscences of the University, Town and Country of Cambridge, from the year 1780*, second edition, in 2 vols (London, 1855), I, 302.
17. William Frend, *Peace and Union, Recommended to the Associated Bodies of Republicans and Anti-Republicans* (1793), facsimile edition (Spelsbury: Woodstock, 1991), p. 43.
18. Gunning, *Reminiscences of the University, Town and Country of Cambridge*, I, 309.
19. Carl R. Woodring, *Politics in the Poetry of Coleridge* (Madison: University of Wisconsin Press, 1961), p. 94.
20. Godwin, *Enquiry Concerning Political Justice*, pp. 252–3.
21. In a review of Jean Mounier, *De L'Influence des Philosophes*, *Edinburgh Review*, I (October 1802), pp. 1–18 (p. 3).
22. Southey to Horace Bedford, 11 December 1793, in *New Letters of Robert Southey, 1811–1838*, ed. Kenneth Curry, in 2 vols (Oxford: Clarendon, 1965), I, 37.
23. Ashton, p. 44.

24. *New Letters of Robert Southey*, I, 56.
25. *The Friend* (CC), II, 147. Richard Holmes points out that there was nothing ridiculous about the idea of collective emigration in itself: 'the Susquehanna scheme did become a reality in other hands', *Early Visions*, p. 89.
26. *The Friend* (CC), II, 147.
27. Joseph Cottle, *Reminiscences of Samuel Taylor Coleridge and Robert Southey* (London: Houlston and Stoneman, 1847), pp. 5 ff.
28. See J. Steven Watson, *The Reign of George III, 1760–1815*, Oxford History of England, Vol. XII (Oxford: Clarendon, 1960), pp. 356–63.
29. *The Speech of John Thelwall at the Second Meeting of the London Corresponding Society, November 12, 1795* (London, 1795), as quoted in Roe, *Wordsworth and Coleridge: The Radical Years*, p. 150.
30. Woodring, *Politics in the Poetry of Coleridge*, p. 91.
31. Southey remembers three lectures; see *New Letters of Robert Southey*, ed. Curry, II, p. 448.
32. As quoted in *Lectures 1795* (CC), p. xxx.
33. *The Friend* (CC), I, 326–38.
34. *Lectures 1795* (CC), pp. 14, 5, 6.
35. *Lectures 1795* (CC), p. 12.
36. *Monthly Magazine*, October 1819, pp. 203–5, as quoted in Holmes, *Early Visions*, p. 93.
37. In an anonymous review of *A Moral and Political Lecture* in the *Critical Review* n.s. XIII (April 1795), p. 455, as quoted in *Lectures 1795* (CC), p. 2.
38. Acts 2, 44–5 (var.).
39. See his sixth lecture 'on Revealed Religion', *Lectures 1795* (CC), p. 229.
40. *Lectures 1795* (CC), p. lv.
41. *Lectures 1795* (CC), p. lxv.
42. As quoted in *Coleridge's Poetry and Prose*, eds Nicholas Halmi, Paul Magnuson, and Raimonda Modiano (New York: Norton, 2004), p. 20, n. 1.
43. *Reminiscences of Samuel Taylor Coleridge and Robert Southey*, p. 74. Cottle was not himself invited, as it happens, because Coleridge already felt himself too deeply in his debt (*CL* I, 174).
44. *The Watchman* (CC), pp. 5, 6.
45. Quoting from an advertisement and the prospectus, *The Watchman* (CC), pp. 380, 5.
46. *The Watchman* (CC), p. 6.
47. *The Watchman* (CC), pp. 269–73.
48. *The Watchman* (CC), pp. 13–14.
49. *The Watchman* (CC), p. 375.
50. Not the £80–90 mentioned in the *Biographia* (*BL* I, 186), though scholars are undecided as to the exact cost.
51. *Reminiscences of Samuel Taylor Coleridge and Robert Southey*, p. 83 and note.

Chapter 3   'A Known and Familiar Landscape': Conversations

1. As quoted in Ashton, p. 86.
2. See my account of Coleridge in Malta in Chapter 6 below.
3. Samuel Johnson, *Selected Writings*, ed. Patrick Cruttwell (London: Penguin), pp. 252–3 (p. 252).

4. Alvin Kernan, *Printing Technology, Letters and Samuel Johnson* (Princeton, NJ: Princeton University Press, 1987), p. 105.
5. In a review of 'Boswell's *Life of Johnson*', first published in *Fraser's Magazine* in 1832, reprinted in Thomas Carlyle, *Critical and Miscellaneous Essays*, in 5 vols (London: Chapman and Hall, 1899), III, 62–135 (p. 102). Compare Macaulay's review of the same edition in the *Edinburgh Review* LIV, no. 107 (September 1831), pp. 1–38: 'At the time Johnson commenced his literary career, a writer had little to hope from the patronage of powerful individuals. The patronage of the public did not yet furnish the means of a comfortable subsistence. ... the age of Mæcenases had passed away. The age of general curiosity and intelligence had not yet arrived' (pp. 22, 21).
6. In a letter to Bennet Langton, quoted in James Boswell, *Life of Johnson*, ed. R. W. Chapman, rev. J. D. Fleeman, The World's Classics (Oxford: Oxford University Press, 1980), p. 231.
7. Carlyle, 'Boswell's *Life of Johnson*', pp. 100, 102.
8. 'For by the common sense of readers uncorrupted by literary prejudices, after all the refinements of subtlety and the dogmatism of learning, must be finally decided all claim to poetical honours', Samuel Johnson, 'Life of Gray', in *Selected Writings*, ed. Cruttwell, pp. 470–80 (p. 480).
9. See Stephen Gill, *William Wordsworth: A Life* (Oxford: Clarendon, 1989), p. 296.
10. See, for example, Paul Korshin, 'Types of Eighteenth-Century Literary Patronage', *Eighteenth-Century Studies*, VII (1973–4), pp. 453–73, and Dustin Griffin, *Literary Patronage in England, 1650–1800* (Cambridge: Cambridge University Press, 1996).
11. Korshin, 'Types of Eighteenth-Century Literary Patronage', p. 464.
12. Korshin, 'Types of Eighteenth-Century Literary Patronage', p. 457.
13. Nigel Cross, *The Common Writer: Life in Nineteenth-Century Grub Street* (Cambridge: Cambridge University Press, 1985), pp. 14, 13, 25–6, 20.
14. As quoted in David Gardiner Williams, *The Royal Society of Literature and the Patronage of George IV* [doctoral dissertation submitted to Harvard University], in 2 vols (New York and London: Garland, 1987), I, 15, 45.
15. Holmes, *Early Visions*, p. 117n.
16. For a study of changes in the conception of poetry and of the poet during the course of the eighteenth century, see M. H. Abrams, *The Mirror and the Lamp: Romantic Theory and the Critical Tradition* (London, Oxford, New York: Oxford University Press, 1953).
17. In *The Statesman's Manual* (1816), *Lay Sermons* (CC), p. 30.
18. The poet Robert Bloomfield published an Aeolian harp anthology in 1808 with the title *Nature's Music*. See *Poetical Works* (CC), I (Part 1), p. 231.
19. The epithet 'governessy' is from Humphry House, *Coleridge*, The Clark Lectures 1951–2 (London: Rupert Hart-Davis, 1953), p. 77.
20. *Lectures on Philosophy* (CC), I, 220.
21. Dorothy Wordsworth to Mary Hutchinson, June 1797, *Wordsworth Letters: The Early Years*, pp. 188–9.
22. *Table Talk* (CC), I, 208 (26 September 1830).
23. *The Prelude* (1805), X, 900.
24. *Lectures 1795* (CC), p. 35.
25. See *Poetical Works* (CC), I (Part 1), p. 350.
26. See the study by Lucy Newlyn of the intertextual echoes and answers in their respective poetry, *Coleridge, Wordsworth, and the Language of Allusion* (Oxford: Clarendon, 1986).

27. Compare the quotation from Plotinus's *Enneads* in the section on self-education in the first chapter.
28. In a note to Southey's edition of his *Poems on Various Subjects* (1797), *Poetical Works* (CC), I (Part 1), p. 232.
29. Written in a friend's copy of his *Sibylline Leaves* (1817), as quoted in *Poetical Works* (CC), I (Part 1), p. 232.

Chapter 4 'The Poet Described in *Ideal* Perfection': *Annus Mirabilis*

1. As quoted in *Thomas Poole and His Friends*, I, 235.
2. Walsh's reports to the Home Office are quoted by Nicholas Roe in his *Wordsworth and Coleridge: The Radical Years* (Oxford: Clarendon, 1988), pp. 258–60.
3. On the French 'invasion' of 22 February 1797 – an invasion largely of 'Irish exiles, prison convicts, *émigrés* on probation and other French undesirables' – see Jennifer Mori, *Britain in the Age of the French Revolution 1785–1820* (Harlow: Pearson Education, 2000), p. 72; Roe discusses it at some length in *Wordsworth and Coleridge: The Radical Years*, pp. 251–7.
4. *Thomas Poole and His Friends*, I, 233.
5. William St Clair, *The Godwins and the Shelleys: The Biography of a Family* (London: Faber and Faber, 1989), p. 228.
6. See Leigh Hunt: 'He recited his *Kubla Khan* one morning to Lord Byron, in his lordship's house in Piccadilly, when I happened to be in another room. I remember the other's coming away from him, highly struck with his poem, and saying how wonderfully he talked. This was the impression of everybody who heard him', *Autobiography*, ed. J. E. Morpurgo (London, 1949), p. 288.
7. Ashton, p. 116.
8. Samuel Johnson, *The History of Rasselas, Prince of Abyssinia*, World's Classics, ed. J. P. Hardy (Oxford: Oxford University Press, 1988), p. 78.
9. See Coleridge's characterization of Robespierre in *Lectures 1795* (CC), p. 35, quoted in the previous chapter.
10. Camille Paglia, 'The Daemon as Lesbian Vampire', in her *Sexual Personae: Art and Decadence from Nefertiti to Emily Dickinson* (London: Penguin, 1991), pp. 317–46 (p. 317).
11. William Hazlitt, 'My First Acquaintance with Poets', in *William Hazlitt: Selected Writings*, World's Classics, ed. Jon Cook (Oxford: Oxford University Press, 1991), pp. 211–30 (p. 217).
12. *Wordsworth Letters: Early Years*, p. 194.
13. See Coleridge's 1828 prefatory note to 'The Wanderings of Cain', *Poetical Works* (CC), I (Part 1), pp. 259–60.
14. In a note dictated to Isabella Fenwick, reprinted in *Coleridge: The Ancient Mariner and Other Poems: A Casebook*, eds Alun R. Jones and William Tydeman (London and Basingstoke: Macmillan, 1973), pp. 24–5 (p. 24).
15. Thomas Percy, *Reliques of Ancient Poetry*, pp. 50–1.
16. See the letter to Joseph Cottle, 24 June 1799, in *Wordsworth Letters: The Early Years*, p. 264.
17. Wordsworth added this in a note to the second, 1800 edition of the *Lyrical Ballads* – see *Lyrical Ballads: Wordsworth and Coleridge*, ed. R. L. Brett and A. R. Jones, second edition (London: Routledge, 1991), p. 276.

18. The classic study of Coleridge's sources for *The Rime of the Ancient Mariner* remains John Livingston Lowes, *The Road to Xanadu: A Study of the Ways of the Imagination*, revised edition (London: Constable, 1930).
19. Bruno Bettelheim, *The Uses of Enchantment: The Meaning and Importance of Fairy Tales* (Harmondsworth: Penguin, 1978), pp. 62–3.
20. Coleridge on 'Ghosts and Apparitions' in *The Friend* (CC), I, 146.
21. As quoted in *Inquiring Spirit: A New Presentation of Coleridge from His Published and Unpublished Prose Writings*, ed. Kathleen Coburn, revised edition (Toronto, Buffalo, London: University of Toronto Press, 1979), pp. 56–7.
22. A convenient modern compilation of rhetorical devices can be found in Richard A. Lanham, *A Handlist of Rhetorical Terms*, second edition (Berkeley, Los Angeles, Oxford: University of California Press, 1991).
23. Richard Holmes, *Samuel Taylor Coleridge: Selected Poetry* (London: Penguin, 1996), p. 311.
24. David Beres, 'A Dream, A Vision, and a Poem', *International Journal of Psycho-analysis*, XI–XII, no. 2 (1959), pp. 97–116, as quoted in *The Annotated Ancient Mariner*, ed. Martin Gardner (Cleveland and New York: C. N. Potter, 1965), 215–17.
25. See *Lyrical Ballads*, ed. Brett and Jones, p. 9.
26. Coleridge in conversation, 31 March 1832, *Table Talk* (CC), I, 272–3.
27. 30 May 1830, *Table Talk* (CC), I, 149.
28. For an important discussion relating the different levels of interpretation in the poem to biblical criticism, see Jerome McGann, '*The Ancient Mariner*: The Meaning of Meanings', in his *The Beauty of Inflections: Literary Investigations in Historical Method and Theory* (Oxford: Clarendon, 1985), pp. 135–72.
29. See the final line of W. B. Yeats's poem 'The Circus Animals' Desertion'.
30. In a letter to Wordsworth, 30 January 1801, *Lamb Letters*, I, 266.
31. I should perhaps add that the 'leg of mutton' was in fact a sail, so named because of its shape.
32. *Coleridge: The Critical Heritage*, ed. J. R. de J. Jackson (London: Routledge & Kegan Paul, 1970), p. 4.
33. Wordsworth, 'My Heart Leaps Up', l. 8.
34. See *Poetical Works* (CC), I, 456n.
35. Holmes, *Early Visions*, p. 91n.
36. The reference here is to Wordsworth's poems 'The Idiot Boy' and 'The Thorn'.

Chapter 5   'The Toil of Thinking': Private Notes and Public Newspapers

1. *Poetical Works* (CC), I (Part 2), p. 1299.
2. William Hazlitt, 'My First Acquaintance with Poets', in *William Hazlitt: Selected Writings*, ed. Jon Cook (Oxford and New York: Oxford University Press, 1991), pp. 211–30 (p. 226).
3. Lamb to Crabb Robinson, 8 January 1823, *HCR*, I, 289
4. *Thomas Poole and His Friends*, I, 192–3.
5. From a MS in the Harry Ransom Humanities Research Center, as quoted in Ashton, p. 155.
6. 'Wordsworth is a very great man – the only man, to whom *at all times* & in *all modes of excellence* I feel myself inferior', Coleridge to Southey 17 July 1797 (*CL* I, p. 334).

7. *Thomas Poole and His Friends*, I, 279.
8. *Thomas Poole and His Friends*, I, 178.
9. *Thomas Poole and His Friends*, I, 279–80.
10. For comment on Coleridge in intellectual debate with his teachers, see Charles Parry's letter home from Göttingen, reprinted in Clement Carlyon, *Early Years and Late Reflections*, in 2 vols (London 1836), I, 100–1n.
11. See *Poetical Works*, I, Part 2, pp. 717–23, where Brun's original and some of the background is discussed.
12. See Gary Kelly, *The English Jacobin Novel 1780–1805* (Oxford: Clarendon, 1976).
13. Text from The Oxford Authors edition of *Byron*, ed. Jerome J. McGann (Oxford and New York: Oxford University Press, 1986).
14. See below, on *The Friend* in Chapter 7 and the *Biographia* in Chapter 8, and for a context, Marilyn Butler, *Romantics, Rebels and Reactionaries: English Literature and Its Background 1760–1830* (Oxford and New York: Oxford University Press, 1981), chapter 6, 'The War of the Intellectuals: from Wordsworth to Keats', pp. 138–54.
15. The most comprehensive and relentless study of Coleridge's plagiarisms remains Norman Fruman, *Coleridge, the Damaged Archangel* (London: George Allen & Unwin, 1972), which it is recommended should be read with Thomas McFarland, *Coleridge and the Pantheist Tradition* (Oxford: Clarendon, 1969). The best way to track Coleridge's plagiarisms is through the individual volumes of the Collected Works, especially, for our purposes, *Biographia Literaria* (CC) and *Lectures on Literature* (CC), both of which address the issue at length in their editorial introductions.
16. The opening line of the fragment known as the Prospectus to *The Recluse*.
17. See Jeffrey's review of Wordsworth's *Poems* (1807), *Edinburgh Review* XI (October 1807), p. 214. This was picked up by an anonymous parodist in the *Satirist* (December 1809), V, 550–2, who entitled a lampoon 'The Bards of the Lake'. Jeffrey later began his review of John Wilson's *Isle of Palms* with the words 'This is a new recruit to the company of lake poets' in February 1812 – *Edinburgh Review* XIX, 373 – and described Horace and James Smiths' parody of Coleridge in *Rejected Addresses* as 'unquestionably lakish' in November 1812 (*Edinburgh Review* XX, 445). Jeffrey's construction of Wordsworth, Southey, and Coleridge as a 'school' from 1802 onwards (a school to which, incidentally, other poets like Wilson and Joanna Baillie were occasionally added) is discussed by David Perkins in his essay 'The Construction of English Romantic Poetry as a Literary Classification', reprinted in his *Is Literary History Possible?* (Baltimore and London: Johns Hopkins University Press, 1992), pp. 85–119 (pp. 88–91).
18. This description from the *Memoir and Letters* of Coleridge's daughter Sara (as quoted in Holmes, *Darker Reflections*, p. 148), while we would hardly expect it to be impartial, is in fact confirmed by other observers, and in a notebook entry Coleridge himself conceded that one 'Can see nothing extraordinary in her', and planned 'a poem noting all the virtues of the mild & retired kind', *CN* I, 1152.
19. Stuart's letter is reprinted in an appendix to *Essays on His Times* (CC), III, 165.
20. For a convenient conspectus of English newspaper history, see Jeremy Black, *The English Press 1621–1861* (Stroud: Sutton Publishing, 2001).
21. *Political Register*, 23 February 1811; as quoted in *Essays on His Times* (CC), I, cxlv.
22. See Chapter 2, above.
23. Jon P. Klancher, *The Making of English Reading Audiences, 1790–1832* (Madison, WI: Wisconsin University Press, 1987), p. ix.
24. *Essays on His Times* (CC), I, lxxi.

25. Southey's best known works include the long poems *Thalaba* (1801), *Madoc* (1805), *The Curse of Kehama* (1810), and *Roderick, the Last of the Goths* (1814); his edited collections *Specimens of the Later English Poets* (1807) and *Select Works of the British Poets, from Chaucer to Jonson* (1831); his biographies of Nelson (1813), Wesley (1820), and the *British Admirals* (1833–7); histories of Brazil (1810–19), Europe (1810–13) and of the Peninsular War (1823–32); literary translations of *Amadis of Gaul* (1803) and the *Chronicle of the Cid* (1808); and literary editions of Chatterton (1803), *Pilgrim's Progress* (1830), Isaac Watts (1834), and Cowper (1835–7).
26. 'Pitt and Bonaparte. Pitt', 19 March 1800, in *Essays on His Times* (CC), I, 219–27 (pp. 219, 221, 222).
27. *Essays on His Times* (CC), I, 220.
28. *Essays on His Times* (CC), I, 219.
29. For a complete record of Coleridge's prevarications over the article on Napoleon, see Erdman's note 17, *Essays on His Times* (CC), I, 226–8.
30. See Erdman's discussion, *Essays on His Times* (CC), I, lxvii–lxxi (p. lxviii).
31. As quoted by Erdman in *Essays on His Times* (CC), I, lxvii.
32. See Erdman's introduction, *Essays on His Times* (CC), I, xcii–xciii.
33. *Thomas Poole and His Friends*, I, 279–80, quoted earlier in the chapter.
34. As quoted by Erdman, *Essays on His Times* (CC), I, lxvii note.
35. Stuart's letter of 29 September 1802 appears as an appendix in *Essays on His Times* (CC), III, 169–71.
36. In a letter to Henry Crabb Robinson, 15 July 1849, as quoted in *Essays on His Times* (CC), I, lxviii note.

Chapter 6   'To Rust Away': The Lost Years 1800–6

1. Lamb to Thomas Manning, 5 April 1800, *Lamb Letters*, I, 191.
2. *Journals of Dorothy Wordsworth*, ed. Mary Moorman (London, Oxford, New York: Oxford University Press, 1971), p. 43.
3. *Lyrical Ballads: Wordsworth and Coleridge*, ed. R. L. Brett and A. R. Jones, second edition (London and New York: Routledge, 1991), p. 276.
4. 'Preface to *Lyrical Ballads*' (1800), in *Wordsworth Prose Works*, I, 124.
5. See the discussion of the *Biographia* in Chapter 8 below.
6. *Memoirs of William Wordsworth*, I, 125.
7. To quote Wordsworth's letter to John Wilson, June 1801, *Wordsworth Letters: The Early Years*, p. 355.
8. These lines are only in the version published in the *Morning Chronicle*, 30 December 1794, see *Poetical Works* (CC), I (Part 1), p. 147.
9. 'Thou shalt not make thee *any* graven image', Deuteronomy 5: 8 (Exodus 20: 4). For Coleridge on idolatry, see *Lectures 1795* (CC), pp. 139–142, 201–2.
10. *Wordsworth Prose Works*, I, 124.
11. *Wordsworth Prose Works*, I, 118.
12. *Wordsworth Prose Works*, I, 124.
13. *Wordsworth Prose Works*, I, 124.
14. David Hartley, *Observations on Man, His Frame, His Duty, and His Expectations*, 2 vols (London, 1749), I, 315.
15. *Observations on Man*, I, 320.
16. *Observations on Man*, I, 287.
17. *Observations on Man*, I, 320.

18. In his 1811 review of Southey's *The Curse of Kehama*, *Edinburgh Review* XVII (February 1811), p. 436.
19. *Wordsworth Prose Works*, I, 128.
20. See *Coleridge's Notebooks: A Selection*, ed. Perry, p. 180.
21. *Poetical Works* (CC), I (Part 2), p. 664.
22. Wordsworth, *The Prelude* (1805), II, 213–15.
23. Meeting Coleridge on Hampstead Heath 19 years later, the poet Keats 'walked with him at his alderman-after dinner pace'; see the letter of Keats to George and Georgiana Keats, 15 April 1819, in *Letters of John Keats*, ed. Robert Gittings (Oxford: Oxford University Press, 1970), p. 237. The letter is quoted at length at the end of Chapter 8.
24. *William Hazlitt: Selected Writings*, ed. Jon Cook (Oxford and New York: Oxford University Press, 1991), p. 225.
25. In a letter to Southey, 26 March 1804, as quoted in Ashton, p. 2.
26. For a recent consideration of Coleridge's addiction by a medical historian, see Roy Porter, *Flesh in the Age of Reason* (New York and London: Norton, 2003), pp. 402–12.
27. On the 'psycho-somatic or psycho-zoic', see his fragment 'On the Passions' (1828), *Shorter Works* (CC), II, 1419–53 (pp. 1444, 1445).
28. Ball's letter to the Secretary of State is quoted and paraphrased by Richard Holmes, *Darker Reflections*, pp. 48–9.
29. Donald Sultana, *Coleridge in Malta and Italy* (New York: Barnes and Noble, 1969), pp. 1–29 (p. 10).
30. For brief discussion of these sonnets in the *Morning Chronicle*, see Chapter 2 above.
31. *Coleridge in Malta and Italy*, p. 19.
32. *The Friend* (CC), I, 535.
33. *The Friend* (CC), I, 535.
34. *Religious Musings*, ll. 44–5.
35. *The Friend* (CC), I, 112.
36. Basil Willey, *Samuel Taylor Coleridge* (London: Chatto & Windus, 1972), p. 115.
37. See *Opus Maximum* (CC), p. ccvi.
38. Willey, *Samuel Taylor Coleridge*, p. 115.

Chapter 7   'The One Proteus of the Fire and the Flood': Critic for Hire

1. Wordsworth to Sir George Beaumont, 8 September 1806, *Wordsworth Letters: The Middle Years 1*, pp. 78–9.
2. Dorothy Wordsworth to Catherine Clarkson, 5–6 November 1806, *Wordsworth Letters: The Middle Years 1*, pp. 86–7.
3. Dorothy Wordsworth to Lady Beaumont, 26 December 1805, *Wordsworth Letters: Early Years*, p. 664. For references to *The Prelude* in process, see Wordsworth, *The Prelude 1799, 1805, 1850*, eds Jonathan Wordsworth, M. H. Abrams, and Stephen Gill (New York: Norton, 1979), pp. 529–40; for a chronology of *The Recluse* and convenient selection of correspondence, see *Wordsworth: The Prelude*, Casebook Series, ed. W. J. Harvey and Richard Gravil (London and Basingstoke: Macmillan, 1972), pp. 33–51.
4. Thomas De Quincey, *Recollections of the Lakes and the Lake Poets*, ed. David Wright (Harmondsworth: Penguin, 1970), pp. 33–111 (p. 45).
5. *Thomas Poole and His Friends*, II, 193.

6. See Holmes, *Darker Reflections*, pp. 70–1.

7. John Morgan to Coleridge, 6 July 1808, as quoted in Holmes, *Darker Reflections*, p. 111.

8. *Lamb Letters*, III, 274.

9. *Lectures on Literature* (CC), I, 16, 122.

10. The Royal Institution required a full text in writing to be available to them if they should choose to consult it. Compare Holmes, *Darker Reflections*, p. 118.

11. Lecture 1, 1808, *Lectures on Literature* (CC), I, 31–4.

12. In a letter to his niece, reprinted in *Lectures on Literature* (CC), I, 143–5 (p. 143).

13. At the Surrey Institution in 1812, Coleridge claimed 'I never once thought of the Lecture, till I had entered the Lecture Box' (*CL* III, 430).

14. Henry Crabb Robinson's MS reminiscences, reprinted in *Lectures on Literature* (CC), I, 410–11.

15. Wordsworth to Sir George Beaumont, 8 April 1808, *Wordsworth Letters: The Middle Years 1*, p. 208.

16. Reprinted in *Lectures on Literature* (CC), I, 145.

17. *Lectures on Literature* (CC), I, 113–16.

18. Lectures 9 and 13, 1818, *Lectures on Literature* (CC), II, 171–3, 217–225 passim.

19. Lecture 9, 1811–12, *Lectures on Literature* (CC), I, xlix, 358 and 358n. Compare Holmes, *Darker Reflections*, p. 279.

20. *Lectures on Literature* (CC), I, lxii.

21. *Wordsworth Prose Works*, III, 69.

22. Though Schlegel's famous study of *Romeo and Juliet* had been delivered in 1797 and available since 1798, and Coleridge knew of Schlegel's Shakespeare criticism in Italy – see *Lectures on Literature* (CC), I, lxi and note 70; Holmes, *Darker Reflections*, pp. 53, 275.

23. *Lectures on Literature* (CC), I, lxxxiii. See the section on 'Texts, Notes, and Reports' in Foakes's introduction, pp. lxxx–lxxxvi.

24. Lecture 1, 1818–19, *Lectures on Literature* (CC), II, 264.

25. Lecture 4, 1808, *Lectures on Literature* (CC), I, 82. Also *CN* III, 3290.

26. Lecture 12, 1811–12, *Lectures on Literature* (CC), I, 386.

27. *HCR* I, 57, and Robinson to Catherine Clarkson, 3 January 1812, as reprinted in *Lectures on Literature* (CC), I, 391.

28. In a conversation on 27 June 1827, *Table Talk* (CC), II, 61; compare *Lectures on Literature* (CC), I, lxxiii.

29. *The Romantics on Shakespeare*, ed. Jonathan Bate (London: Penguin, 1992), pp. 307–11 (p. 309).

30. *The Romantics on Shakespeare*, ed. Bate, p. 317.

31. As quoted in *Shakespeare Criticism 1623–1830*, ed. D. Nichol Smith (Oxford: Oxford University Press, 1916), pp. 170n. and 172n.

32. See Coleridge's annotations to Oliver's speech in *As You Like It*, I, i, 145–54 in the Samuel Ayscough 1807 edition and to Aufidius's speech, *Coriolanus* I, x, 10–24 in the 1773 Theobald edition in the *Marginalia* (CC), IV, 784 (compare p. 697), 730.

33. Lecture 9, 1811–12, *Lectures on Literature* (CC), I, 366–7.

34. *Marginalia* (CC), IV, 784.

35. Lecture 9, 1811–12, *Lectures on Literature* (CC), I, 362–3.

36. For the Aristotle quotation, see *Ancient Literary Criticism*, ed. D. A. Russell and M. Winterbottom (Oxford: Clarendon, 1972), p. 126; for Coleridge, see lecture 5, 1818–19, *Lectures on Literature* (CC), II, 317.

37. Lecture 1, 1813, *Lectures on Literature* (CC), I, 520.
38. Lecture 6, 1818–19, *Lectures on Literature* (CC), II, 326–8.
39. From the supplementary records for Coleridge's 1808 lectures, *Lectures on Literature* (CC), I, 134.
40. Lecture 1, 1818–19 Lectures on Shakespeare, *Lectures on Literature* (CC), II, 265–6.
41. *Coleridge: Shakespearean Criticism*, in 2 vols, ed. Thomas Raysor (London: J. M. Dent & Sons, 1960), I, 53.
42. Lecture 1, 1818–19, *Lectures on Literature* (CC), II, 264.
43. 'Treatise on Method' as published in the *Encyclopaedia Metropolitana, Shorter Works* (CC), I, 625–85 (p. 681).
44. Lecture 7, 1811–12, *Lectures on Literature* (CC), I, 306.
45. Lecture 4, 1818, *Lectures on Literature* (CC), II, 120.
46. Lecture 12, 1811–12, *Lectures on Literature* (CC), I, 387.
47. Lecture 12, 1811–12, *Lectures on Literature* (CC), I, 387.
48. *Shorter Works* (CC), I, 655.
49. See, for example, *Lectures on Literature* (CC), I, 519, and the end of Coleridge's unpublished letter on plagiarism, 15–21 December 1811 (*CL* III, 361).
50. Notes for lecture 4, 1808 Lectures on the Principles of Poetry, *Lectures on Literature* (CC), I, 86–7.
51. Compare Richard Holmes: 'perhaps the single, most influential phrase and critical concept that Coleridge ever produced', citing seven examples of its use in the media during one week of 1997, *Darker Reflections*, p. 130n.
52. Lecture 3, 1813, *Lectures on Literature* (CC), I, 543.
53. The letter to Wordsworth is not extant; see *Wordsworth Letters: The Middle Years 1*, pp. 239–45 and 239n.
54. See the account of Coleridge's first visit to the Lake District in Chapter 5 above.
55. Compare the table talk of Coleridge's noted by Henry Crabb Robinson 29 March 1811, *HCR* I, 28–9, and on the Scotch 'feelosophers' in *The Courier, Essays on His Times* (*CC*), II 275–6, 289–92, 316–17.
56. *The Friend* (CC), I, facing p. xl and II, facing p. 2; cp. *The Watchman* (CC), pp. xxxii and facing. See the discussion of *The Watchman* at the end of Chapter 2 above.
57. De Quincey, *Recollections of the Lakes and the Lake Poets*, p. 81.
58. *Wordsworth Letters: The Middle Years 1*, p. 350. Compare *Lamb Letters*, II, 287–8.
59. See Deirdre Coleman, *Coleridge and* The Friend *(1809–1810)* (Oxford: Clarendon, 1988), p. 3 (and on Sara Hutchinson, Chapter 2, pp. 27–40).
60. The numbered issues ran to 27, but Coleridge produced a '*supernumerary Essay*' on 11 January 1810 (*The Friend* (CC), II, 271–84) that was addressed in part to subscribers and defined the terms of their continued acquisition of the periodical.
61. *The Friend* (CC), II, 16–20 (pp. 16–7).
62. Southey to John Rickman 18 January 1809, *Selections from the Letters of Robert Southey*, ed. John Wood Warter, in 4 vols (London: Longmans, 1856), II, 120.
63. Francis Jeffrey to Coleridge, 28 December 1808, reprinted in Deirdre Coleman, 'Jeffrey and Coleridge: Four Unpublished Letters', *The Wordsworth Circle* XVIII, no. 1 (Winter 1987), pp. 39–45 (p. 44).
64. Quoted in my discussion of the advent of William and Dorothy Wordsworth in Chapter 3 above.
65. No. 11, 26 October 1809, *The Friend* (CC), II, 151–2.
66. No. 8, 5 October 1809, *The Friend* (CC), II, 117.
67. No. 11, 26 October 1809, *The Friend* (CC), II, 151.

68. See nos 6, 11, 12, 19, 25, *The Friend* (CC), II, 89–96, 147–8, 156–8, 170–1, 258–9, 334–46.
69. Recorded as for 27 April 1823, though not in the original MS notes – see *Table Talk* (CC), II, 41 and I, 40 note 3 (and compare editorial comment, I, xcii). Whether by 'flashes of lightning' Coleridge meant just that, or whether he was referring to the slang for 'shots of gin', as has been suggested, the point is the same: both suggest fits of illumination only, nothing sustained.
70. See, for example, Coleman, *Coleridge and* The Friend, Chapters 6 and 7.
71. The passage on imagination quoted above at the beginning of the Prologue, for example.
72. See Norman Fruman, *Coleridge, The Damaged Archangel* (London: George Allen & Unwin, 1972), p. 174.
73. No. 8, 5 October 1809, *The Friend* (CC), II, 112–13, 116.
74. Robinson's comments are reprinted in *Lectures on Literature* (CC), I, 410.
75. In an unsigned, pre-emptive review of *The Statesman's Manual* in the *Examiner*, 8 September 1816, reprinted in *Coleridge: The Critical Heritage*, pp. 248–53 (p. 249).
76. See Coleman, *Coleridge and* The Friend, Chapter 5 (especially pp. 103–6).
77. Dorothy Wordsworth to Catherine Clarkson, *c.* 12 April 1810, *Wordsworth Letters: Middle Years 1*, p. 399.
78. Dorothy Wordsworth to Catherine Clarkson, *c.* 12 April 1810, *Wordsworth Letters: Middle Years 1*, p. 398.

Chapter 8   'To Preserve the Soul Steady': The Sage of Highgate

1. Richard Holmes's explanation for the otherwise inexplicable support offered by the Morgans and Charlotte Brent seems irresistible: 'the Morgans were simply and essentially kind', Holmes, *Darker Reflections*, p. 263.
2. See the Prologue above.
3. *Lamb Letters*, III, 61–2.
4. *The Tragedy of King Lear*, IV, i, 28 in the Folio version, in *King Lear: The 1608 Quarto and 1623 Folio Texts*, ed. Stephen Orgel (London: Penguin, 2000).
5. Holmes, *Darker Reflections*, p. 222. Holmes himself remarks on Coleridge's powers of self-resuscitation on a number of occasions throughout his two-volume biography.
6. *Wordsworth Letters: The Middle Years 1*, p. 188.
7. *HCR*, I, 16.
8. Coleridge's literary lecturing is discussed above, in Chapter 7. For Coleridge's digressions, see Crabb Robinson's comments to his brother, 16 December 1811, reprinted in *Lectures on Literature* (CC), I, 409–10.
9. 5 December 1811, *HCR*, I, 53. On the second lecture as 'a vast improvement on the first', see the entry for 21 November 1811, *HCR*, I, 52.
10. 'Coleridge informs me his tragedy is accepted at Drury Lane. Whitbread admires it exceedingly, and Arnold, the manager, is confident of its success', Crabb Robinson's note of 3 November 1812, *HCR*, I, 112.
11. See Gillian Russell on 'Theatre', *Oxford Companion to the Romantic Age*, pp. 223–31 (p. 228).
12. As quoted in Penny Gay, *Jane Austen and the Theatre* (Cambridge: Cambridge University Press, 2002), p. 13. Prior to the fire of 1809, Gay notes, Drury Lane's capacity had been a staggering 3611 patrons; in 1813 it was around 2800.

13. 23 January 1813, *HCR*, I, 117.
14. *Coleridge: The Critical Heritage*, p. 7.
15. As quoted by David Erdman in his introduction to *Essays on His Times* (CC), I, cxliv.
16. 'We hold these truths to be self-evident, that all men were created equal, that they are endowed by their Creator with certain unalienable Rights, that among these are Life, Liberty, and the pursuit of Happiness', 'The Unanimous Declaration of the Thirteen United States of America, 4 July 1776', reprinted in *Revolutions 1775–1830*, ed. Merryn Williams (Harmondsworth: Penguin, 1971), pp. 44–53 (p. 45).
17. See my discussion of Coleridge and German Thought in Chapter 5.
18. Marilyn Butler, *Romantics, Rebels and Reactionaries: English Literature and Its Background 1760–1830* (Oxford and New York: Oxford University Press, 1981), p.146.
19. A. S. [John Thelwall], *The Champion*, 21 December 1818, as quoted in *Lectures on Literature* (CC), I, 276.
20. Norman Fruman, *Coleridge, the Damaged Archangel* (London: George Allen & Unwin, 1972), p. 101; George Watson, in the introduction to his edition of *Biographia Literaria*, third edition (London: J. M. Dent & Sons, 1975), p. xix.
21. For a long time the standard approach was set by George Whalley in his 'The Integrity of *Biographia Literaria*', *Essays and Studies*, new series, VI (1953), pp. 87–101.
22. Jerome Christensen, 'The Literary Life of a Man of Letters', in his *Coleridge's Blessed Machine of Language* (Ithaca, NY: Cornel University Press, 1981), pp. 118–85 (p. 121).
23. Quoting Wordsworth's *The Excursion*, I, 79.
24. Wordsworth, *The Prelude* (1805), X, 969.
25. *Wordsworth Letters: The Middle Years 1*, pp. 228, 230–1.
26. See the opening of Chapter 6 on Wordsworth's indifference to Coleridge's 'supernatural' poetry.
27. The following words and phrases from Jeffrey's review of Wordsworth's *Poems in Two Volumes*, *Edinburgh Review* XI (October 1807) set the tone: 'silliness', 'Childishness' (p. 214); 'infantine' (p. 217); 'plebeian nurseries' (p. 218); 'Silly Sooth' (p. 219); 'namby-pamby', 'a professed imitation of one of Mr Philips's prettyisms' (p. 220); 'childishness and insipidity' (p. 231). The cry was taken up by other reviewers.
28. In the words of the Preface to *Lyrical Ballads*, Wordsworth *Prose Works*, I, 128.
29. To quote John E. Jordan, *Why the 'Lyrical Ballads'? The Background, Writing, and Character of Wordsworth's 1798 Lyrical Ballads* (Berkeley, Los Angeles, and London: University of California Press, 1976), p. 158.
30. Review of Wordsworth's *Poems in Two Volumes*, *Edinburgh Review* XI (October 1807), p. 218. Compare Jeffrey on Wordsworth in his review of Samuel Richardson's 'volume of Familiar Letters for the use of persons in inferior situations', *Edinburgh Review* V (October 1804), pp. 23–44 (p. 31).
31. Review of Southey's *Thalaba*, *Edinburgh Review* I (October 1802), pp. 67, 66.
32. Review of *Poems in Two Volumes*, *Edinburgh Review* XI (October 1807), p. 218. Twentieth-century commentators have followed Jeffrey in remarking that, in the words of T. S. Eliot, Wordsworth's 'own language was as capable of artificiality, and no more capable of naturalness, than that of Pope — as Byron felt, and as Coleridge candidly pointed out', in *The Use of Poetry and the Use of Criticism*, second edition (London: Faber & Faber, 1964), p. 26.

33. In the review of *Thalaba*, *Edinburgh Review* I (October 1802), p. 65.
34. William Hazlitt, 'Mr. Wordsworth', *The Complete Works of William Hazlitt*, ed. P. P. Howe, in 21 vols (London and Toronto: J. M. Dent & Sons, 1930–4), XI, 86–95.
35. *The Satirist*, I (November 1807), pp. 188–191 (pp. 188–9).
36. See *BL*, I, 71.
37. See the discussion of the Preface to *Lyrical Ballads* in Chapter 6 and Coleridge's letter to William Sotheby of 13 July 1802, in which he confesses his suspicion that 'there is, somewhere or other, a *radical* Difference' between his and Wordsworth's opinions on poetry (*CL* II, 812).
38. Proper 'poetical diction', according to Johnson, was composed entirely of words 'at once refined from the grossness of domestick use and free from the harshness of terms appropriated to particular arts', in Samuel Johnson, 'Life of Dryden', *Lives of the English Poets*, World's Classics, in 2 vols (London, New York, Toronto: Oxford University Press, 1952), I, 420.
39. See the section on the Preface to *Lyrical Ballads* and the Birth of the Critic in Chapter 6 above.
40. 'Swift's style' Coleridge believed to be, in this line, 'perfect; the manner is a complete expression of the matter, the terms appropriate, and the artifice concealed. It is simplicity in the true sense of the word', in his lecture 'On Style', Lecture 14 of the 1818 lectures, *Lectures on Literature* (CC), II, 236.
41. *The Excursion*, V, l. 392, *Wordsworth Poetical Works*, V, 166.
42. 'THE CLERISY of the nation, or national church, in its primary acceptation and original intention comprehended the learned of all denominations', *Church and State* (CC), p. 46. For an earlier expression of Coleridge's belief in the necessity for a guiding class, see Coleridge on the 'thinking and disinterested Patriots' in his 'A Moral and Political Lecture' (and in *Conciones ad Populum*), *Lectures 1795* (CC), pp. 12, 40 (above, Chapter 2).
43. From the Advertisement to *Lyrical Ballads* (1798), in *Wordsworth and Coleridge: Lyrical Ballads*, eds R. L. Brett and A. R. Jones, second edition (London: Routledge, 1991), p. 7.
44. See the discussion of the Preface to *Lyrical Ballads* in Chapter 6 above.
45. See, for example, *Diary, Reminiscences, and Correspondence of Henry Crabb Robinson, Barrister-at-Law, F.S.A.*, ed. Thomas Sadler, in 3 vols (London, 1869), I, 304–5.
46. See the review of *Thalaba*, *Edinburgh Review* I (October 1802), p. 65, and the review of *Poems in Two Volumes*, *Edinburgh Review* XI (October 1807), p. 216.
47. Most of Wordsworth's poems were dismissed as 'unfortunate experiments', in the words of the *New Annual Register*, 'on which genius and labour have been misemployed', notice of the *Lyrical Ballads* (1798), *New Annual Register for 1798*, XIX (1799), pp. 309–10 (p. 310). Lucy Aiken's final, summary explanation for her review of the *Poems in Two Volumes* could stand, in its content and magisterial tone, as a collective statement for many reviewers of the *Lyrical Ballads* and *Poems in Two Volumes*: 'we were anxious to combat a system which appears to us so injurious to its author, and so dangerous to public taste', *Annual Review*, VI (1808), pp. 521–29 (p. 529).
48. Review of *Poems in Two Volumes*, *Edinburgh Review* XI (October 1807), p. 228. There were precedents – see, for example, the review of *Lyrical Ballads* in the *New London Review*, I (January 1799), pp. 33–5: 'so far from these poems being entirely written in the eccentric principle he proposes, we shall find, that he has many exquisite thoughts exquisitely expressed' (p. 34) – after Jeffrey's review, however, all the magazines and reviews took up this cry.
49. *Critical Review*, XVI (1763), p. 449.

50. Alvin Kernan, *Printing Technology, Letters and Samuel Johnson* (Princeton, NJ: Princeton University Press, 1987), p. 6.
51. See the discussion of Literary Patronage in Chapter 3 above.
52. Edmund Burke, *Reflections on the Revolution in France: A Critical Edition*, ed. J. C. D. Clark (Stanford, CA: Stanford University Press, 2001), p. 238.
53. William St Clair, *The Reading Nation in the Romantic Period* (Cambridge: Cambridge University Press, 2004), p. 164.
54. Two influential critical studies challenging a Wordsworth-centred Romantic literary culture were Marilyn Butler's *Romantics, Rebels & Reactionaries* in 1981 and Jerome J. McGann's *The Romantic Ideology: A Critical Investigation* (Chicago: Chicago University Press, 1983).
55. *Byron's Letters and Journals*, Vol. 4, ed. Leslie A. Marchand (Cambridge, MA: Belknap, 1975), pp. 318–19, 324. Not only did Moore not review Coleridge's *Sibylline Leaves* in 1817 but it may well have been Moore who wrote the attack on the *Christabel* volume that came out in 1816. See *Coleridge: The Critical Heritage*, pp. 226 and ff.
56. *Sibylline Leaves* did not include the three poems published by Murray in 1816 – that is, *Christabel*, 'Kubla Khan', and 'The Pains of Sleep'.
57. *Coleridge: The Critical Heritage*, p. 9.
58. Conventionally dated from John Gibson Lockhart's review of Coleridge's poetry in *Blackwood's Edinburgh Magazine* in October 1819, in *Coleridge: The Critical Heritage*, pp. 436–51.
59. *Lay Sermons* (CC), pp. 29–30.
60. As Coleridge promised in his *Aids to Reflection* (1825), as quoted in *Opus Maximum* (CC), pp. ccv–ccvi.
61. Keats to George and Georgiana Keats, 15 April 1819, in *Letters of John Keats*, ed. Robert Gittings (Oxford: Oxford University Press, 1970), p. 237.
62. Gillman, p. 271.
63. Gillman, pp. 271, 272, 273.
64. In his *Life of John Sterling* (1851), as quoted in *Lives of the Great Romantics II: Keats, Coleridge and Scott by Their Contemporaries*, Vol. 2, *Coleridge*, ed. Ralph Pite (London: Pickering & Chatto, 1997), p. 279.

Epilogue

1. *Letters, Conversations and Recollections of S. T. Coleridge*, in two volumes (London, 1836), I, 112 as quoted in *Lives of the Great Romantics II: Keats, Coleridge and Scott by Their Contemporaries*, Vol. 2, *Coleridge*, ed. Ralph Pite, p. 125.
2. In a letter to Wordsworth, 23 September 1816, *Lamb Letters*, III, 225.
3. Lamb to Wordsworth, 26 April 1816, *Lamb Letters*, III, 215.
4. Burnett's degradation, tellingly, evoked a bizarre and uncharacteristically cruel response from the vulnerable Coleridge, becoming the displaced object of his self-contempt: 'For myself, I have no heart to spare for a Coxcomb mad with vanity & stupified with opium'; 'I grieve that there should be such helpless self-tormenting Tormentors' (*CL* II, 1068, 910).
5. 'Samuel Taylor Coleridge', in Thomas De Quincey, *Recollections of the Lakes and the Lake Poets*, ed. David Wright (Harmondsworth: Penguin, 1970), pp. 33–111 (p. 97). The poem De Quincey quotes from is Wordsworth's 'Resolution and Independence', ll. 40–2.

Further Reading

The following is a list of books recommended for those who would like to follow up on any one or more of the many aspects of Coleridge's life and literature touched on in this study. It is not a bibliography for the study, bibliographical details of each text quoted having been included in the endnotes. Having said that, the reader will find that there is not surprisingly a large overlap.

Coleridge Texts

The Collected Works of Samuel Taylor Coleridge, Bollingen Series LXXV, that have been coming out from Routledge & Kegan Paul and Princeton University Press since the earlier 1970s have become the authoritative text for all Coleridge's writings. As the full bibliographical details of the volumes relevant to this study have been recorded in the List of Abbreviations at the front, there is no need to repeat them here. The same is true of Coleridge's collected *Letters* and *Notebooks*.

Palgrave Macmillan are bringing out a comprehensive multi-volume selection of *Coleridge's Writings* under different subject titles: Vol. 1 *On Politics and Society*, edited by John Morrow; Vol. 2 *On Humanity*, edited by Anya Taylor; Vol. 3 *On Language*, edited by A. C. Goodson; Vol. 4 *On Religion and Psychology*, edited by John Beer; Vol. 5 *On Shakespeare*, edited by E. S. Shaffer (1991–).

As all these are readily available only in libraries, however, I would draw your attention to two representative single volume anthologies of Coleridge's selected works: one edited by H. J. Jackson and now available in the World's Classics series of Oxford University Press under the title *Samuel Taylor Coleridge: The Major Works* (2000; available since 1985 in The Oxford Authors series). The other is *Coleridge's Poetry and Prose* in the Norton Critical Edition series, edited by Nicholas Halmi, Paul Magnuson, and Raimonda Modiano (New York: Norton, 2004), which is a generous and informed selection from Coleridge's works with critical essays at the end, though it does have the annoying editorial policy of faithfully reproducing the first published version of each work under its original title, even when the later, more familiar version is better.

Otherwise, paperback volumes of the poems abound – Penguin, for example, offer *The Complete Poems*, ed. William Keach, as well as *Selected Poetry*, ed. Richard Holmes – and single paperback editions of the *Biographia Literaria* can usually be found (the Collected Works edition, eds Engell and Bate, is available as two volumes in one, for example, and until recently there were two Everyman editions, an older one edited by George Watson and a more recent and complete edition edited by Nigel Leask). For a convenient edition of Wordsworth's and Coleridge's famous joint volume, including the Preface and poems Wordsworth added in 1800, there is *Lyrical Ballads: Wordsworth and Coleridge*, eds R. L. Brett and A. R. Jones, second edition (London: Routledge, 1991).

On the period

Abrams, M. H., *The Mirror and the Lamp: Romantic Theory and the Critical Tradition* (London, Oxford, New York: Oxford University Press, 1953).

Butler, Marilyn, *Romantics, Rebels and Reactionaries: English Literature and Its Background 1760–1830* (Oxford: Oxford University Press, 1981).

Butler, Marilyn (ed.), *Burke, Paine, Godwin, and the Revolution Controversy* (Cambridge: Cambridge University Press, 1984).

Christiansen, Rupert, *Romantic Affinities: Portraits from an Age 1780–1830* (London: Cardinal, 1989).

Christie, Ian R., *Wars and Revolutions: Britain 1760–1815, A New History of England*, Vol. VII (London: Edward Arnold, 1982).

Curran, Stuart (ed.), *The Cambridge Companion to British Romanticism* (Cambridge: Cambridge University Press, 1993).

Dickinson, H. T. (ed.), *Britain and the French Revolution, 1789–1815* (Basingstoke and London: Macmillan, 1989).

Eagleton, Terry, *The Function of Criticism: From* The Spectator *to Poststructuralism* (London: Verso, 1984).

Everest, Kelvin, *English Romantic Poetry: An Introduction to the Historical Context and the Literary Scene* (Milton Keynes and Philadelphia, PA: Open University Press, 1990).

Gaull, Marilyn, *English Romanticism: The Human Context* (New York and London: Norton, 1988).

Hobsbawm, E. J., *The Age of Revolution, 1789–1848* (London: Weidenfeld and Nicolson, 1962).

Jarvis, Robin, *The Romantic Period: The Intellectual and Cultural Context of English Literature, 1789–1830* (Harlow: Longman, 2004).

Jones, Howard Mumford, *Revolution and Romanticism* (Cambridge, MA: Harvard University Press; London: Oxford University Press, 1974).

Klancher, Jon, *The Making of English Reading Audiences, 1790–1832* (Madison, WI: University of Wisconsin Press, 1987).

McCalman, Iain (gen. ed.), *An Oxford Companion to the Romantic Age: British Culture 1776–1832* (Oxford: Oxford University Press, 1999).

McGann, Jerome J., *The Romantic Ideology: A Critical Investigation* (Chicago and London: University of Chicago Press, 1983).

Mori, Jennifer, *Britain in the Age of the French Revolution* (Harlow: Pearson Education, 2000).

Murphy, Peter, *Poetry as an Occupation and an Art, 1760–1830* (Cambridge: Cambridge University Press).

Murray, Chris (ed.), *Encyclopedia of the Romantic Era, 1760–1850* (New York and London: Fitzroy Dearborn, 2004).

O'Neill, Michael (ed.), *Literature of the Romantic Period: A Bibliographical Guide* (Oxford: Clarendon, 1998).

Pirie, David P. (ed.), *The Romantic Period*, The Penguin History of Literature, Vol. 5 (London: Penguin, 1994).

Roe, Nicholas (ed.), *Romanticism: An Oxford Guide* (Oxford: Oxford University Press, 2005).

St Clair, William, *The Reading Nation in the Romantic Period* (Cambridge: Cambridge University Press, 2004).

Watson, J. Steven, *The Reign of George III, 1760–1815*, Oxford History of England, Vol. XII (Oxford: Clarendon, 1960).

Webb, R. K., *Modern England from the Eighteenth Century to the Present*, second edition (London: Unwin Hyman, 1980).

Williams, Merryn (ed.), *Revolutions 1775–1830* (Harmondsworth: Penguin, 1971).

Williams, Raymond, *Culture and Society 1780–1850* (London: Chatto & Windus, 1958).

Wu, Duncan (ed.), *A Companion to Romanticism*, ed. Duncan Wu (Oxford: Blackwell, 1998).

On the life

The respective editorial introductions to the individual numbers in the Collected Works of Samuel Taylor Coleridge invariably contain extensive biographical detail gleaned from a rich variety of primary sources that is relevant to that particular work. Together they amount to a comprehensive if discontinuous literary life of Coleridge.

Ashton, Rosemary, *The Life of Samuel Taylor Coleridge* (Oxford: Blackwell, 1996).

Bate, Walter Jackson, *Coleridge* (London: Weidenfield and Nicholson, 1969).

Beer, John, 'Samuel Taylor Coleridge', entry in the *Oxford Dictionary of National Biography* (Oxford: Oxford University Press, 2004–6).

Campbell, James Dyke, *Coleridge: A Narrative of the Events of His Life* (London: Macmillan, 1894).

Cornwell, John, *Coleridge: Poet and Revolutionary, 1772–1804* (London: Allen Lane, 1973).

De Quincey, Thomas, *Recollections of the Lakes and the Lake Poets*, ed. David Wright (Harmondsworth: Penguin, 1970).

Gillman, James, *The Life of Samuel Taylor Coleridge* (London: William Pickering, 1838).

Hazlitt, William, 'My First Acquaintance with Poets', in *William Hazlitt: Selected Writings*, ed. Jon Cook (Oxford and New York: 1991), pp. 211–30.

Holmes, Richard, *Coleridge: Darker Reflections* (London: HarperCollins, 1998).

Holmes, Richard, *Coleridge: Early Visions* (London: Hodder & Stoughton, 1989).

Lefebure, Molly, *The Bondage of Love: A Life of Mrs Samuel Taylor Coleridge* (London: Victor Gallancz, 1988).

Perry, Seamus, *S. T. Coleridge*, The British Library Writers' Lives (London: The British Library, 2003).

Perry, Seamus (ed.), *S. T. Coleridge: Interviews and Recollections* (Basingstoke: Palgrave, 2000).
Pite, Ralph (ed.), *Lives of the Great Romantics II: Keats, Coleridge and Scott by Their Contemporaries*, Vol. 2, *Coleridge* (London: Pickering & Chatto, 1997).
Robinson, Henry Crabb, *Henry Crabb Robinson on Books and Their Writers*, ed. Edith J. Morley, in 3 vols (London: J. M. Dent & Sons, 1938).
Roe, Nicholas, *Wordsworth and Coleridge: The Radical Years* (Oxford: Clarendon, 1988).
Sandford, Mrs Henry [Margaret E.], *Thomas Poole and His Friends*, in 2 vols (London: Macmillan, 1888).
Sultana, Donald, *Coleridge in Malta and Italy* (New York: Barnes and Noble, 1969).
Willey, Basil, *Samuel Taylor Coleridge* (London: Chatto and Windus, 1972).
Wordsworth, Dorothy, *Journals of Dorothy Wordsworth*, ed. Mary Moorman (London, Oxford, New York: Oxford University Press, 1971).

On the literature

Abrams, M. H., *The Correspondent Breeze: Essays in English Romanticism* (New York: Norton, 1984).
Badawi, M. M., *Coleridge: Critic of Shakespeare* (Cambridge: Cambridge University Press, 1973).
Barfield, Owen, *What Coleridge Thought* (London: Oxford University Press, 1972).
Barth, J. Robert, *The Symbolic Imagination: Coleridge and the Romantic Tradition* (Princeton, NJ: Princeton University Press, 1977).
Beer, John (ed.), *Coleridge's Variety* (London and Basingstoke: Macmillan, 1974).
Bostetter, Edward E., 'The Nightmare World of *The Ancient Mariner*', *Studies in Romanticism*, 1 (1961–2), pp. 241–54.
Brett, R. L. (ed.), *S. T. Coleridge*, Writers and Their Background Series (London: G. Bell & Sons, 1971).
Burwick, Frederick (ed.), *Coleridge's* Biographia Literaria: *Text and Meaning* (Columbus: Ohio State University Press, 1989).
Bygrave, Stephen, *Coleridge and the Self: Romantic Egotism* (Basingstoke and London: Macmillan, 1986).
Calleo, David P., *Coleridge and the Idea of the Modern State* (New Haven, CT and London: Yale University Press, 1966).
Carlson, Julie A., *In the Theatre of Romanticism: Coleridge, Nationalism, Women* (Cambridge: Cambridge University Press, 1994).
Christensen, Jerome, *Coleridge's Blessed Machine of Language* (Ithaca, NY and London: Cornell University Press, 1981).
Coburn, Kathleen, *The Self-Conscious Imagination: A Study of the Coleridge Notebooks in Celebration of His Birth 21 October 1772* (London: Oxford University Press, 1974).
Coleman, Deirdre, *Coleridge and* The Friend *(1809–1810)* (Oxford: Clarendon, 1988).
Colmer, John, *Coleridge: Critic of Society* (Oxford: Clarendon, 1959).
Cooke, M. G., 'Quisque Sui Faber: Coleridge in the *Biographia Literaria*', *Philological Quarterly*, 50 (2) (April 1971), pp. 208–29.
Davidson, Graham, *Coleridge's Career* (Basingstoke: Macmillan, 1990).
Eilenberg, Susan, *Strange Powers of Speech: Wordsworth, Coleridge, and Literary Possession* (Oxford: Clarendon, 1992).
Everest, Kelvin, *Coleridge's Secret Ministry: The Context of the Conversation Poems 1795–1798* (Hassocks, Sussex: Harvester; New York: Barnes and Noble, 1979).

Fruman, Norman, *Coleridge: The Damaged Archangel* (London: George, Allen & Unwin, 1972).

Fulford, Tim, and Morton D. Paley (eds), *Coleridge's Visionary Languages* (Cambridge: D. S. Brewer, 1993).

Goodson, A. C., *Verbal Imagination: Coleridge and the Language of Modern Criticism* (New York and London: Oxford University Press, 1988).

Hamilton, Paul, *Coleridge's Poetics* (Oxford: Basil Blackwell, 1983).

Hamilton, Paul, 'Coleridge', in *The Romantic Period*, The Penguin History of Literature, Vol. 5, ed. David P. Pirie (London: Penguin, 1994), pp. 185–220.

House, Humphry, *Coleridge: The Clark Lectures 1951–2* (London: Rupert Hart-Davis, 1953).

Jackson, J. R. de J., *Method and Imagination in Coleridge's Criticism* (London: Routledge and Kegan Paul, 1969).

Jackson, J. R. de J. (ed.), *Coleridge: The Critical Heritage* (London: Routledge and Kegan Paul, 1970).

Jackson, J. R. de J. (ed.), *Coleridge: The Critical Heritage, Vol. 2: 1834–1900* (London: Routledge and Kegan Paul, 1991).

Jones, Alan R., and William Tydeman (eds), *Coleridge: The Ancient Mariner and Other Poems: A Casebook* (London and Basingstoke: Macmillan, 1973).

Kitson, Peter J., and Thomas N. Corns (eds), *Coleridge and the Armoury of the Human Mind: Essays on His Prose Writings* (London: Frank Cass, 1991).

Leask, Nigel, *The Politics of Imagination in Coleridge's Critical Thought* (Basingstoke: Macmillan, 1988).

Lowes, John Livingston, *The Road to Xanadu: A Study in the Ways of the Imagination*, rev edn (London: Constable, 1930).

Matlak, Richard, *The Poetry of Relationship: The Wordsworths and Coleridge, 1797–1800* (Basingstoke: Macmillan, 1997).

McFarland, Thomas, *Coleridge and the Pantheist Tradition* (Oxford: Clarendon, 1969).

McFarland, Thomas, *Romanticism and the Forms of Ruin: Wordsworth, Coleridge, and Modalities of Fragmentation* (Princeton, NJ: Princeton University Press, 1981).

McGann, Jerome J., 'The Meaning of *The Ancient Mariner*', *Critical Inquiry*, 8 (1981), pp. 35–66, reprinted as '*The Ancient Mariner*: The Meaning of Meanings', in his *The Beauty of Inflections: Literary Investigations in Historical Method and Theory* (Oxford: Clarendon, 1985), pp. 135–72.

Mill, John Stuart, *Mill on Bentham and Coleridge*, ed. F. R. Leavis (London: Chatto & Windus, 1950).

Morrow, John, *Coleridge's Political Thought: Property, Mortality and the Limits of Traditional Discourse* (Basingstoke: Macmillan, 1990).

Newlyn, Lucy, *Coleridge, Wordsworth and the Language of Allusion* (Oxford: Clarendon, 1986).

Newlyn, Lucy, *Reading, Writing, and Romanticism: The Anxiety of Reception* (Oxford: Clarendon, 2000).

Newlyn, Lucy (ed.), *The Cambridge Companion to Coleridge* (Cambridge: Cambridge University Press, 2002).

Parker, Reeve, *Coleridge's Meditative Art* (Ithaca, NY and London: Cornell, 1975).

Perkins, Mary Anne, *Coleridge's Philosophy: The Logos as Unifying Principle* (Oxford: Clarendon Press; New York: Oxford University Press, 1994).

Perry, Seamus, *Coleridge and the Uses of Division* (Oxford: Clarendon, 1999).

Richards, I. A., *Coleridge on Imagination* (London: Kegan Paul, 1934).

Sultana, Donald (ed.), *New Approaches to Coleridge* (London: Vision; New York: Barnes and Noble, 1981).

Taylor, Anya, *Coleridge's Defense of the Human* (Columbus, OH: Ohio State University Press, 1986).

Wallace, Catherine, *The Design of the* Biographia Literaria (London: Allen & Unwin, 1983).

Wendling, Ronald C., *Coleridge's Progress to Christianity: Experience and Authority in Religious Faith* (Lewisberg, PA: Bucknell University Press, 1995).

Whalley, George, 'The Integrity of the *Biographia Literaria*', *Essays and Studies*, n.s. 6 (1953), pp. 85–101.

Wheeler, Kathleen M., *Sources, Processes and Methods in Coleridge's* Biographia Literaria (Cambridge: Cambridge University Press, 1980).

Woodring, Carl, *Politics in the Poetry of Coleridge* (Madison, WI: University of Wisconsin Press, 1961).

Wylie, Ian, *Young Coleridge and the Philosophers of Nature* (Oxford: Clarendon, 1989).

Index

Printed in the United States
97594LV00001B/93/A